DON'T JUST FLY, *Soar*

The Inspiration and tools you need to rise above adversity and create a life by design

Kelly Markey

Endorsements

This triumphant narrative is a must read for anyone who has struggled to find their identity and voice relationally in church settings, business boardrooms and autonomous friendships. From the hinterland of South Africa to New Zealand and Australia, Markey unmasks the truth about the greatest paradox in history – that authentic identity can only be found in Christ Jesus. The more we cede our lives to Him, the more powerful we are to conquer our past, prophetically change our present, and re-engineer our destiny. This book is more than a collection of Markey's rollercoaster compass points of an ethnic female of colour, sister, co-labourer, and journeywoman searching for wholeness; it is a beacon of hope that Christ, the Hope of Glory in you, is real, and He restores vision, thus transforming lives.

Fepulea'i, F. Ulua'ipou-O-Malo Aiono: Founder – The RapHa Seed, Auckland, New Zealand.

This book is written about a life lived with the purpose of achieving GOLD. Kelly shares her life, feelings and decisions, the principles learnt and the resulting values. In each experience she has found friends, family, and strength to help her to continue living, be human and staying resilient. Now taking the next step, Kelly shares tools to help others examine their lives and find their own GOLD. This is a book I would recommend to anyone who is hoping to find the worthwhile lessons from their own experiences. Experience is better than an ocean of theory and Kelly has a ton of experience under her belt – REAL GOLD that you do not have to dig to find!

Carol Seeto, Sydney, Australia

Kelly recounts the details of many moments in her life that were both shocking and painful. Readers will be surprised at how much Kelly has endured, and the tragedies she has witnessed. But within the pages of Kelly's story there is not just pain, there is also the overcoming of extreme abuse and great loss. Kelly addresses the emotions involved with feeling rejected, abandoned, hopeless, angry and afraid. But she also shares moments of true sisterhood, genuine compassion and a faith that ultimately carries her through many storms. As you read through the pages there is the treasure of discovering one woman's truth. Kelly draws the reader to growing up with apartheid, then relocating halfway across the world only to discover that discrimination is a worldwide epidemic. And while this is the story of one woman's ability to return to faith, hope and love again, I can't help but believe readers will find practical bits of wisdom that will help them on their own path.

Nicole Bingaman: Author, Falling Away from You, BrainLine Blog, Permission to Tell the Truth and Facebook: Team Taylor. Pennsylvania, United States of America

Kelly's story is a true testament to the power of a woman who lives with hope and fate. Regardless of what life threw at Kelly and wounded her soul and body, she turned her wounds to be her superpower and shares that with the readers so they can do the same with their life. Her story is powerful and inspirational to many. Her story reminded me of a poem of a great Persian Poet: *'Woman is the radiance of God, she is not a creature, and she is a creator'* Rumi.

Azita Abdollahian: Author of the book 'Breaking Free' Amazon #1 Bestseller, Award winner and the founder of Azita Academy and School of Resiliency and Emotional Wellbeing. Sydney, Australia

Life's most important question is: WHY AM I HERE? No adventure or ambition in life can be fulfilling without answering this important question. When this question is answered, we can face the future with fearless confidence and the adventure would be worth it because it would be purposeful and meaningful. In this book, Kelly Markey stresses the need to realise purpose is a journey through the lens of her own story. I believe our personal stories are sources of transformation for others. She is not telling you to do what she has not been through or take you where she hasn't been. The pages of this book echo her daily walk and the principles she's lived by to discover her purpose in life and to be fulfilling it. This book will transform your life and birth a new you. Congratulations on picking it up

Dr Samuel Ekundayo: Author, Preacher, Teacher, Life Coach and Motivational Speaker. Auckland, New Zealand

First published by Ultimate World Publishing 2021
Copyright © 2021 Kelly Markey

Find us on Facebook @KellyMarkeyAuthor and Instagram @Author_Kelly_Markey

ISBN

Paperback: 978-0-6451968-0-1
Hardback: 978-0-6451968-2-5
Ebook: 978-0-6451968-1-8

Kelly Markey has asserted her rights under the Copyright, Designs and Patents Act 1988 to be identified as the author of this work. The information in this book is based on the author's experiences and opinions. The publisher specifically disclaims responsibility for any adverse consequences which may result from use of the information contained herein. Permission to use information has been sought by the author. Any breaches will be rectified in further editions of the book.

All rights reserved. No part of this publication may be reproduced, stored in or introduced into a retrieval system, or transmitted in any form, or by any means (electronic, mechanical, photocopying, recording or otherwise) without the prior written permission of the author. Any person who does any unauthorised act in relation to this publication may be liable to criminal prosecution and civil claims for damages. Enquiries should be made through the publisher.

For both professional and moral reasons in some instances the names of characters have been edited. The author is mindful of the fact that this is her journey and does not presume to narrate the account of others who feature in this story.

Cover design: Giselle Dadios Pulido
Layout: Dave Markey
Typesetting: Ultimate World Publishing
Photographer for internal page images: Kelly Markey
Diagrams: Dave and Kelly Markey

Ultimate World Publishing
Diamond Creek,
Victoria Australia 3089
www.writeabook.com.au

Dedicated To...

The Spirit of the living God that has guided, protected and blessed me exquisitely in every season of my life. Each time I encounter Him, I am struck anew by Him. My inspiration and philanthropy are modelled on Him.

Foreword

As I read this book, my thoughts drifted to the life of an eagle. At age 40, the eagle has to make a very tough decision, live or die; at this age, the eagle can no longer survive, its talons are no longer flexible enough to hold onto a prey for its food, its beak is no longer sharp but bent, its wings are no longer swift but heavy and a burden for it to fly. Live or die: a decision the eagle has to make! The process of change is a tough one. The eagle flies high on a mountain, just him and his creator, and it is here that his body goes through a painful process of transformation and rebirth. One hundred and fifty days later this bird emerges more powerful and more resilient with a life span of another 30 years, with a sharper beak, stronger talons and swifter wings.

So, too, has God prepared Kelly Markey for an amazing journey with Him, like the Eagle who had to endure a painful process, so too has Kelly, her journey has been hurtful, disappointing, exceedingly challenging, she has endured tears, deep sadness, and loneliness. During her time of despair, God was designing and shaping her, she was going through a time of rebirth and transformation, today she has emerged, strong and resilient: *'But those who hope in the Lord will renew their strength. They will soar on wings like eagles; they will run and not grow weary; they will walk and not be faint'* Isaiah 40:31. This book is powerful; it will teach you, it will equip you and it will shape you for a healthier walk in life. God has bestowed Kelly with much wisdom and insight. I have so enjoyed reading the journey of this remarkable woman; I have cried, smiled, laughed out loud, and I was tickled too, and so will every reader! What an extraordinary journey and experience that turned out an exceptional woman of our era.

Liz Naidoo: Founder and Editor of Woman of Faith Magazine. Durban, South Africa.

Preface

Everyone who knows me on a personal level knows that my heart beats to cultivate hope, especially when life seems bleak. I believe the pain and learning curve of each experience in my life was not just limited to my transformation. Every intense period of growth was orchestrated to help me reach my apex so I can pass on these insightful gems to you, the reader. May each experience touch and change you with the same magnitude I experienced. As you unravel each new layer within yourself, I beseech you to seek growth and purpose with each newfound revelation. May you be educated with critical dissent that ignites your own journey to your true calling and destiny for an enhanced you and a greater enlightened humanity.

My life has carried me across the world and brought me face to face with many characters and events, both positive and negative. This afforded me the impeccable choice to determine exactly who and what deserves a seat at my table of life. No one can foresee what tomorrow brings, so let's all begin with today, here and now. Be the best version of yourself despite the dilemmas that come your way.

This book devotes significant consideration to both the motivation and confidence that you need to reach your true potential. It's about my first-hand experiences, and I share my journey curves with you to propel you to fan your flames no matter how dim life may seem. It will model options to heal your personal breaches by tangentially and directly choosing better behaviour. Thus, throughout this book you will see many references to the strain and inequity that lie within humans – the seeds they toss to others so unjustly. The historic thread will bring you to my personal encounter with compassion, tolerance and choices of liberation.

I would not be here writing this book had I given up every time a hurdle came my way. People quit after being knocked off the peak a few times. Some shy away when the slightest indication of hardship sets in. My response to life, as you will read in this book, is a testament to what happens if you refuse to quit. Shake the burden, but never let the load tremble you. I had the zeal to zoom in and transcribe this book in just ten days because I lived it. It's tangible. I did not have to wait for inspiration to arrive – my life is a blueprint that echoes inspiration. I share from my practical experience, not generic theory or plagiarism. Your energy is valuable, so be strategic in deciding where it goes. My personal choices unravelled where my energy patterns mounted in conditions beyond the herd mentality.

The sterling moments when you walk through the wildfire of capability can shape and influence others who watch you. A drop of experience speaks louder than an ocean of theories. I invite you to explore my life's knowledge, which will shape you with a new culture of curves and equip you to battle injustices – it may even inspire you to take a courageous heart tour and revolutionise your sparks of empathy. My life has been riddled with catastrophes, and what I share today is the shining aftermath of the mess, transcending my life to a finer message a one-of-a-kind masterpiece created by spending over two decades living in international countries. Away from my birthright nucleus, life created a vortex that compelled my survival. These pages will show you how to harness life when you have no harvest left.

I know without a shadow of doubt that you also don't want to just survive life, but you want to excel in every facet. My voyage will prove to you that if a mere mortal like me can turn every predicament of life into a testimony of courage; then you can tap into the same power. All you have to do is find that flame and fan it to burn brighter than the force that tries to smother it. I have an adoration of living life to the brightest potential, and I wrote this to help you find the same light of hope and perseverance. My voice is raw and naturally seeping with life as it happens. It is not a photoshopped and edited experience curated to brand an image. It is simply life in all its glory of tribulations, triumphs and forging forward in every context.

Sometimes life seems like an obstacle course by default. Take heart, for these pages will give you the glimmer of hope, motivation and zeal needed to ignite your soul. Don't let life hold you hostage. Find the tiny flame and fan it so you can go out and show the world just how the fig tree dried up, so the masses don't have to imagine it. My life, captured in this memoir, will show you it does not matter what comes your way; the key is how you rise above. I am a by-product of the apartheid regime and numerous other personal transgressions, but I don't live with those tags defining me. **The heart of this memoir echoes choices – the choices we design by our own resolve to sink, swim or soar.** I tapped into the resilience applying my modus operandi from life and my core values and beliefs to chart through the mayhem of life. This book is an experience of perseverance to transform life's standards even when the crushed heart has no atonement. My euphoria after emerging from the burning furnace like a phoenix will envelop and inspire you to build your own bridges of fortitude.

This book will pull you into a transformational force that will grip you like a vice. Bursting with strength, resilience and tenacity from a young bud to a blossomed woman – an experience to benefit the reader with practical and approachable insights from my remarkable voyage of life. Demonstrating that we can all transcend every facet of our lives and overcome any obstacle. Exercising our choice wisely is a therapy that we can all master! These pages describe a life whittled by the dire awareness that discrimination has no international borders; a life encased with authentic forgiveness, resilience, profound pain, healing of deep wounds and prevailing victory. This book unmasks exactly how to use your mind efficiently to thrive in ways that far exceed your expectations. A well-weighted journey comes with a belt of experience – the best teacher.

You too can create a grand future despite your current predicament. This book contains twenty five potent tools that will assist you to realign your life and style yourself to be a better you. These tools will spur rich pondering questions that will crack through your external veneers and hopefully mandate you to shed some layers. Most importantly, my testimony will challenge you significantly to realign to your true authentic north. I invite you to grasp the threadbare fabric of my life's experiences and take a long pause to let the thousand years of customs and perceived normal behaviours pass through your mind. Then evaluate your heart and question how you wish to fan your own flames.

Break the control that dictates that you do not have a better choice. No matter how tiny the flame of hope is – fan it like your life depends on it. Giving up behaviours that do not add value is easier said than done. I have included my life experience to inspire you by the fact that I had no map to life and yet I had to create a path in the wilderness – by the choices to fan a flame. Resolve what you wish to fan in your life. Two roads diverge in the woods and choosing to take the road less travelled may make all the difference. One of the greatest gifts you give to yourself is the power to live an authentic life, grow from your setbacks, and rise up stronger, before legitimately enhancing the world with your personal learnings.

My expressions will give you insights to what and who matters in this life and the future. We all have our own expressions of life; let this book help you to intentionally reform and revive your expressions in a meaningful way. My text draws attention to the nature of human unconsciousness and consciousness and the conflict of choices to make a wholesome experience for both an individual and humanity at large. I will invite you to **not** explore external restorations but to trace your own mind and heart to conjure up the colour of your real world and true heart. When the silent enemy of life chases you down relentlessly, these chronicles will spark hope that will create a zeal to compel you to find your own steadfast foot in a season of change.

As you read these words and feel my genuine tears, you will be set free in remarkable ways. These revelations will empower you to stand on a mountain even while the vine is stripped bare in your life. This is not an eloquent poem. I say this with conviction as I've walked this terrain of clout. Just as my setback exhibits a comeback, You, too, will see a lustrous tomorrow for yourself by the power of my testimony. My voice will help you remove malarkey that no longer serves you and focus on what truly matters. It will tug you to introspect on the crevices of your life that you never paid attention to before. This book will show you that life is never about what happens to you but all about how you design your life to personally soar or descend.

This is not just a print to take up space in the library. This is my delicate life: I open up my bruised and healed heart to allow you a glimpse of what hope and restoration looks like. My usual candour will deepen your quest to confirm if your thoughts, deeds, and actions are figuratively Sanskrit and what you may need to realign to your true north. This plot will help you find yourself even if you are not aware you are lost. You will find answers to questions that you may have never pondered on before: Discover the purpose and vision of your life, reach a point of forgiveness, ascertain what your blind spots are, identify risk factors, design a mitigation plan for your life, plan how to achieve alignment with your life, tap into the art of palpable growth and renew the mind positively.

It will reveal a person who is fiercely resilient, helping you with reconciliation to transform to a better version in an unfair world, helping you find courage to succeed in things that really matter. This is a map that will inspire you to leave your current state of life, remove bias from your compass, and transform to a new enhanced version of your authentic self. It will compel you to step up, take control and create a mental resilience. I envision this book as a passport to a new, exciting destination. Dive in and stay driven for distinction. Fasten your seatbelt as this may get bumpy but stay focused on what really matters. Research *why* you feel the bump and hunt for the solution. Determine what cures you!

My illustrations will define fresh directions for your subconscious mind to aid your healing. This book will drive you to surgically transform your consciousness and confidence for a greater good. It will showcase how you can achieve the radiant success that is hidden in the studio of your mind and the trunk of your heart. My steadfast personal expressions will optimistically help you realise your bias coercions to affirm improved waves of harmony with the sea of people you touch in prominent and humble tides of life. Offering you the over powering hunch to shed layers and grow anew tomorrow. My chronicles will thrust readers on a pursuit to ponder why egalitarian epitomes are so desolate in their habitual hearts.

'If you fall, fall like a seed to germinate and bring forth life. Not like a leaf to wither and die.' Unknown

Contents

Endorsement iii
Foreword ix
Preface xi
Introduction 1

Part One – My Voyage 7
   Chapter One – Resilience 9
      Protection in a Catastrophe – NOT 9
      Relentless Roar to SOAR 14
      Essence of FAITH 19
   Chapter Two – Vicissitudes of Life 22
      Untainted Intrigues 22
      Unflinching Results 25
      Growing Deeper Affiliations 28
      Man With Double Standards 32
      Cultivate Your Circle Especially in the Difficult Seasons 36
   Chapter Three – Internal Fortitude 40
      Super Saturated and Then… 40
      Purview of the Cosmos 46
      Separate the Wheat from the Chaff 49
   Chapter Four – Prototypes for Deeper Connection 57

The Trudge to Forgiveness	57
Glean, Grow and Glow	66

Chapter Five – A Virtuous Woman 73

Shaping Life Despite Invisible Pain	73
Prophetic Word	76
Know Your Value	79
Defining Your Brand…Stride	82
Mental Dexterity – HOPE	85
A House Is Not a Home	87
Mother With a Worthy Influence	90

Chapter Six – You Cannot Give a Shattered Heart........................96

Divorce Stigma	96
Breaking Soul Ties	101
My Boaz Prayer List	104
Wolf in Sheep's Clothing	107
Chalk and Cheese	109

Chapter Seven – Litmus Test for True Alliance 114

Best Friends Since Sliced Bread	114
The Deed of Giving and Taking	118
Thankful Progress is Priceless	121
Bonds That Beckon, Forty Years and Counting	127
No One Is Invincible	133

Chapter Eight – The Rollercoaster Extravaganza 135

Killing the Bird With Broken Wings	135
Craft Your Own Lifeline	140
One Day or DAY ONE – Your Resolve	146
A Golden State of Mind in a Pandemic	149

Chapter Nine – Highlight Your Core Beauty 151

Sweet Life of a Giver 151
Forgotten Seed That Still Thrives 153
Shine the Light 156
Ethics Are Not Limited Edition 159
Be a Voice Not An Echo 162
Eradicate the Green-Eyed Monster 165
How to Wake Up Pretty 168

Chapter Ten – We All Have CHOICES 171
Chronicles That Ignite Choice 171
Decision Flow Between a Victim Mindset Versus the Choice to Transform Your Mind 176
The Charisma of Choice and Courage 178
The Choice to Cultivate Prayer Patterns 187

Chapter Eleven – The Unconscious Bias 193
Inherent Prejudice 193
Developing with Apartheid 206

Chapter Twelve – The Best Has Come and It Prevails 222
Living My Truth 222
Let Your Success be the Noise 224
Sisterhood That Anchors Strength 226
Tap Into a Deeper Well 235

Part Two – The Art of Transformation 239

Transition From Scarred to Healed 240
Mental Resilience 244
How to Renew the Mind 247
Personal Journaling 249
Steps Towards Authentic Self-Assessment 251
Self-Care Enhancements 256

Improve Your Radar	259
Ascend Above the Predicament	261
The Roaring Difference Between Change & Progress	267
Implementing Change in Your Life	267
Change Cycle Methodology	269
Wisdom to Know the Change Difference	271
Change Factors That You Can Control	271
Change Factors That You CANNOT Control	272
Work to Reach the Promised Land	273
Moving to the Next Level	276
Discovering Your Purpose	279
Purge List	281
How Content Are You With Your Life at Present?	283
Setting Goals	285
Strategic Vision	289
Why You Need a Vision Plan For Your Life	289
Key Benefits for a Vision Plan	290
Let the Vision Begin	291
Vision Plan	293
Process the Unprocessed Pain	295
Love Map	297
Proactively Discover Your Blind Spot	299
What Does Utopia Look Like for You?	300
Elements for Success	302
How to Monitor Your Personal Growth	306
Balancing the Equation of Sowing and Reaping	308
The Ladder of Ascent to Transformation	312
Personal Ascension to Transformation	313
Beauty or Afflictions? You Choose	316
Reducing Learning Cycles	320

    Consecrated and Concrete Standards 323
        1. Hannah Pours Her Heart to God in Prayer (1 Samuel 1 – 15) ... 324

        2. The Wrestle of Jacob (Genesis 32: 22 – 32) 324

        3. The Revival Prophesy of Ezekiel (Ezekiel 37: 1 – 14) 326

        4. Jesus sweating Blood (Luke 22: 44) 326

Conclusion 330

Acknowledgements 335

About the Author 338

References 341

Introduction

Christmas 2019, we sojourned to Finland and Norway. Upon our return flight in January 2020, we had a five-hour stopover in Hong Kong. A blaring announcement broke the jetlag a few times in an accent that was really hard to discern, but no danger was decoded. It was a routine announcement that I'd heard many times during my previous travels. Fast forward to life back in Sydney, Australia – a pandemic unleashed itself on the world, life as we knew it was shaken, rattled and rolled globally, and the reverie of our Nordic escape was well and truly over.

I felt frustrated that this virus was noxious and spreading, yet it was mismanaged and treated like a fiasco with no regard for our lives and exposure to its threat. I had sat in transit for five hours where I could have contracted the virus and perished, merely shrinking into another statistic with no compassion from the board of mismanagement gurus to create a moral code of conduct. Gloomily, we have all become victims of this regime. I watched in sheer horror as the world grappled with the crisis and many lives were thrown into what seemed like uncalculated disarray.

We reached these milestones because someone made choices – choices in their own best interests but devoid of introspection to ponder on the fate of the rest of the world. As the metaphoric applecart toppled worldwide, most people were struggling to cope and make better choices. I have not lived through a pandemic before and I have no clue about the mandated 101 standard operating processes, but I had so much experience under my belt dealing with catastrophe that I felt like my default resilience button had been kicked in, telling me precisely what to do. I found myself talking to people from different parts of the globe and I watched the news and social media with intent mania only to find a common theme of belligerent despair – most people did not have the basic coping mechanism for life in general, let alone a pandemic!

Cognitive dissonance prevailed in this unprecedented stretch. Granted that I too was in lockdown, still I decided to channel my energy positively to give to the masses a gift that would help them glean how to cope and transform amidst anything that life may throw – cultivate HOPE in any facet of life so you can tap into it like a prescribed drug. I wrote this book in ten days; I also dusted off my culinary skills, preparing meals to the fine distinction of Martha Stewart's perfection. Multitasking in the stride of a pandemic – bring it on! As I concluded my manuscript, the 'Black Lives Matter' movement unravelled and this compelled me to write about my experience growing up in the apartheid regime and immigrating to find a better life… only to discover discrimination lives everywhere.

Given that we all have a finite time on earth, we need to make our metaphoric transition from caterpillar to butterfly sooner rather than later. Make every moment in life significant, no matter what the season is. This book will give you a vivid insight into my personal voyage, the courage, strength and tears I had to muster to get back on the horse and try once more. We all have a distinctive Garden of Eden bliss paved path, the position where we would like our life to be. How do we reach our destination? We all have inborn needs: subsistence, love, power, independence, and pleasure. The entirety of our behaviours, whether operative or unproductive, is constantly an endeavour to fulfil one or more of these needs. Most of us stumble as the path is not clearly defined. There is no pre-constructed Google map.

The minimum you can do is confirm which direction you want to head toward before you step onto the busy freeway. Plan and have a basic vision to avoid a vortex of harsh realities. Tame the whirlwind and cultivate hope so that your life will emerge by **designed choice.** Resilience on steroids is cultivated from marvels dragged by decent choices, and great things come to those who choose wisely. Tarry with the absorption of resilience and hope to define your own swag. Only you can punctuate your life with purpose and hope. The grandest personality is shaped by the huff and puff of transformation guided by your choices. Reign as you build a real inheritance and legacy of hope. This book will demonstrate all of the above to you in a human relatable format.

Be the change mafia. Fashion your success by design as you embrace the power of choice and shape your enthusiastic identity with sheer hope even among all the muck and mire. No matter what tries to pull you up short, constantly distinguish your right of passage with both your natural and spiritual heart – the muscle which cultivates hope. This book delves into the insights that I gleaned from my trials and tribulations. It offers perceptive takeaways for others to grow in every season of life and build motivational power amid adversity. The intent is not only to focus on the power of the prominent promise in the transformation but to share the prevailing themes of struggles and victories from my life. Even though my struggles left me raw, I did not remain in this state. Naturally, life plays havoc with everything that is ordered and predicable. Draw fresh air in and get ripe with adventure to precariously brave every pesky intrigue.

Life took me on a journey that I did not want to buy a ticket for, and this can normally rob away the joy in your life. However, I tapped into my radar of resilience and found hope that prevailed. My journey shaped me – harshly but strategically, I love who I am – scars and all. In my lower dimension and higher element of life as it unravelled, I discerned that it is not about getting on track but instead about creating or finding the next path that brings joy, contentment, and peace with all the remnants that ruin the so-called mapped out myths of how life should pan out. This profound realisation stemmed from witnessing that not all the characters on this life stage have the same script in hand. There is absolutely no predictability how anyone will behave or how life unfolds. The best armour anyone can have is the ability to adapt and transform. Wherever you may be in your life right now, rest assured you have room for improvement. Pick this book up to change your life for the best and define your fulfilment.

One evening, as a young adult living in New Zealand, I returned home from a day's work. I flicked on the news and started preparing dinner with great gusto only to stop in my tracks as I listened to what made the top headline on the news. *'Kids in a parked school bus had to get trauma counselling.'* The parked bus had rolled a few meters. I felt sorry for those kids' harrowing experience. Instantly, a sliver of memory glimmered and opened the floodgates to my personal experience as a ten year old child. Most would attest to the fact that life in a developing country like South Africa is not the average walk-in-the-park life. I recalled a lunch break at school that was surreptitiously peculiar and unusual. I did not notice any of my cousins on the playground (and I had hundreds of them). I shrugged it off as a figment of my over analytical imagination.

Class was now in session and my teacher was fashionably late. He was a dark-skinned Indian, yet he looked contrastingly pale, as if he had just seen a ghost. He informed us that two thirteen year old boys from our school had been gruesomely murdered. He began to relate the explicit details... one boy was beheaded and the other had his eyes gouged out and genitals cut off. Their body parts had been placed in a bag and left in the sugarcane field near the boys' home. Police were now looking for the rest of their remains.

This news knocked the breath out of me, and I was already gasping when the teacher mentioned the names of the two boys. I was now in deep shock. They were my first cousins, my mum's nephews. I understood then why I did not see my cousins in the playground that lunch break. They were definitely there in the morning break. My relative had fetched all my cousins that lived in the vicinity of this catastrophe but had clearly forgotten about me, since I lived in a different suburb. I had to literally scrape up courage to leave the classroom when school concluded. I was upset that the teacher had so eagerly and recklessly shared the gruesome details of the crime with his students only to abandon them to callously process the horrifying truth by themselves. Even on a day such as this one, the school was simply expecting the children to walk home alone.

I had to now walk six kilometres home, by myself. It was the most terrifying journey of my life. I thought about the last time I saw my cousins, the last encounter with them when they had been happy, and then the reality of thinking of their final moments. Tears streamed down my face, and I cried like a little girl – oh wait! I was a little girl. I was poignantly aware that the only person I could depend on was me, myself and I. I have come a long way from when I was ten but through all the roles I have taken on in my adult life – sister, daughter, sister in Christ, wife, friend, church leader, sister-in-law, professional colleague, aunty, bestie and godmother – I've experienced so many life changing events that have all reinforced this stark reality. I can only depend on me, myself and I.

That being said, my intrepid voyage with the progression of vast time enabled me to glean that I don't have to be solely dependent on me, myself and I. The cycles afforded me a tribe of people whom I grew to trust, love, and depend on. Rest assured they have my back. God sent people from all walks of life to help me at pivotal points when I least expected it and that has made all the difference in my destiny. It is God-incidence, not coincidence. Rejection and abandonment bite and leave lifelong bruises. With this, I grew a sense of belonging. God showed me His love in tangible and profound ways, so that I knew without a shadow of a doubt that He had me in the palm of His hand. He sent people to hold my hand in the storm.

This testimony of my life probes into some of these encounters. Most importantly, it is a chronicle of choices and what I've gleaned from them. I share my journey so others may reap the wonderful benefits without the same painful experiences. I put pen to paper to intrinsically motivate you to become the best version of yourself, to dive headfirst into your challenges, to introspect on your daily walk and to empower you to keep going no matter how disheartening your predicament is. No life is a linear equation, so take heart to find solace and solution to your personal pain right here in these pages. My tears and grace will give you strength to find your own resolve.

Most of the time when we are experiencing catastrophe, the well that we drink from makes us more dehydrated and exhausted, leaving us with no strength to carry on and no hope for a better outcome. This creates a perpetual cycle of despair. This book will steer you to dig deeper to find a better source to drink from and nourish your soul in a way that really matters. It will encourage you in profound ways to master the art of overcoming hurdles. Victory is always part of the equation; setbacks are just learning curves to take you higher.

I have four siblings: two sisters and two brothers, and I am the youngest. My brothers were typical lads growing up, playing male games such as marbles, darts, tops, yoyo and the indigenous card game called *Thunee*. They were passionate about always winning, as kids normally are inclined. Often, in sheer desperation to win the battle, they would pull me in as an unsuspecting guinea pig to practise their skills with.

Being younger and a female, I had no aptitude for these games. Sadly, dashing their egos, I became the competition, causing them to practise with each other to take me down. This gave me insight at a very young age that we can all teach ourselves new skills, no matter how foreign they may be, and we most definitely can excel at them. Spiralling up is giving ourselves the opportunity to try new things. Consider yourself sensationally charged to learn, especially when it is an unfair plot that lands in your life.

This book is my journey of life mostly in chronological order with piles of experience captured in twelve chapters. It has a wealth of knowledge netted in the sections captioned 'my journey gleans.' This book is gorgeously punctuated with photographs to afford the reader a more vivid experience. The format of all highlighted text denotes inclusions from another source. Part two encompasses the tools that I custom designed to aid transformation in every facet of life. I have curated and developed diagrams from my personal growth to illustrate my point in a crystal clear and jargon free manner, so you can glean, grow and glow from these powerful illustrations. I wrote this book in ten days during COVID-19 lockdown to offer the community and humanity a ray of hope.

As you meander to the self-help transformation tools, I beseech you to persevere with completion of this exercise – just as life has no quick fix; transformation lacks a flick-switch approach as well. Investing in a better version of yourself will take time but pay you rich dividends as well. You may deem some aspects of this book irrelevant to you, but I encourage you to read them nonetheless as some pearls of wisdom may leap out at you and enhance your personal growth in a profound way. We can live life through many filters; as you read this book, you can glean some of my filters. Our heart starts an unhealthy pounding when we have no compass, filters, or even-minded vision.

When you are between a rock and a hard place, do you stagnate or adapt, or both? When you transition to the next realm, what will be your exit signature? Perhaps just a bouquet of red roses on your grave? But don't you want more? The line that we only live once is a myth – the correct outlook is we die once, and we live **EVERY DAY**. Make each day, hour, and second count. Read on to ignite your passion of hope as you embark on designing a new you and soaring to new levels.

'Valour is stability, not of legs and arms but of courage and the soul.' Michel de Montaigne

Part One

My Voyage

Chapter One

Resilience

Protection in a Catastrophe – NOT

In the midst of Christmas 1996 cheer, a group of workers next door to me in Tugela, South Africa, were murdered. They were sabotaged on the Mandeni steel bridge. Premeditated and maliciously massacred.

February rolled on and I was at work, my first ever job. A well paid civil servant! It was a Friday afternoon, and my cousin rang me to confirm that he would drop in at work to fetch me and we would kick start the weekend vibes at the movies. The yard at work was full of displaced locals who were affected by flooding in Tugela village. These were poor indigenous people living in shacks, their homes now under water. With nowhere to go, they sought refuge on higher ground.

The flood victims were sprawled across the yard with their meagre assets – nothing more than a few plastic bags of dirty belongings. The saturated African sun seemed to offer all the relief they desired from the rain that finally abated after many days. The undertone of poverty was rife and tangible. They stood to a lengthy pedigree of inflictions passed down generations with no real halt to the curse. The indigenous society was gradually being cast off by piecemeal, strategic development as if the regime considered these people unimportant in the apartheid rhetoric. Even though apartheid ended by legislation; the strong trace of the regime had and still has long lasting effects. The trials of deficiency and disparity remain unaddressed in South Africa to date. The race had steadily and systematically been rejected from their mother land in so many profound ways. Hope diminished if they ever had hope...now that their homes were eroded by the natural flood.

The building where I worked belonged to the local government, so people housed themselves wherever they could: on the balcony, on the side street, in the car park or in the local clinic. Kids were crying all day. Nothing but despair reigned as I made my plans for the coming weekend. My heart felt heavy for these people. I helped by giving them fresh water all day and distributing milk and food hampers to the kids. A well dressed teenage boy sat on the external bin all day looking rather disillusioned with life – an undercurrent that contradicted everyday life in an unfathomable style.

My male cousin, many years older than I pulled in excited to fetch me and leave the working week behind. I worked in the health department in the morning and in administration in the afternoon. I locked up the administration office and began walking with my cousin to my morning office to drop off my radio and say goodbye to my colleagues. Even in my wildest dreams I could not have predicted what would unfold. The teenage boy who had been sitting on the bin all day approached us. I was not fazed, as I assumed he wanted to bum a cigarette from my cousin. Next thing he pulled out a gun and stuck it into my side, demanding me to go back to the office to open up the Strong room and hand over all the cash.

We both walked back to the administration office then. Keep in mind this was peak daylight and literally hundreds of people were in the yard, including guys that work for the same government organisation as I looked at them, trying to communicate the unspoken by the sheer distress painted on my face. No one moved to run for help. Ignoring my pleading eyes, they placidly continued their mundane tasks. I was shaking with shock and threw my handbag to my cousin to grab the keys and open the door. The boy then put the gun to my head and said, 'You open the door 'coz you know how.'

Slowly opening the office door, my cousin and I stepped inside. The gunman stood outside, screaming at me to open the Strong room. Thinking of the workers killed on the steel bridge a few months before, I wondered if that was also my fate. As this guy was not wearing a mask, I could identify him and so he would not let me live! I could see myself in a coffin and my family directing my funeral. This vision flashed vividly in my mind, as if I were having an out of body experience. I started to unlock the door of the Strong room, just waiting to turn the megastrong latch open with all the strength I could muster.

I wondered yet again, why did my colleagues from next door not do any James Bond moves to rescue me? I was still standing at the entrance of my office when I noticed an older flood victim who was seeking refuge in the yard had gone into the clinic to alert them of my plight. As my cousin was with me, they found it hard to believe I was being robbed at gunpoint. They were all outside trying to gain a million dollar look at what was going on. My mind went into overdrive again. Once he gets the money, he will shoot us both, I thought. In the meantime, back at the ranch (aka my office), my cousin ducked behind the bullet proof glass and then hid under the cubicle behind a stone wall.

I made the instant decision not to go out without a fight. I caught the enquiring eye of my colleague from across the yard, and I screamed with all the voice I could rally, 'CALL THE POLICE!' The gunman turned to them waving the gun in the air, screaming, 'No police.' They all got super charged and ran into the building. I now plugged the office door shut but could not lock it as the key was unreachable in the Strong room. I was standing behind a wooden door that could not protect me against bullets. I was holding the doorknob shut with all the strength I could gather to prevent the gunman from opening it. My cousin told me, 'Come, and hide here.' My awareness went in overdrive again as it struck me that my older male cousin was crouched behind a bulletproof glass and stone wall, whereas I, a defenceless young woman, was clutching at this door latch to keep the gunman at bay.

I survived the ordeal, but life never trickled back to normal. Living in a small country town meant I was acutely aware that anyone could find my home and place a gun at my head and demand I hand over the office keys in my handbag. Once again, I was intensely conscious this is not a country that values me, and I did not want to get comfortable with adding worth to this land. My immigration was now a certainty.

My Journey Gleans

On that day I learned many things. When catastrophe befalls your loved ones and strangers fail to shield you in a crises. People you work with and have expectations of in real time of need will look the other way and choose to not get their hands dirty by trying to save your life. I acutely concluded that I can only depend on me, myself and I.

This incident was my wakeup call that I could not carve out a life for myself in South Africa. I embarked on a journey to relocate to New Zealand and discover the vicissitudes of life. Unknown to me, this traumatic event set the benchmark for a sense of immunity to all future curve balls life planned to hurl at me. Oh boy, some of those curve balls left me spinning, some left me under a rock for a decade and some I am still grappling with.

The key is to trudge on no matter how difficult life gets. The seasons most definitely change. Some days I could not find *fine* even with binoculars. Tell your heart to keep beating and stand strong, and eventually you will bounce back to see colour in the world.

Jeremiah 12:5 – If you have raced with men on foot and they have worn you out, how can you compete with horses? If you stumble in safe country, how will you manage in the thickets by the Jordan?

As I grew older and richer in experience with more painful lessons stashed under my belt, I understood what this scripture really meant to me. As a child I did not start in a 'safe country.' The thickets of the Jordan were thrust upon me as a child. I moved to New Zealand at the age of twenty two, a foreign country with absolutely no family. Yes indeed, bring forth the perils of the thickets by the Jordan, let's see what you got and the grit I am comprised of. I had been subconsciously preparing for a foreign land void of loved ones long before I even knew I was going to leave the country of my birth.

A few weeks before my immigration, my mum and dad were sitting on the porch having casual banter with my neighbours, siblings and extended family – a spot we often congregated at and shared life stories, laughs and so much more. Both my parents began crying when the topic of my departure surfaced. I exclaimed, 'I am just moving to another country, I am not dying.' Later I realised why my parents cried, and then I cried. Nothing ever goes back to the way things used to be, so consciously cherish the time you have with people who give you the opportunity to love and create memories.

'Strength does not come from physical capacity. It comes from an indomitable will.' Mahatma Gandhi

Relentless Roar to SOAR

With a qualification from Auckland University in 2000, New Zealand gave me zeal. I had blissful optimism of having a successful future. It was the usual dreaded commute to the city, to a pharmacy where I was due to embark on my all important practical assessment and then sign on the dotted line for an internship, provided I passed the practical examination. The night before, while I cleaned up after dinner, I got my head in the zone to prepare for my practical examination and asked my significant other to ensure the car had enough fuel as we would have no time in the morning for this errand. His ego was bigger than the room and he hated being told twice. We did not even reach the freeway before the low petrol light came on. My blood pressure naturally escalated, and we exchanged heated words.

Back in South Africa, service stations had been manned by underprivileged teenagers who could not afford to attend school and instead tried hard to make a buck. They provided a set of services: check the tyres, clean the windscreen, and fuel the car. So in essence the driver never left the car. We would tip them for their assistance and in return they earned a livelihood. As a result, I never had any experience doing this by myself.

Mr. Macho knew precisely how important this day was to me and how necessary that I present myself on time. So he pulled over to the side of the road and exclaimed he was catching a bus home and I could take the car myself. Here I was in a new country, no real driving experience there, I had never ever filled petrol at a New Zealand service station, parking in the city was premium and I had no clue where to park. Looking at the rear view-mirror, I saw him standing by the back of the car expectantly waiting for me to grovel at him and beg him to drive me to the city to this all important milestone.

Time was scarce and slipping away fast, so I decided to focus on my practical exam. This was well before the days of a smart phone so there was no Google Maps to the rescue. The thread of his behaviour was woven with contempt and he probably thought I would plummet flat on my face and perish in a foreign country. He was as predictable as a Bollywood movie. I hopped in the driver's seat with sweaty hands, thinking, I was born alone and would die alone and the only person I could depend on is me, myself and I. I passed the exam and served a successful internship with a pat on the back that I had accomplished something with my own grit and wit.

Arguments with him grew more frequent after that and they eventually escalated to violence. One day I was in bed and he climbed on the mattress and kicked me numerous times with his steelcapped boots. I cried and tried hard to develop selective amnesia. Many hours later a mutual friend rang and guessed from the onset that something was amiss. She enquired what was wrong. I briefly mentioned what had happened and she said, 'Why don't you call the police?' I hung up and called the police. My face and body was blue and purple, crusted blood coagulating on my clothes and skin. I was still in shock, pain, trauma and disbelief.

The police arrived and took numerous pictures. They prepared a statement of the precise events. Mr. Macho eventually returned home, and the police asked if he was responsible for the acts of violence inflicted upon me. They arrested him. Three days later he was released but life was never the same. He dared not get violent again, but it was abuse on a whole new level. He knew I hated smoking, so he would deliberately light up in our home and pointedly blow the smoke on my face. He worked four days on and four days off, and on his off days while I was at work in Auckland, he would disappear to Palmerston North to hang out with his sister without the courtesy of letting me know.

According to New Zealand legislation, when the police is summoned to a domestic violence incident, the case is owned by the state. It is mandatory to present at court. This was implemented as the net result of numerous deaths during domestic violence. Hence, I was scheduled to appear in court to testify against him. He did not want the matter to go to court. He begged me to liaise with the police to drop the charges. The police informed me of the mandatory legislation and the fact that it will go to court. They also advised that by law the court cannot make a wife testify against her husband. So the onus was upon me to act. Twenty four years young, farm fresh and with a pliable heart full of kindness, I did the noble deed and forgave him. I turned the other cheek, and he was not subpoenaed to court. Phew!

The day of reckoning finally arrived. I had no idea that vindication was on its way. The pair of us had applied for New Zealand citizenship, so on the day of our citizenship meeting we arrived at the stipulated office. I had my grilling session first, followed by a pleasant gesture of welcome to New Zealand as my application was approved. Mr. Macho's turn and the officer informed him that given his history of violence his application was denied.

Oh my word, this was a day to celebrate as this girl from the fragment of Tugela had just got awarded citizenship in New Zealand. But he made my life beyond miserable. He was anger personified, bitter that I received citizenship and he did not. He kept yelling that we were in this together and given the fact he had been denied citizenship I should also reject mine. He said I should wait to celebrate with him, not celebrate by myself. The fiascos continued and I then decided to move to Australia.

My Journey Gleans

Don't ever let another person abuse you in any way, shape or form. Refrain from feeling sorry for the abuser as this is not love. Love is a verb. Love acts as love is. Expecting you to look the other way when they break the law is not acceptable either. Rise up. Shake off the pain and trauma. Wash off the crusted blood. Trade your sorrows for a brand-new day – only you can decide when that new day will come. Only you can decide how tight your cord to the past will be and how long it will last. Rise up and be the phoenix that you are meant to be.

Romans 8:31 – What then shall we say in response to these things? If God is for us who can be against us?

Protection on my life and God's ability to vindicate even when I was so young and forgiving. No abuser can intimidate me! Beg me to change what the law dictates and truly perceive to be the victor. We always have the victory. Know your worth, never settle for less than you are destined for and NEVER ever tolerate someone who disrespects you.

I had to wipe off the tears and empower myself to live my best life. We all deserve to be respected, loved and cherished. I first enjoyed the rush of relaxation when this wisdom was engraved in my heart. Maturity begins with the acceptance of responsibility. I got buck wild about my duty. Love is a verb; it is who we bring into the relationship equilibrium – our baggage and energy included. Love does not self-destruct; we congest it with hostile disputes and erode it with hollow assurances. Blessed are those that keep love thriving particularly when the seas of life turn rough. Walt Disney proclaimed, 'All our dreams can come true, if we have the courage to pursue them.' The fundamental essence here is to really distil your heart and know what your dream is. How much do you value yourself?

I know women who stayed in a relationship when they were cheated on and disrespected because their dream centred on what society would say, because they enjoyed the man providing for their needs and the money he contributed to the equation. Self-worth is not a myth, and an abusive relationship will make you question your value. When we fail to recognise our own substance, we let others define us in accordance with their finite perceptions. Therefore, tap into understanding yourself, enrich your acceptance, boost your self-love, and recognise your self-worth. This is the only dream worth living as a reality. It is a pretence to assume we are living our dreams when our individuality is in a cage. Surround yourself with people who make you happy, folks who reliably care about you. They are the ones that are worthy of custody in your life.

Take all the time you need to dabble out your destiny and be intentional about the path you are sculpting. Do not flog yourself over misfortunes; hold your head up even when you are beaten and bleeding – seasons change, make the shift to facilitate it. Disparaging moments do not define and confine us. Do not get stuck in a life where you feel uncelebrated constantly. You cannot restore and heal in the same environment that made you ill. It is difficult to heal with the same people and atmosphere that triggered your trauma, sorrow and agony. Understand the magnitude of your pain and create a healthy distance to ignite the healing process. Allow yourself the capacity and freedom to speak, to vent your frustration, without anyone telling you how you should feel, what you ought to do and inflict their box of cures on you. Find your own healing path.

'I can be changed by what happens to me. But I refuse to be reduced by it.' Maya Angelou

Essence of FAITH

One day in Auckland I was on the quest for inner peace and found myself in a Buddhist gathering. I met a lady from India who had recently moved to New Zealand and was trying to find her feet. She needed a place to stay, so I offered her my spare bedroom for a few months. When I told her I was relocating to Australia and knew no one there, she gave me a phone number of a friend in Melbourne and said, 'If you get stuck, call John.'

Fast forward a few months and I was a bag of bones thrown unceremoniously into work at The Alfred Hospital in Melbourne, Australia, in 2001. Catching the refreshingly new tram to and from work in the bustling city with people addicted to the rat race, the climate felt significantly divergent to the South African land I was accustomed to. I was almost invisible in this new landscape and completely cut away from anything familiar. If you need a hint why life felt like sheer existence; it is because the fairy tale wedding and immigration to a new country did not pan out as the script my mind had conjured up. I was in an unfamiliar country living a different reality void of any real human connection.

It took me in excess of two hours to consume half a glass of milk and a banana. My family telephone conversations were brief, light hearted and superficial. I painted a picture of getting on with life, when in reality I was like a water droplet at the edge of a leaf ready to disappear into the expanse. My family painted a pretty picture for me as well. My dad was diagnosed with terminal colon cancer, but they made the executive decision to shield me from the diagnosis. They assumed I could not manage another thing on my plate while living so far from my nucleus and natural habitat.

I could barely assemble enough strength to get out of bed on most mornings. Once, while having a shower, I was so weak I just collapsed to the floor. I cried from the bottom of my heart, 'God, I cannot do this, I have no strength to go on.' I had reached rock bottom and was now figuratively drowning, I was sinking, and I cried to God and he heard me. A voice said from the passage **'I will not leave you, I will not let you die, and I will save you. TRUST IN ME.'**

I got up with a jolt to see who was there: no one and I was still alone. But the voice had been clear as a bell. I felt a sense of equanimity and composure, and I knew that was a real encounter with God! So I said, 'Ok

God, let's see how we are going to navigate out of these waters.' Then I fell asleep, only to be awoken with a loud knock on the door and a man screaming my name. 'Wow, God are you that quick?' I remember myself thinking.

It was John, my friend's friend. I had called him a few days earlier to introduce myself. He had asked where I lived and exclaimed it was just a block away from his place. He was now at my doorstep. He took one look at me and knew I was not in good shape. He helped me get my appetite back and took me to apply for a Medicare card, gave me company until I felt human again.

I was bouncing back to life when I got a rude awakening one morning as the world awoke to 11 September 2001. I could not fathom what was going on in this world. My pain was real, yet it seemed to vanish in the mass of this reality.

Psalm 120:1 - In my trouble I cried to the Lord and he answered me.

My Journey Gleans

This scripture revealed to me that even though I was not yet a Christian, God had found me in the depths of my despair. He made Himself known to me when the world was in a mess. He took the time to orchestrate my healing and recovery. He lifted me out from my wretched position so I could gain clarity of vision and a hope of my future. He made me a warrior, not only fit for battle but also empowered to be an overcomer in His authority. He used every situation in my life to both draw me close and keep me closer.

The fundamental lesson I learned is that healing is a process. The journey may be painful, and most people hate the process but there is no quick fix. If you desire long lasting deeper enhancement to your life, then a quick fix will not suffice, and neither will it pay dividends in the long term. Struggles are necessary to create a strident character.

A caterpillar forced out of its cocoon prematurely will die, but when the natural process of metamorphosis occurs a beautiful butterfly emerges. We need to go through the same process of transformation. It gives us perspective so we can thrive like the butterfly rather than endure the plight of the caterpillar. My destiny is certain and so is reaching it. I thank you, Lord, for my salvation. You suffice and you are to be revelled in.

'Success doesn't come to you, you go to it.' Marva Collins

Chapter Two

Vicissitudes of Life

Untainted Intrigues

Early November 2002, the real picture hit the surface with a vengeance while I was living in Melbourne, Australia. My dad was admitted to the hospital and my family told me he had less than two months to live. Overwhelmed with shock, I resigned from my job and decided to go home to South Africa for a visit.

On my way to South Africa, I first made a pit stop at New Zealand for a few days as the knocks of life had left me a tad frazzled. I needed to refuel my emotional tank before I embarked on a journey to say my final goodbye at his funeral. My heart was heavy about going home in such circumstances and with such raw emotions. I shared this with a close friend. I poured out the abundance of my heart. We prayed for my dad's healing and recovery from cancer. I believed in his healing one hundred percent, but I doubted that God could take away the gigantic pain I was feeling.

I accompanied my friend to church one Sunday while in Auckland. The message spoke to me and I responded to the altar call. I prayed the Sinners Prayer:

Lord Jesus, for too long I have kept you out of my life. I know that I am a sinner and that I cannot save myself. No longer will I KEEP THE DOOR closed when I hear you knocking. By faith I gratefully receive your gift of salvation. I am ready to trust you as my Lord and Saviour. Thank you, Lord Jesus, for coming to earth. I believe you are the Son of God who died on the cross for my sins and rose from the dead on the third day. Thank you for bearing my sins and giving me the gift of eternal life. I believe your words are true. Come into my heart, Lord Jesus, and be my Saviour.

Amen.

I received a new believer's starter kit which included many things, chief among them a pocket-sized Bible. I had a new lease on life and was excited by the milestone.

Romans 8:28 - And we know that in all things God works for the good of those who love Him AND have been called according to His purpose.

My Journey Gleans

This scripture especially resonated with me. My natural birth date is 8:28. It was an anchor for me – springing forth a new spiritual life.

The same wind blows on us all, winds of disaster, opportunity, change and zeal. However, it is not the blowing wind that determines our direction in life but the fundamental task of setting our sails. To achieve this, I focused on a vision and enhanced my spiritual growth. This required cognitive behavioural change and an active desire to change.

'What we fear doing the most is usually what we need to do.' Timothy Ferriss

Unflinching Results

When I arrived in South Africa in 2002, my dad had acute Alzheimer's and he initially did not recognise me. Every day that I went to the hospital, he acted like he was seeing me for the first time. He asked the same questions about my flight and time of arrival. It broke my heart seeing him in this state. I wished I had come home earlier but there was no wishing well to turn back time.

My sister had pre-booked a Christian conference for herself and my mum, but she had a date clash at the last minute and asked me to take her place. I had not shared my newfound faith with anyone in my family. The guest speaker at the conference was great. During the intermission, I was sitting underneath the shade of a huge tree, deep in wondering how my dad was doing and how my mum was coping with all this. I began to weep. I shared the burden of my heart with God, asking Him to heal my dad and my broken heart.

The conference resumed. The preacher looked at me squarely in the eye and said, 'God has granted you the miracle you cried for.' I was still a doubting Thomas, and my mental response was, 'Show me.' Working in the health industry, I was abreast with industry standards, protocols and mandatory standard operating processes. Still, nothing could have prepared me for this. When I walked straight to my dad's hospital ward bed, I found him unconscious and lying in a pool of blood that was slowly congealing. He had a drip inserted incorrectly and his blood was back flowing out of his body. He had been unsupervised for so long that no clinical staff could note the malfunction.

I was shocked and upset that clinical care was so deplorable, and malpractice was so rife. My aunt and uncle were present, and I exclaimed that I would be pursuing this further. My uncle was vexed with my first-world zeal and told me to calm down. He warned me that the staff would intentionally inject the patient and their family with HIV if I reacted. I was mortified.

I waited for what seemed an eternity for my dad to regain consciousness. He opened his eyes, looked at me and smiled. I moved closer, my hand clutching at the pocket Bible in my handbag. I asked him if I could pray for him and he nodded. My prayer had more tears than words, and I concluded with the Bible in his hands and my hands over his.

Decades ago, I had witnessed my dad spin into a frantic state and mislay the plot when my sister converted from Hinduism to Christianity. I knew without a shadow of a doubt this was a sensitive subject and I needed to proceed with utter caution. Yet peace prevailed in my heart. Tears streamed down my cheeks and he broke the silence, saying, 'I believe in the Bible.' My heart jolted with sheer delight and I said, 'Great! You can keep this to read.' He assured me he would.

I left the hospital and when I arrived at my aunt's house, I cried my heart out. Stillness hung in the air thicker than nectar oozing from a honeycomb, life and death seemed grey. Something had happened that I could not explain. My mum began to cry too when she saw me crying, and we both sobbed together until an utter peace prevailed, surpassing all understanding. Peace that had been absent in my life for a long time. I knew without a shadow of doubt that my dad was headed for a better place and this calmed my soul.

I went to spend the night at my cousin's home. I was awake at the crack of dawn just lazing in bed and chatting with my niece. When I eventually got up and went out, my cousin informed me that my dad had passed away during the night. They were arranging the funeral for the next day. I still had peace.

Acts 16:31 – Believe in the Lord Jesus and you will be saved, you and your household.

My Journey Gleans

The prodigal daughter returned to a milestone fearing an imminent demise. Nonetheless, in the eye of the storm I found peace. The words at the conference finally made sense. I got the miracle of healing, while my dad got something far greater than healing from cancer. He was blessed with salvation, which is eternal life.

To date, I have travelled the globe, attained accolades, been lavished with kudos and I lack no good thing. If I have to pick one thing to bless my loved ones with, it is the joy of salvation. The reassurance of reunifying with their soul for eternity outweighs any material gift. Just because I did not see a way, doesn't mean that God did not have a way.

'Be a rainbow in someone else's cloud.' Maya Angelou

Growing Deeper Affiliations

I moved back to New Zealand from Australia in 2003. I was attending Mount Zion Church and Pastor Elaine was preaching a sermon entitled, 'Who will fend for you when you cannot defend yourself.' She shared a memory from her recent holiday experience in America. They had witnessed a riot from a hotel window. People were bashing each other. A guy was knocked unconscious in the middle of the street and lay precisely where he landed on the ground. People just stepped over him with no regard for his welfare.

This brings the story of the Good Samaritan to attention. So Pastor Elaine watched on intently to see who would rise up and fend for him. When mayhem arrives, who will fend for you? Is it your loved ones? They may not be around! We need to trust God to bring the Good Samaritan to us. After a few minutes of people trampling a fellow human for their own cause to riot, a man stopped in his tracks. He carried the prone man to the side and sat with him until an ambulance arrived, then he walked away. She concluded by asking us, 'Who will fend for you when you cannot?'

My friend Jo was sitting beside me at church, heavily pregnant. She turned to me and said, 'I have many friends and while I will not put my neck on the block for most, I will definitely put my neck on the block for you.' I just looked at her speechless. My mind drifted to the words of my husband – now Mr. Ex who portrayed an image to make Jesus look like he slacked on creating the apt LinkedIn profile. I had a vivid recall of when Mr. Ex had told me to not trust people as they would let me down when I needed them. He told me to only trust God, a groom that was not really so groomed once hindsight met reality. My friend repeated, 'I mean it, I will put my neck on the block for you.' I still had no reaction.

Two weeks later, Jo died during childbirth. I am the godmother of her daughter, Joycinda. Many people told me these would be big shoes to fill – implying that I need to step up to support a motherless child. Still in deep shock and trying to reconcile the sequence of events, I felt traumatised that I had not shared my heart with Jo when she was alive. Hindsight makes the picture clear as crystal.

Jo was a wonderful person. I regret to this day that I never told her just how much I loved and cherished her and how surely, I too would put my neck on the block for her. But it was too late to cry over the past. I was at her graveside saying my final goodbye and I was grateful for our season of friendship. Our sisterhood had been brief but rather deep. I learned so many life enriching things from her. She left a legacy that remains forever etched in my heart. I closed my eyes and apologised for not being the friend I should have been. I promised both Jo and God I would be the best true friend to every person God brought to my path from that day forth, that I would not wait for a better day to be a better friend. It all starts from day one.

Ecclesiastes 9:10 - Whatever you do, do well. For when you go to the grave, there will be no work or planning or knowledge or wisdom.

My Journey Gleans

This scripture was Jo's favourite, and I have grown to love and live by it. It challenges me to live a better life and be a better friend. Since then, I have met many people whom I have given my all to, and some of them have just used me as a resource centre. It hurts but I rest assured and have peace that God created me to be a giver. I am a cheerful giver and I always do my best to be a real friend. I have also made peace with having no expectations of the other party and how they behave. They are ultimately accountable to God. Aim at augmenting your life with the broader circle that moves you to think and live better. Time moves with a vengeance, so the personal vendetta is yours – feel anything but deprived when your time ends

'If we did not sometimes taste adversity, prosperity would not be so welcome.' Anne Bradstreet.

I have seen a montage of pictures in my lifetime, yet this is a picture that will forever be seared in my heart. My god daughter Joycinda clinging to the tomb stone of her mother that she never shared life with. I live my life to bring lavished hope to precious people like Joycinda, being a blessing is a small effort when someone's world is shattered. Go add some intentional love and colour to this world despite your personal pain. Society has no inkling of the weight on each person's shoulders; therefore, rather than reacting to people with a dose of sugar, spice and all the emotions in between, learn to cognitively respond with unreserved empathy.

Photograph:
New Zealand, Auckland
2013

Man With Double Standards

A couple of months after Jo's death and a few weeks away from commencing IVF, I was driving to work with Mr. Ex one morning. The radio was tuned into a Christian radio station talking about IVF. The announcer advised IVF was against Biblical beliefs and claimed the Pope had spoken against IVF. He continued by adding he had Biblical scripture to highlight this truth. Naturally, the volume was turned up in the car. Mr. Ex pulled into the driveway of his work and I began to get in the driver's seat to drive to my work. He kissed me goodbye and said, 'Right, that's it. I am not going ahead with IVF. We need to cancel this treatment.' Shocked, I tried to reason but he spoke over me. 'I am the head of this family and I say no discussion. I am not going against God's Word.' When I responded we need to confirm if it is God's Word first, his face contorted with sovereignty of his own reality.

I got to work in a huff and Googled the radio station. I then sent a message addressed to the announcer. I related the scenario of our circumstances and asked him for the precise scriptures he made reference to. I received a reply almost instantly. He did not give me any scriptures; instead, he gave me details for family counselling. I was ready to punch him. If you want to make a statement about a sensitive subject, then be ready with the core facts to back it up. After we had a conclave with our pastor about the situation, he advised that he did not think IVF was against The Word of God. So Mr. Ex confirmed he would give it a go with one caveat. No freezing of eggs, as he believed that life forms at the point of fertilisation and he was not comfortable with the freezing and discarding of life.

Scientifically, eggs that are fertilised in a dish, then transferred to a new habitat, may not like their new habitat and refuse to thrive. So in essence, we needed a few spares to have another go. But I had no say once the leader of the household had spoken with authority, acutely reminding me it is so as he is the head of the household but he certainly had no sermon stuffed down my throat about great understanding of the situation or excess fondness for my emotions. I had a positive conception on strike one, but a few weeks later I began to haemorrhage uncontrollably. My mind was struggling to align with the reality of the symptoms of my body. I shared the news with my church family. A few friends, including the men, were fasting and praying for me. In light of Jo's death during childbirth, most were praying for God's will to prevail and not my desire.

The IVF clinic scheduled an ultrasound for me a couple days later. That morning, Mr. Ex was getting routinely dressed for work when I asked, 'Are you coming to the hospital with me?' He said, 'No, I cannot afford to lose a day's pay.' I was shocked. Later that day, I drove myself to the hospital alone to tackle the ultrasound. When I looked at the black-and-white screen as the radiographer performed the scan, I was overwhelmed with grief. I knew without a shadow of doubt that I had lost the baby. She passed me the tissue box. I asked her about the results, and she said the clinic would inform me, adding gently that I could take as long as I wanted to get dressed before meeting her at reception. The IVF clinic was expecting my imminent arrival. I was consumed by distress, tears gushing down my cheeks, as I walked along the corridor and random people stared at me. I ran into a toilet cubicle and shut the door.

Was this a conscience stricken dream? When would I wake up? I could hear other people talking as my mind slowly got a grip of reality. I presented myself at the clinic where the assigned nurse greeted me and said she had just rung my husband. I sat and waited for what seemed like an eternity. She finally called me in and gave me the spiel.

I began a slow walk to the car and called Mr. Ex. I said I had just finished at the clinic and… 'I know,' he said. 'The nurse rang me with the news and asked me to come to the hospital. I could not make it.' My shock slipped into a deeper level as the pain intensified. He worked just five minutes away from the hospital that I was at. I cried uncontrollably as I pleaded to him to please come drive me (or just give me a hug or hold my hand). But he pulled out his authority hat again and said, 'Get a grip on yourself. Don't believe what the doctors say to you. Trust in God's Word and His promise to us. I cannot leave work now, so drive yourself home and be strong.'

I got home cold as a slab of ice. I curled up in my bed and slept to escape this reality of intense pain. Eventually, I got up to prepare dinner. When he finally got home, he had a shower and went straight to pray for a few hours. At dinner, all he would say was for me to stand firm on God's Word. Every time I tried to talk to him about the pain, he would shut me down.

With the progression of a few months, we tried IVF again. Halfway through the process of injections, the specialist summoned us to his office. He said, 'Your body is not responding to the highest dose of drugs and we need to cease the treatment immediately as this may be due to the fact your ovaries have stopped producing eggs. Your only option now is an egg donor or surrogacy solutions.' Mr. Ex flatout refused to even consider an egg donor or a surrogate.

The pain prevailed. Meanwhile, New Zealand was in a recession. We decided to move to Australia with me going there first to secure a job. He would remain to wrap up the sale of our home. He made arrangements for me to sign over the power of attorney to him so he could oversee the sale of our home without me having to take time off work and fly back. One of our church friends, Earl, was a Justice of the Peace, so we went over to his home to complete the legal process. I signed the power of attorney form and handed it to Mr. Ex and said, 'I've now signed everything to you.' Earl looked at me and said, 'That piece of paper means nothing. What is more important is that you are married and have God as part of your life, and He will direct all your paths.'

After two months of him in New Zealand and me living apart in Australia, it was Christmas and the house had still not been sold. We decided to temporarily rent it out so he could join me for Christmas in Brisbane, Australia. After six months of living in Australia our marriage was on the rocks of divorce.

Many years later he visited one of his sisters in New Zealand and she challenged him on a few things. He called me out of the blue and I was caught off guard. I had so much to say, but who can think of soul destroying acts at the drop of a hat? I said the thing that hurt me the most was his lack of support when I lost the baby. He said, 'You need to get over it, it was just an egg not a baby,' and hung up.

After all that fuss following the radio announcer's enlightenment, the man of the house with authority mandating me to only fertilise one egg as life starts at that point – it was a tad hypocritical to now say it is just an egg because we lost it and I should just get over it!

My Journey Gleans

I gleaned that Mr. Ex could not have such dichotomous beliefs about IVF. I was travelling through life with my rose-tinted glasses on and did not care to see the writing on the wall. He had checked out of matrimony for other reasons long before I was brutally aware of the situation. He only noticed me by the corner of his existence and loved listening to the decibels of his own voice.

I crawled under a rock and stayed there for almost a decade. But I did not stagnate. I shut my heart to love and trust, but I grew as a person. I explored the world, read books, attended seminars and conferences. I joined a book club. I attended connect groups in the church. I was discovering what makes my heart beat and what makes me happy, and I pursued that happiness. I enhanced myself for me.

Be determined to embrace all that comes into your life. Learn the lessons required in every situation and search for blessings too. If you learn the lessons the first time around, you will save time and energy. You will prevent yourself from going around the same bush again. Trials are part of the journey but never our permanent destination. Focus beyond the setbacks and see the vision, promise, goal, future, and outcome. Even if all you can manage are microscopic steps, don't stagnate, and keep going forward.

'The best teacher is your last mistake.' Unknown

Cultivate Your Circle Especially in the Difficult Seasons

Fresh off the plane in Australia in 2008, I had settled into a church in Brisbane CBD, just starting to connect and discover Australian fellowship. A few months after I started my new job in Australia, I was promoted and had to travel to Adelaide to work on a project at a public hospital. I received an email from Mr. Ex saying he had sold our home in New Zealand and was leaving. He informed me we had broken the fixed term contract with the bank and thus had to pay the bank to be released from the contract, and there was no profit from the home as it was sold below what was owed to the mortgage.

He said he was leaving the marriage, leaving me, and forbade me from contacting him again. I was shocked and heart broken. I still had another week onsite with this project. I had so many new things to grasp. My head was spinning. I needed a timeout, but I could not just pull the plug on work. I also did not want to discuss my personal issues, afraid I would be deemed unfit to perform my role. I had to remain professional and do a high paced job with no sleep while being a broken mess inside. My professional confidence reigned, and the cracks seemed concealed.

I returned home a week later. Mr. Ex had taken some assets and personal trimmings and vanished. When the bill of having our assets shipped to Australia arrived, it became painfully clear that the coins in my purse would not suffice, ouch! The sense of betrayal was oh-so-tangible.

My heart was bleeding as I dragged myself to church. After the service, I was in the lounge and a lady I had met a few times came up and spoke to me. Maureen asked how I was doing, and I burst into a gush of tears. I unloaded my troubles onto her, which gave me a sense of relief. I felt better for it. I did not know her from a bar of soap. I had no friends or support network in Australia. Maureen prayed for me, then held my hand and said, 'I will stand with you in this storm no matter how long it takes.'

The rubber hits the road when you walk the talk. This lady from church is one of distinction and integrity. I kid you not: it is incredible for her to say that to a person she did not know and follow through. God was teaching me that I did not need me, myself and I. He had appointed the right people to come walk the journey with me. She and I had many encounters of sweet fellowship, dine outs, holidays, movies, walks, laughs, cries, deep conversations, prayers, fasting, day trips...and I gleaned so much from her experience and pearls of wisdom.

One thing that still sticks to my mind like glue is an analogy that she shared with me. I was wallowing in pain and asking the why questions for the millionth time. She proceeded to tell me this:

> *Two guys were walking on the deck of a ship and the wind blew the cap off one guy's head. He did not lose his stride and just kept walking with no visible care. The other guy was anxious about the cap and ran to the side of the ship to look for it. He turned to the man and said, 'Are you not worried about your cap?' The guy responded, 'What can I do about it as I know it is in the water and I cannot retrieve the hat with ease. It is not worth diving into the water to risk my life for something that is not worth my life.'*

We need to adopt the same attitude with life situations. Don't lose peace and sleep over something you cannot change. Don't risk your precious life for something that is worth far less than your life. Whenever I feel overwhelmed, I let this sink in and I proclaim scripture over my life.

When I started my new role in Australia, another guy started work the same day - Simon. We did our orientation together. He had some health issues, so people kept him at arm's length. I was friendly towards him, so he gravitated towards me. We became close friends. I invited him to my Bible study group. He would rock up with a tall bottle of beer in his hand as the rest of us did our study. Everyone was friendly and accepted him. He cursed me every time I played worship music. For Christmas I gave him a Bible and he swore at me, telling me giving presents to someone is meaningful only when you get them something they like!

Proverbs 18:24 - There are friends who destroy each other but a real friend sticks closer than a brother.

My Journey Gleans

The concept of friendship is a strong one in Proverbs. This Proverb is rather jarring, for there are ways that a friend can be more faithful than a brother. Our era of social media promotes many superficial acquaintances who are called 'friends.' Even the most connected can be lonely. A friend is someone who is steadfast, loyal and trustworthy. I am blessed to have found these qualities and so many more in many of my friends who are closer than siblings. I do not need to depend on me, myself and I. I have real friends in South Africa, New Zealand, Brisbane, Sydney, Orange and some in heaven. I also found a best friend in my new and wonderful husband. Some people have left, confirming that I did not need them to fulfil my destiny or to soar in life. Sometimes we are led by limitations of the people we lose. This was one of the most harrowing sagas of my life and I was hurt deeply by the person that I trusted the most, yet I made real friends who anchored my soul in this storm. Random people whom I had no vows or affiliations with.

Trust your scars to find who they need to heal. Understand that people will leave your life and make allowance for it, no matter how unwilling you are to let them go. Resist the notion to fall apart every time someone leaves. When you orchestrate someone's free will, you may bind them to you, but you cannot bind their loyalty and focus.

'If you feel like you are losing everything, remember that trees lose their leaves and still stand tall and wait for better days to come.' Unknown

It is a challenge to be a yes person: to say you are going to do something and follow up on it right until the end. I did not know Maureen that well and she proved to be a yes woman. Her fine example has enhanced our friendship in so many tangible ways. Your integrity impacts lives in many untold ways. Without the integrity to follow through, your words are futile and worthless. My dear friend Maureen travelled from Brisbane to Sydney – we attended the colour conference then conquered the Sydney Harbour Bridge climb on a cold, wet and windy day. Terrified of heights but together we conquered and prevailed to tell the tale.

Photograph:
Sydney, Australia
2017

Chapter Three

Internal Fortitude

Super Saturated and Then...

Mr. Ex turned into a replica of Houdini in Australia, no matter how desperately I searched for him. It was 2009. His birthday and our wedding anniversary were approaching, and I missed him and longed for closure. I planned a holiday to India to keep me preoccupied. I wanted to escape life, escape the pain. I booked a guided tour with a small cohort. I was the only Indian in this group. At some point on the tour, I mentioned to the guide that I would like to visit a church. He contacted a friend of his in one of the towns we were due to reach.

He introduced me to a young lady, saying she is a Christian and would take me to a church. She and I proceeded on foot to a little village in North India. Not once had I ever seen squalor to this intensity even in the movies. This was the reality that people lived, and it was all they knew. The guide had earlier joked that the government employed thousands of workers to clean up the yards. He pointed us to local pigs eating the muck on the grounds. This new village that I was walking through was drenched with the sound of swines. The constant grunts were overwhelming and arduous at the same time. I had a brand new pair of hush puppies on. Once I reached the hotel that evening, I removed and discarded them directly in the bin.

The Christian lady took me to a church that was part of this couple's home. It had a mud floor and was tiny, dark, musty and sparsely furnished. They offered me a drink and I politely refused. I explained that I was visiting India and just wanted to visit a local church for prayer. They launched into prayer. The Pastor then proceeded to give me a prophetic word saying, 'God will use you to bring comfort to, heal, restore, and make dreams come true for many people.'

I felt overwhelmed with pain because these were precisely all the things I needed for myself right then. Tears gushed forth and his wife held my hand and whispered, 'God will do amazing things through you.' I took it with a grain of salt. I reached into my bag and pulled out an envelope filled with cash – my life savings – and handed it to her to use for God's work. I had lost the zeal for life and thus found no real need to have savings; it could not buy me what my soul was yearning for. I wanted to disappear from this broken world.

Night yanked the sun below the horizon, silencing the world with its absence, but my mind was not silenced. I tossed and turned that night with sleep eluding me. I eventually got up and thought of my brand new hush puppies in the bin – then it hit me like a ton of bricks. I was blessed and privileged enough to throw away a brand new pair of hush puppies, and around me were many who had never even owned a pair of shoes in their life.

I discovered that someone had already taken the shoes from the bin. I then began leaving all my clothes near the bin each day after wearing them, and they were also taken; people saw it as a blessing. This made me realise despite the pain I was feeling that I was already bringing a bedrock of hope and helping others in a way. The Word I received earlier that day became a light guiding my feet. It propelled me to not focus on my own pain but to focus on helping others. Giving others a better day and making a small difference in other lives.

I concluded the tour and returned home to Australia. Life was not void of pain from that point. I still struggled and cried. I was alone in a foreign country and I discovered who my real friends were. I had some good days and I trudged along.

I recall watching the movie *Cast Away* starring Tom Hanks. He was stranded on an island after a plane crash. After a tormenting time, he tried to find a way off the island. He built a raft. He made an imaginary friend, Wilson, by painting a face on a ball. This sense of companionship gave him hope and kept him sane in conversation even though it was monologue.

He tried to make an escape via the deep blue sea, but the wind was a force to be reckoned with and the current of the merciless sea tossed him like a rag doll. He was malnourished and exhausted both physically and mentally.

His imaginary friend, Wilson, was perched safely on this raft for the great voyage home. As Mother Nature tossed the raft about ruthlessly, Wilson came unfastened and toppled into the wild waters. Tom cried his heart out as Wilson drifted away. He was holding firm to the rope of the raft, his lifeline. He was tormented as he watched his friend Wilson drift further away.

Even in such rigorous circumstances, he had tangible hope, a raft that is his lifeline to hope, an option to live. On the other end of the spectrum, he had a 'friend' in Wilson, who is in essence a figment of his imagination, but he relates to him as a source of comfort in his darkest season, bringing him a glimmer of hope and taking him to a happy place.

Cognitively, Tom was aware Wilson could not get him home and that is the reason why he built the raft. The raft was real, though it offered no guarantees to get him to his destination safely. Yet Tom let go of the raft and gave up on his life to go after Wilson. He risked his life for something that could offer him only false comfort. So he perceives this to be the best thing in his life at that moment, and he does not want to give up on that flicker of good solace and consolation even if it is just a figment of his imagination.

Numbers 17:8 – The next day when Moses went into the tent, flowers and almonds were already growing on Aaron's stick.

My Journey Gleans

This scripture reminds me of how I felt like a dead piece of wood, and then the spirit touched me, and I sprouted to life just like this dead staff of Aaron's sprouted with almond buds when it was in the Holy presence of God. If God can make a dead piece of wood bloom, then rest assured you and I have hope too. So often in life, as we navigate difficult circumstances, we lose our ability to see logically and look at the broader picture to make informed decisions for our greater welfare. We focus on the quick fix. We want what feels right for the moment even when it does not correlate with logic and reason.

There is no instant fix in life as everything is a process. We need to give God the opportunity to work with us. Have faith that He will find a way. Faith without corresponding action is dead. Tom had faith that he could find a way home, but his corresponding action did not align to his faith. I chose to deliberately take actions that aligned with my faith to find my way out of the wilderness. Both Tom and I had a choice and so do you. Our choices constitute our therapy.

We are creatures created for connection and sweet fellowship. Trauma rewires our psyche to go into protective and reclusive mode. That is why wounded people struggle with making wholesome choices. When I reached the crossroads, I had to choose between two paths: one that led to my demise or one that led to eternal life. We all have to make choices every day. Some life choices are less dramatic than others.

Trauma changes us forever, so be kind and accepting of yourself; deliberate and plan all your healing. Prioritise your boundaries and implement your vision map to be the person you want to be. You deserve a wonderful, blessed and fulfilling life. No one is going to hand that to you on a platter; you must go out and carve it out for yourself. Remember, you are not a victim unless you wear that hat and sing that song. Isolation and depression are real struggles, and the flesh can only find the remedy as the finite mind deems, and sometimes the outcomes of the flesh are limited and off the mark.

When God is our refuge then He prevails. He knows the plans He has for us and nothing can stop them; not even our flesh acting out of pain. So it is best to be directed by God rather than try to find the answers on your own when you are sinking. We do not have to struggle through strife alone and then come to His presence. We waste time, possibilities and strength when we flounder around. We need to come into His presence just as we are, as quick as we can, so He can start the process of healing sooner rather than later. We need to remain in His presence, come hell or high water. Keep your eyes fixed on Him. Period.

I had to learn to show God my vulnerabilities even when I had tons of victories in the world. I had to take my fear and process it into courage. I had to take small steps and sear into my mind that I am not a quitter. I had no one's faith to tap into – so I had to build my own faith. I built this faith one step at a time, with one trauma and victory at a time. It is easy to run after 'Wilson' like Tom, chasing things that are not really worthy and have very little capacity to add value to our lives.

Unfortunately, there is no quick fix. God is building character in us all, and that takes a lifetime to master. Life may have derailed you, but rest assured that the master excels in restoration. There will inevitably be highs and lows, but strength, grace and enablement are distributed as required. Reaching your God-ordained position and destiny is certain if you follow the directions. Go take your territory and retain it. This is the greatest season of your life as you leap forward.

Grapes must be crushed to make wine. Diamonds are formed under prolonged pressure. Olives must be pressed to release oil. Seeds lie dormant then burst forth with life in the apt season – they grow in darkness. All of these fine products have a process, a process of refinement for creating a superior end product. When you feel crushed, under pressure, pressed and in darkness, rest assured you are in a powerful place of transcending. Trust the process to refine you.

Jesus performed His first miracle at a wedding in Cana in John 2:1-11. He turned water into wine. People do strive to be more like Him. They transform some things better than others – transforming their salary into wine with no real miraculous attributes. However, the deeper significance of this scripture is that the end product – the wine He produced from water – was far superior in quality than the wine that they ran out of. Additionally, He broke all the natural laws of time taken to percolate the wine during the all important transformation stage.

Just as wine, diamonds, olive oil, and seedlings require time to transform by changing phases, we also transform in the same fashion – but we can also transform in an instant, transcending from strength to strength when we are aligned to the right position. Therapy and transformation is a CHOICE, you can go through the normal process of shedding each layer at a time which has its merits, or you can align yourself to be a Jesus miracle and get the instant transformation of a superior product that is not on any other shelf – your resolve.

My life is now pregnant with meaning; God in the equation is sacred. When you lose something that is more important than money, you mislay hope and that is a dangerous place to camp at. Do not let others judge you, especially when they have never known this season. They may not handle the situation with the same amount of finesse as you. Talk is cheap, our real pluck is revealed in mayhem. Miracles occur when your back is up against the wall, when you reach the end of yourself and are at the cusp of the coup de grace, then God lifts you up. A miracle does not happen when your life is dandy. If you are blessed to never experience perils that permeate your soul, then stay blessed and more importantly cast no judgement onto others.

'If you hear a voice within you say you cannot paint, then by all means paint and that voice will be silenced.' Vincent Van Gogh

Purview of the Cosmos

The brutal ending of a marriage with no communication or closure cuts deep! My wedding ring was still stuck on my finger and I could not remove it. I was still signing my married name. People still asked me where my husband was. It was 2010 and even the Australian society probed.

My friend Maureen and I decided to hold a day of fasting and prayer to seek God to help direct my path. In essence I needed to know if I should keep praying for restoration with Mr. Ex or close that chapter and move on with life. While we were fasting, we both felt the strong presence of God. The words we read seemed to speak to us as if they were literally alive. I was distressed as I was hoping for restoration. Maureen read to me and the scriptures were like a balm to my soul, and I then read my daily devotional reading for the day and found all the answers I needed – the writing was on the wall. She said God would reveal everything that was done in darkness to you. We concluded with a nice lunch out and said goodbye.

Later that day I received a phone call from another friend who confirmed that Mr. Ex had moved on and was pursuing another relationship. My heart sank. I had worked so hard to feel emotionally better after my trip to India, but this process was breaking me. Hindsight confirmed God was preparing me for greater destinations and blessings.

I called Maureen and relayed what I had discovered. She said, 'Thank you, Lord, for answering our prayers so quickly. This is what we prayed for, for God to show us where Mr. Ex was at and what you should do.' The sign of the times stood potent. Man speaks even in the form of Houdini – it is communication. The communication is always there; however cryptic the message, or we choose to stick our heads in the sand to avoid reality. Schedule your passion to reign and get real to discern the communication even if it is ineffective or you have to decipher it. Otherwise, it will manifest as an insidious demise.

God does not always speak so clearly, and this was the confirmation I needed. I made an appointment with a jeweller to cut the ring off my finger. I had to remind myself to not be ashamed and focus on how far I had come, to count my blessings rather than my setbacks. No one has immunity in life. No one can protect us from drama and trauma. We cannot live in denial and we have to actively trade our pains for joy. We have to go through a process to heal, to live again, to laugh again, and to smile again. To get back on the horse, love and live with more intent. Only you can make that choice.

I had no family around, but I had a new network of friends. There were days when I felt like I just wanted to stay in bed and have a cup of tea brought to me or someone to hand me tissues when I cried, or make me chicken soup when I was sick, or do the laundry. The reality was that I had no one. I had to depend on me, myself and I. Even when I felt like I could not go to work to contend with the corporate jungle another day, I had no choice. The process was breaking me. But there amidst the anguish, I started to feel human again. The process was making me whole again.

Eager for a distraction from the emptiness within, I decided to move to Sydney for work, for a project based in Singapore. When I broke the news at work, my colleague Simon was disappointed. Apparently, I was the only real friend he had. For the first time he had experienced acceptance and fellowship without any judgement, and he did not want to lose it. He asked me not to move and stay in Brisbane. I did not realise the impact of our friendship.

Simon asked me for a worship compact disk, saying he had come to enjoy the music and would miss it. I used to give him a lift to and from work, and he would complain bitterly about my choice in music, to avoid listening to my music he had bought me a few compact disks by mainstream artists. And now he wanted me to leave my music with him, this coming from a guy who swore at me for buying him a Bible. The seed was planted, and I flew to Sydney. Before I departed, I met with Maureen for lunch. We sat for a while and had a bit of a yarn and she prayed, then we hugged. As I was leaving, she said, 'Maybe you will meet your soul mate in Sydney.'

Luke 8:17 - For there is nothing hidden that will not be disclosed and nothing concealed that will not be known or brought into the open.

My Journey Gleans

This scripture put my feet upon a rock. When I had so many question marks in my head, uncertain and stuck in limbo, these words became tangible in my life. I had no answers and no closure, so I turned to God to bring forth the truth and take me down a discovery lane. I gleaned so much about Mr. Ex that I was unaware of. I could now make informed decisions. The cards might be on the table, but it was still a process to come to terms with.

I had to work with the pain layer by layer. I also decided to discover myself, to shed the pain and brokenness, to uncover what makes me smile. I found the butterfly within me and I was finally free to fly anywhere I wanted. Only we can ultimately control our lives, so refrain from over complicating it. Listen to your inner voice to establish what brings you peace and the compass of confidence, then go chase after it and give yourself more grace than usual.

Be steered by the Holy Spirit and not by your circumstances and be fiercely independent to start from a new canvass if you need to. We all have strength; what sets us apart is perseverance and favour. We master our lives by mastering our perception. Life is not what happens to us but how we manage what happens. Find a way to rise above and not remain stuck. Your foremost priority and resolute responsibility is YOU.

'Moving on is a simple thing. It's what is left behind that is difficult.'
Dave Mustaine

Separate the Wheat from the Chaff

Sydney, 2011 – an amazing city, a hive of bustling activity that makes the Piccadilly Circus look a bore in the slow lane. Thrown in the mix, my job was in Singapore, which meant I travelled there frequently while Sydney was my home base. Getting connected and finding fellowship was a difficult affair. I would fly to work and upon my grand return to church no one would recognise me. I eventually found a small community church that offered great connection and fellowship. They even kept in touch when I was at work in Singapore.

Life was busy and started to get dandy again. The new prototype hospital that I worked at in Singapore was the first model of its kind in the world. It kept me engaged and stimulated, but pain still bubbled under the surface. I had relocated from Brisbane for this job, but after a year I was made redundant. I felt perplexed but I trusted God knew what He was doing. I then landed a contract role for the State Government. My income grew exponentially as God granted me the dream to purchase my own home in Sydney, a market where it is almost impossible to purchase property on a single income. God worked the redundancy out for good.

During a holiday in South Africa, I was overcome with abdominal pain. A medical specialist confirmed that I required an operation immediately to remove ovarian fibroids and scar tissue. Granted my first-hand experience when my dad was in hospital and an expected six week recovery period post-surgery, I decided to fly back to Sydney to get the required care. I had to redo the tests and scans in Sydney and wait for the results so my specialist could make her own informed decision.

Post-surgery I was not allowed to drive, cook or perform any strenuous tasks. My mum and aunt had planned a trip, but the visa application process confirmed that they would only arrive a few months after my surgery. So my church family stepped in and made me feel like I had a family in Sydney. They rostered a meal drop-off sometimes during my six week recovery. It was true that I did not have to depend on me, myself and I. Amazing people stepped into my life to take care of me. Even the church men helped in thoughtful ways.

I met a young lady from Africa at church. She was going through her own struggles, so I tried to be a lighthouse in her storm. We had fellowship, spoke our hearts out, laughed until our bellies ached, cried a few rivers and developed what I deemed was real sisterhood. We were strolling through The Rocks market one day and I bought a few things. Her eyes landed on a dress and beamed like fluorescent bulbs. She tried it on and loved it but confessed to me that she could not afford it. This broke my heart, so while she was getting changed, I bought it for her. I had similarly on many occasions offered her presents including clothes, handbags, shoes, and lavish dinners. Most of our fellowship was either at my home and I cooked or at a restaurant which I paid for. I was now unable to fend for myself. I was starving and she came to visit me with no food and did not offer to drive for a meal – it was evident that she did not care about my circumstances. I remember crying after she left.

As I was a good friend to her and had acted with generosity and thoughtfulness at every turn, I learned the hard way we are all not cut from the same cloth. It bemused me how she could take so much but had no capacity to give. She could not even give me support when I needed medical care. A healthy friendship is a give and take. We build a sisterhood so that when we cannot fend for ourselves, a sister will step in and fend for us. Both Jesus and Judas came from the church, so we are setting ourselves for pain if we only expect the Jesus encounter. We need to develop the skillset, character and tools to deal with the Judas calibre too.

The Word declares that when we give to someone, we should not expect anything in return. Our reward is in heaven. The disadvantage of being a Christian is that people take advantage of kind and generous people. The world has many people who are self absorbed and in love with acquiring material wealth at all costs. They constantly take advantage of others to advance their own agendas. We ought to reprimand those who take advantage of kind and generous people.

Even the disciples did not extend material help to everyone who extended their hands: Peter said in the book of Acts 3:6, 'Silver and Gold have I none, but such as I have I give thee: In the name of Jesus Christ of Nazareth rise up and walk.' I had to learn from this example and then ensure that as a friend you teach a man to fish and feed him for life, but when you give him a fish you feed him for the day. I had to stop handing out fish to everyone who wanted one. This especially hit home when someone I had been so kind to and I could not even get comfort when I was sick and weak. Yes, we are called to help, but we are also called to help with wisdom and discernment. A life gem I acquired the hard way.

My neighbour was a Buddhist living in Sydney with no family either and we soon became friends. We had many deep conversations that enhanced both our lives. We looked out for each other and took care of each other when we took ill. We had real sisterhood. This made me realise that great hearts are everywhere and not limited to those that are Christian. Some have the Christian tag, but they do not walk the talk. I am not professing to be a paragon, but I have developed a level of self-awareness to be salt and light in this world. I had to seek to understand my destiny.

My quest uncovered so many amazing fundamentals that made me grow into a better version of myself. I urge you to go on your own quest to discover your purpose and destiny. I am going to take the liberty to share one moment of truth with you. After reading the Bible I decided to look at the insight of each chronicle to glean what I could learn from it. The story of Lot as found in Genesis Chapters 13, 14 and 19 aligns so purposefully with destiny. More specifically the destiny of Lot's wife. Her sole identity as Lot's wife concludes that was her predetermined destiny. Coupled with destiny is the fact that we all have the free will to choose. We can partner with God and adhere to his direction for our life, or we can make our own free choice.

The Bible does not give us a background or history of 'Lot's wife.' She is simply called Lot's wife.' That is all we can ever know about her. She was perhaps destined to be someone's wife.' I have repeated this to ensure you do not miss the call of her destiny. God gave her explicit instruction not to look back. Did the woman adhere? Did she fulfil her destiny? Did she listen to God's direction? Did she exercise her own free will? Yes indeed, she exercised her own free will and turned back to take a look when she was instructed to not look back. She turned into a pillar of salt. Did the story end there? No!

Lot and his two daughters ended up living in a cave in the mountains. His daughters feared that they were the last humans on earth. So they got their father drunk and lay down with him. The older daughter gave birth to Moab and the younger daughter gave birth to Ammon. Two ungodly nations were created from Lot's daughters. Do you think these daughters would have resorted to incestuous rape of their father if their mum were still around? Do you think the mother failed her assignment and destiny as a mother and wife?

Lot's wife looked back because she cherished what she was leaving behind. There is absolutely nothing in this world worthy of giving so much that it costs you your eternal life and derails your family's descendants. Her sheer gaze back revealed her appreciation for the things of the world. Scripture reveals that where the heart is, there also is the treasure. Her treasure was in Sodom, the city of sin, hence efforts were made to remove her from Sodom, but it was in vain as Sodom could not be removed from her and at this juncture lies one of the greatest lessons in history. So be wise and discerning about where your treasure lies, you may be rewriting history in a positive way or disrupting it for yourself and future generations.

John 3:16 - For GOD so loved the world, that He gave His only begotten SON, that whosoever believeth in Him should not perish, but have everlasting life.

My Journey Gleans

One particular day when I was recovering from my surgery, I did not have any food and I assumed the 'friend' who visited that day would deliver me a meal. To my disappointment she did not. This hurt me as I could not drive or cook. I cried out, all I really have is me, myself and I. I got up and prayed and the above scripture reminded me that God had my life in the palm of His hand. Helping others in a time of need demonstrates the love of God in a very real and powerful way. Never underestimate the power of a simple gesture. Preach the gospel all the time and use words only if you have to.

A simple harmless gaze back by Lot's wife resulted in repercussions. Is this where we need to introspect upon our own lives? When we are in the thick of things, do we let our free will take over. Well, I was guilty. I now stop and cognitively ask God for direction. Make a decision to live the destiny God fashioned for you.

A few months later I travelled to New York and visited Central Park's 'Strawberry Fields' where John Lennon's cremated ashes were reportedly scattered. At this memorial someone had written on the opposite side in white chalk a scripture 'John 3:16.' As soon as I saw this, I felt a sense of the tangible reality that God wanted me to grasp. I was never alone due to my belief in the Son, and I did not have to depend on me, myself and I. I was finally trusting God to take care of me. I took a picture at that site to mark that day.

I do not have to maintain all friendships, especially the ones where I am doing all the heavy lifting. Depths of mystery are found in human behaviour. It can be a lifelong pursuit to understand why people behave the way they do. I had a few more times of fellowship with this African lady and noted sadly that things were not so fine. Then the penny dropped when she said that she intentionally found a church because she knew people would help her. She was pleading poverty constantly despite having a professional job. She was using her income to build a home in Africa and expected her church family to sustain her locally.

I have no problems helping anyone attain their dreams, but one must be real and honest about their intentions. She added no value to me, she was just taking. I gathered so much worthy longitudinal data from our fellowship that it is noticeable enough not to ignore. When the dust settled, I realised the value and quality of friends is far more valuable than the quantity of friends. It is better to have a few amazing friends that can be substantial in all facets of life than having many fair weather friends. Good friendships are reciprocal.

I tried to gently alert her to be a giver and not just a taker but noted no positive response. You can still be a giver even if you have no money. Our time is a gift as well. I began to feel used as the hand outs were strategically only for her convenience. I certainly did not feel like a priority at any point, and I observed that my peace was robbed after spending time with her. I took active steps to establish healthier boundaries for my wellbeing.

If a friendship is difficult and the other party takes no ownership of their behaviour or is unwilling to change, then it may be time to end the friendship. Be honest and kind while still prevailing with your decision. Chalk it down to experience and move on. We all need to pray for discernment so we can actively take steps to look inward and discover why we do what we do. We need to get acquainted with how other people view us and why. Identify if we have a blind spot and remedy it. Take steps to discover how you are configured:

- a) Are you a giver or a taker?
- b) Are you a peacekeeper or peace maker?
- c) What do you bring to the table as a friend, daughter, son, wife, husband, sister, brother, mother, or father and to the kingdom of God?

The greatest witness we can give another is grace. Showing mercy and grace is a privilege. Do you have the capacity to exhibit this? Sadly, the world that we live in today is populated with people who take the mercy, grace and blessings for granted, and develop a habit of grabbing more. Do not be discouraged by this behaviour and stop helping others. Be true to your destiny and calling. Those that use you selfishly are ultimately accountable to God.

Upon my return from New York, I read a book on how to establish healthy boundaries and this gave me the strength and acumen to remove this so called friend from my life. I had to purposely make my circle of friends stronger by removing the ones that brought no value to my life. Sometimes people must be escorted out from your life for your own welfare.

A freeloading relationship is unhealthy where one person does all the giving and the other does all the taking. A healthy relationship is one that is mutually beneficially to both parties. Redefine and purge your circle of friends if you have to. It is not about the size of your circle; it is about the calibre and loyalty of the circle that defines the true richness of friendship. I created a 'do and don't' list for my friendships:

The Dos

- ✓ Love is the most important ingredient in a friendship, and you should be showered with this especially when you need it.
- ✓ We rise to new horizons when we lift others up.
- ✓ Cultivate self-awareness and understand how we impact the world.
- ✓ Grow integrity – value and treat others as we prefer to be treated.
- ✓ Change – become a better version of yourself.
- ✓ Be grateful – be thankful for what others do for you. (Remember Jesus came to serve and not to be served)
- ✓ A friend that is closer than a brother will never let you down. This is my new benchmark. I dispense this to my friends so those that cannot do the same move into the purged status.
- ✓ Do watch people's actions and not their words, because actions have a far more difficult time lying to your face.

The Don'ts

- ✓ Do not let the ugly in others kill the beauty in you.
- ✓ Do not permit anyone to mock or insult you. Friends do not do that. Beautiful things have dents and scratches too.
- ✓ Do not despise the little you have, be a blessing with your limited resources and see how God multiplies that seed you plant.
- ✓ Do not avoid change – you may rob yourself of a new horizon and new blessing.
- ✓ Do not be afraid of failure – it is personal development and the series of lessons learned will propel you into a better destination with experience.
- ✓ Do not let people make you feel like you are holding a grudge. Setting healthy boundaries is for your emotional well-being and constant happiness.
- ✓ Do not let a few minutes of recklessness ruin years of character.
- ✓ Abstain from lingering in the consequences of a stalemate; move on swiftly to what brings you peace and edification.
- ✓ Find your identity, don't copy it. You cannot bring the same shade of experience to the table as anyone else.

'You cannot stop the birds from flying over your head, but you can certainly stop them from building a nest in your hair.' Unknown

Chapter Four

Prototypes for Deeper Connection

The Trudge to Forgiveness

While living in Sydney I actively attended connect group every day of the week, trying to glean as much as I could like a sponge. This overload aided my ability to stay all fuelled up from the vine when I flew to work in Singapore. I was all soaked up with The Word and fellowship. I also planned a lot of activities for the church members to connect with each other. I earned the nickname 'social butterfly.'

One day I got a text from a connect leader saying a new lady, Bella, was joining us that night. I dashed to the local bakery and got a cake with a personalised 'welcome' and her name written in chocolate icing. Bella soon started dating a guy from our connect group. He was going through a bad patch with his business and was otherwise distracted. They broke up and then decided to have another go, trying to make it work the second time. When they finally broke up again, she was distraught and shared her raw emotions with me. I lent her my ear and shoulder. I opened up my home for fellowship. Sometimes she stayed over, or often she left very late. I shared some of my past traumas with her to encourage her to stay strong.

My 40th birthday was approaching, and I asked a few international friends if they would like to accompany me on a trip to New York, followed by a celebration in Hawaii. It was 2014. Not only was it a milestone birthday, but my divorce was also granted on my birthday, so I wanted to focus on the celebration rather than feeling desolate. Only Bella decided to join me on this holiday. At the airport I gave her a card with words of affirmation and aspirations of a great holiday, then we flew off to New York.

Many small things spoilt the atmosphere, but I did not address them. I showered her with grace and mercy. I was mindful that she was still nursing a broken heart. The morning of my birthday got off to a beautiful start; she presented me with a video of my church family wishing me a happy birthday. I was blown away. We went to the US Tennis Open, then madly dashed downtown to grab a helicopter to have a tour of Manhattan from above. It was exhilarating.

It was a scorching hot day and the tar on the tarmacked surface had melted. As we disembarked from the helicopter, she stepped into the oozing melted tar. She went to the bathroom to wash up. The cold water made the tar hard and sticky and difficult to remove. She then explained she needed to go to a pharmacy to buy a solvent to remove the tar and off we went. We eventually got back to our hotel and I dressed up for our dinner reservations for my milestone birthday celebration. She went into the bathroom and two hours later, she still hadn't come out.

I left the room and went downstairs to the lounge to respond to my birthday wishes online. After another half an hour, she came down and asked me if I still wanted to go out for dinner. It was now several hours past our reservation. I asked the concierge to call the restaurant and confirm if we could still present for dinner. I was hurt but I decided to make hay while the sun was shining. We went out and had a great time.

Many other incidents occurred that hurt me and baffled me yet again, but I decided to choose my battles and so left them unaddressed. We were on our final leg in Hawaii, and I needed time for myself. So I strategically planned to go horse riding alone, while she chose her own activity according to her interests. I loved that day, pottering around and able to enjoy anything that pleased me. We both presented to the hotel and Bella was in a foul mood because she had forgotten her souvenir pictures on the bus. She was having an intense discussion with someone on the phone about it.

I was grateful I spent the last day by myself and had regained the positive energy vibes. I was packed and ready for our 5:00am airport shuttle pickup. The next morning at 4:45am, I was leaving the room while Bella was still sleeping. I woke her up, informed her of the time of our pickup and told her I was going to check out.

I checked out and waited outside with my bags. After a short while the shuttle arrived and parked in the driveway. There was a steep downhill descent and I had to navigate my several packed bags myself. I lifted them into the shuttle, then took a seat. The shuttle was empty. The driver asked, 'There are two of you, right?' When I nodded, he enquired where the other one was, and I told him she was still coming. He said he could not wait any longer as he had other passengers to pick up. He waited another five minutes, then said he had to go. He shut the door and proceeded to drive off. As he was pulling out, I saw Bella step out from the elevator. I asked him to stop and go back as she had come down.

The driver went back and stopped at the exact same spot. Bella appeared with her bags in a huff and began to yell and abuse the driver for not carrying her bags. He responded he was only there to drive, not carry bags. She gave him more lip. He got off the shuttle and said, 'Lady, here is the money you prepaid for the shuttle. Find your own way to the airport.' He left her there and drove off with me in the shuttle.

I was standing in line to board my flight when Bella barged her way through to me and started yelling at me and accusing me of leaving her behind. She then proceeded to demand money from me because she had no money to pay for the taxi that she had to catch because I got the shuttle driver to leave without her. I was bamboozled. With all I endured the entire holiday, this was the last straw, and it seemed like the grace I showed her was misconstrued for acceptance rather than tolerance. I opened my wallet and gave her all the cash I had and told her to leave me alone.

Once we landed in Sydney, she grabbed my bags off the carousel and came to me saying her mum was waiting for us. I asked her to hand over my bags, refusing her invitation and caught a taxi home. I wrote her an email with all that I tolerated, the disappointments and hurts, and the absolutely shocking behaviour with the shuttle driver, blaming me for her getting left at the curb side and demanding money from me.

Her response was bitter and angry, but this line stood out most for me: 'You're a horrible person, that's why your husband left you.' After all I did for her, she had stooped to a new low. I launched into verbal and viral combat mode. I did not want to see her until she took ownership for her behaviour and took responsibility for her actions and repaid all the money she owed me. An apology would be nice – I was delusional. Awareness is a profit that not all of us harness.

This church was now my family, but I stayed away because I was so hurt. The elders spoke to me and assured me that the issues would be addressed. A lot more happened with this church than I care to write about. They asked me to be patient and understanding as she came from a broken home and had many things on her plate.

I had been nothing but understanding with her from day one. I was patient even when she mucked up my 40th birthday. I showed her mercy and grace when she hurt and cut me so deeply. The church members had no capacity to address the situation. They just shoved it under the rug and hoped it would go away.

Because I did not wear my heart on my sleeve, they perceived I was professional and blessed with a fine life and could handle being cut off. Most people who I deemed as my church family and sowed into, blessed and had sweet fellowship with, made no effort to maintain the fellowship or friendship. You cannot climb the top of the mountain with friends that don't give you oxygen.

Matthew 7:3-4 - Why do you look at the speck of sawdust in your brother's eye and pay no attention to the plank in your own eye? How can you say to your brother, 'Let me take the speck out of your eye,' when all the time there is a plank in your own eye?

My Journey Gleans

My soul wrestled with this scripture for a long time. I reached a point where I was consumed by it. Thinking Bella was walking around with a plank in her eye but had the audacity to point out a speck in my eye. Hindsight is a wonderful thing. Ignorance is sheer bliss when we don't know the fundamentals any better.

God is sovereign and it rains on the just and unjust alike. Most importantly, vengeance is for God. I let my peace depart by a sequence of events. It is human nature to act oblivious about the blind spots in our own life but magnify the shortcomings of others. Another important lesson here too: when you have a falling out with a friend, don't share what was discussed in confidence. Walk away with all your dignity and integrity intact. When someone confides in you, refrain from turning it into a conspiracy to give yourself leverage.

When someone points out a flaw or something negative in our lives, rather than reacting we should give credence to the fact that there may be some truth to it. I personally want to be the best version of myself; thus, I am open to enhancing my character by purging what I need to. It takes a lifetime to establish character, create values, define goals, build a vision and carve out beliefs - so give yourself the time to become a polished and distinguished character.

If someone wants to help speed up the process by highlighting your flaws without your request, it can rub you the wrong way, but my advice is to glean from it, absorb what you need to and discard the rest. You do not have to take everything to heart. Evaluate it objectively and honestly, then act in accordance with your beliefs. Correct a wise man and he will be wiser.

Eventually I accepted not knowing why my ex-husband had left. It was his loss, and it was his prerogative to exercise his free will to break the solemn promise made to God despite what the world may think. I also developed peace with the world not knowing my side of the story. My soul is well with that. I have since evolved enough to grasp and live by God's fundamental Word. We must all prepare to be judged. Jesus was judged and scorned and shouted at, *'You are just Joseph's son.'* We need to reach a healthy plateau where we can respond rather that react when we are judged.

A golden oldie song comes to mind: *'Sticks and stones may break my bones, but words will never break me…'* This song is a lie and utterly misleading, because words have enormous power to both make and break a person. The Word says the tongue is like a rudder on a ship. Your tongue steers your life by the words it shapes. Words spoken by your tongue determine the direction of your life, just like the rudder of a ship determines the direction the ship will go. So imagine the impact of your unseasoned words on another person. Your words can and do inflict pain, so tread with caution. Your words are either a blessing or a curse – you can choose how you want to serve it up.

The miserable fact of life is that we all love to judge others and while we must prepare to accept this norm, it is equally important to note and live by The Word in Matthew 7:2 *'For with whatever judgement you judge, you will be judged and with whatever measure you measure, it will be measured to you.'* So choose your words wisely, especially when you are in an altercation! What we procreate with our mouth and deeds will surround us and sometimes drown us. Does it make you feel prettier to point out someone's pain? What makes criticism so destructive is that there is nothing else we do that will so suddenly and peacefully make the criticised party acutely aware that there is a huge difference between an attack and an apology.

I found that when I developed the art of forgiveness, I was able to release my pain and move on with my life. Tomorrow is a new day so start afresh leaving the hurts behind and try again. It is better to try and fail than fail to try. If you dwell on the negative it will drag you down.

I am an intelligent professional with accolades and kudos in my archives of achievements. Yet when thrown into new territory of soul rocking conflict, I had to learn to stay afloat and develop new coping mechanisms. I had to teach myself to let go of anger, annoyance, resentment, and refrain from creating a chronological laundry list of all the wrongs and stop highlighting the irrational and illogical behaviour of others. Resentments and unforgiveness do not occur from the other party in the altercation, though they occasionally ignite there.

Resentment remained as I was unwilling to end the altercation with an offering of love and authentic forgiveness. Even though I was wronged, I had to dig deep to end the hostility so that kindness and goodwill could transcend and prevail. I had to practice being a giver and not a taker. I gave unto God and my reward is in heaven, not from the recipient's heart, hand or mouth. I had to pray for God to help me bring pardon where there was injury. I had to teach myself to refrain from judgement and enhance my world by substituting judgement with agape love.

Remaining magnanimous concerning those that hurt you is mandatory if you want to enjoy God's promise of restoration and an abundant life. Jesus forgave while he was on the cross of crucifixion, so who am I that I cannot forgive? It is totally acceptable to forgive others and still deny them access to you. The person who hurt you may never take responsibility, may never ever apologise, may refuse to make restitution, and that is tolerable. Forgiveness is for you to move on and heal. There is no forgiveness without rage, so I had to allow myself to feel angry. To feel the emotions and then choose how to respond to the pain, ensuring never to get trapped in this terrain. When there is no acknowledgement of the pain, the rage feels like wildfire. Only you can snap out of it and release yourself from the suffering, a gift to yourself that no one else has the power to give. Crawl, cry and create your mantra of forgiveness.

When we suppress our true emotions with premature forgiveness, we create an alpha error with the false notion of a constructive outcome. The real pain is subdued in a self-styled peace, and we harm the natural beneficial flow of healing. Rage will permeate the air like a bad perfume. Develop tangible and authentic self examination so the staple of your being thrives with discerned reliability. I am not a perfect human by any stretch, but I strive every day to improve. A certified diamond requires excessive work before reaching the status of certified. Do the work to reach your desired status. Healing does not equate to overlooking the pain but rather to reframing your experience to add worth to your growth in life. When our buttons are pushed, we must be willing to have mature and responsible dialogue and maybe monologue to our self – get curious about your emotions and thus find essential remedies.

John and Ross, two of my friends affiliated with the past church, stood by me in this tough time. They supported me and offered shoulders to lean on. They kept my spirit going strong. Some friends have the capacity to be there when you need them. They will be real and help you when you need their support. I learned that not everyone had my back. Most people are fair weather friends. As long as they can benefit from you in some way, they will be happy. People disappear when turbulence hits. It is critical that you find your tribe. I now know who will support me and be there in my storm, so when I am ready to celebrate it is those people who I reach out to first. Circumstances will reveal to you who your true friends are. Be sure to pay attention. When you find a true friend do not break the bonds by breaching trust – It's like having a fine China plate shattered then picking up the pieces and using super glue to stick the fragments together. The plate can never be the same and the same is applicable to human relations.

'Caesar fought heroically until Brutus, his beloved friend, struck. Then, impaled by criticism as much as by the blade, Caesar gave up. If we can become aware of the extent to which criticism is always associated with severe loss of control, we will make effort to learn to deal more effectively with frustrations in our relationships. Criticism is a luxury I believe none of us can afford.' William Glasser.

Choose your friends a la Carte: choose wisely, for not everyone that wears the friend badge is a friend. Both John and Ross proved their loyalty and level of friendship when the rubber hit the road. I am blessed to have them in my circle of friends. What you bring to the friendship matters and it creates deep roots to anchor us all for life. From left to right: John, Dave, Kelly and Ross.

Photograph:
Sydney, Australia
2020

Glean, Grow and Glow

Organised religion is roughly dogma, rules, traditions, dominance and authority. It lacks the vital ingredient of authentic connection to the sufferings of humanity. God is not an institution. Faith is practical. Verity, realness and God are synonymous. God is the way we treat and love people; it's about our horizontal and vertical relationships. My wings were already broken, and I was just learning to fly again. Then the incident with Bella felt like I was engulfed by flames. I was left like a pile of burnt ash. I tried a few other churches but found that a burnt child dreads the fire. I could not get my mojo back. I was hurt when I landed in Sydney and post my revelations from my trip in India. I was ready to be the best friend I could be. Despite my efforts I was treated like I did not matter.

Unfortunately, Christians do shoot the wounded sometimes. This is a reality of the world we live in. When a person is hurt, they tend to hurt others as well. Life can be hard to live when every day is overwhelming. When I had no support, I felt disillusioned and displaced. My faith in God remained strong but the pain was real too. I trusted God for healing, but often it felt like my ton of bricks was swapped for a ton of stones. The pain was still just as intense. I read many books specifically on establishing my personal boundaries. I talked to my tribe of friends that were most definitely concerned for my wellness and healing.

I had to cognitively choose to forgive friends that took sides, so called friends that showed no support when I needed them the most. To forgive the church for saying they would address the situation but doing nothing to remedy the situation or pain. To forgive people who only listened to one side of the story and drew up conclusions. It was a royal road of hardship filled with tears, and I had to learn the art of purging people who were toxic for me. The church was all about peacekeepers. Sadly, they did not understand the difference between peacekeepers and peace makers as denoted in The Word.

My numbness slowly evaporated with the progression of time. I discovered that no one would really be committed to the truth or my welfare. I needed to get up and change my life. Only I could focus on my best interests and live a blessed good life. So I had to scrape up the courage to drag myself off the floor, wipe away the tears and find a new church.

The pain dissipated as I chose to walk in a new day, a new beginning and new mercies. I listened to online sermons. I devoted one Sunday to praying specifically for my healing and the ability to forgive Bella. I had a long session of prayer where I talked to God about the hurt and overwhelming pain. I opened my eyes, and a white feather was floating right in front of me and then it landed on my lap. This was peculiar as I had no open windows to allow its entry into my home. Nonetheless, I felt nothing but peace in my heart after a very long time.

That peace started to grow in proportion. Every time I recalled a situation or hurt, I would remember the emotion of peace, the feather and my prayer, and this anchored my soul in peace. I was healing. Know that sometimes you are the only person committed to your healing. Stay focused on the bigger picture, ensure that you are on the path to health and restoration. No one will draw up a care plan for your recovery. You need to champion and own the recovery plan and partner with God. You may feel alone but just as God was with me, even when I was disillusioned for over a year, when I got real with God He showed up and most importantly He cared, and He was definitely committed to my healing.

I saw the hand of God even though Bella owed me money from this trip and refused to return it. I had to learn to let it go. I had to live by The Word of God with reference to Matthew 5:40. *'If your brother takes your shirt, give him your coat too.'* I let go.

One day after church, I went to lunch with a group of ladies. While we chatted, an older lady that I met for the first time shared how she travelled on public transport in the peak of winter and at the crack of dawn to help refugees. She said she was saving, praying and trusting God for a car. When I was on my way to exit at the checkout, the cashier confirmed that the older woman had already paid the bill. I was blown away! Most times I am the generous one that picks up the bills, and people very rarely return the favour. This is a lady that I did not know at all; she was a pensioner struggling to save for a car.

Mainstream Sydneysiders find it difficult to penetrate the Sydney property market, yet God unbolted doors for me to purchase my own home with a single income. After this random lady paid my bill, I felt utterly blessed that good people with great hearts still existed. I offered to give her my car so she could work with the refugees at ease. She was blown away by the gesture. We still keep in touch and she prays for me. I was then blessed to afford a brand new car. So often people protract the wonder with personas of KINDNESS by either sticking a feather in their own cap, having a bumper sticker or a tag attached saying they are this or that, but they rarely do the genuine deeds that exhibit kindness.

I learned to remain true to who God created me to be. A giver, as The Word says in the book of Acts 20:35. *'It is better to be a giver than a taker.'* Even when people hurt me and I felt derailed, God prevailed in my life. There were still random strangers generous enough to bless me, and I could still be a blessing despite my past hurts and pain. I did not let the negative experience change my personality. Even though I lost my shirt and coat metaphorically, I still had the capacity to give, and God further enhanced my glory.

Matthew 5:9 - Blessed are the peace makers for they will be called the children of God.

My Journey Gleans

This scripture gave me emotions like weevils burrowed into my brain and made me feel like the church did not practice what it preached. I did not want a bar of it. I prefer to not dwell in a house filled with peacekeepers; people who did not acknowledge the hurts and wrongdoings in order to maintain their so called peace. They lacked the courage, skills and acumen to manage the situation and to foster greater peace for all parties concerned. The church stepped into this equation without an invitation from my part, yet they found no remedy as per their intentions. The pain would be minimal if they maintained a professional boundary. Unfortunately, bias does exist in the foyers and hearts of the church.

Ultimately peacekeeping was to firstly eradicate the facade of peace making *(ability to engage professionally amidst the tension, to achieve a solid resolution)*. In essence it was a shallow effort of peace making *(will not tackle the bull by its horns, instead they avoided it as they have no real experience to deal with disagreements effectively)*. This approach of peace making by the church made me angry. It reminded me of the words by Mahatma Gandhi 'I like your Christ, but I do not like your Christians. Your Christians are so unlike your Christ.' Even though these Christians kept me out of church for over a year, my relationship with Christ prevailed. God did not quit on me. I wrestled with this, day and night. I tossed and turned at night as I had no church family. I grew more disillusioned with Christians until one day I read the following from my daily devotion:

'Men of genius are as rare as icicles in summer. Abraham was not one of them. Abraham learned to trust God and God revealed to him the paths of peace. In his day, cities existed by military might and were founded by bloodshed. God gave Abraham a new vision of a city of peace whose builder and maker was God (Hebrews 11:10). Abraham was the first to discern the paths of righteousness, paths in the sea and ways in the wilderness. The paths of righteousness and peace have been found. These paths are marked and are known. If we trace them back, they would bring us to the flattering tent

> **door of Abraham where God said 'walk before me and be perfect'.'**
> **Genesis 17:1**

I reread this and cried. I felt a balm soothe my soul as I was letting go of what felt like injustice to me for the first time. The above scripture literally washed over me as I learned that there is no 'right' way of doing things, only right principles which are drawn from The Word of God. Not everyone has the ability to draw from The Word of God. People act based on their level of edification, spiritual growth, ability to refute the negative, respect for others' skillset to handle disagreement, maintain a passive approach or sometimes they just don't care about doing what is right.

The greatest lesson I learned from this experience was not to stumble just because those around me had limited scope. It dawned on me that I was scratching around in the wrong camp. I was an eagle created to soar. Once I discerned that, I soared despite my broken spirit. We develop a Godly character by following the example of Jesus who is the prince of peace. We need to cultivate a lifestyle of peace and go the extra mile to be an extravagant peace maker leaving no stone unturned. In our situations we need to always ask ourselves, 'What will Jesus do?' Jesus is the ultimate mediator, and we need to walk in His footsteps.

May our disapproval of the issue never outweigh our impact to the resolution! God has anointed us to do more than perform analysis. He has anointed us to construct what has been ruined and repair what has been tarnished. We exhibit our faith not by appreciation of doctrine or status of our title at church. We demonstrate our faith to labour and illustrate our grace factor to the world and what righteous justice looks like in the Kingdom of God, and model this to the rest of humanity in a tangible and relatable fashion. You can only model what you have instilled in your own character – hurt with relish is not character. Moreover, you cannot force anyone to respect you, but you can refuse to be disrespected. Love yourself enough that you can find the courage to respect yourself and create a new path when your welfare is not welcomed and prioritise. 'A fish rots from the head down' leakage of destructive emotions penetrates emotions of a fellowship circle as well. Make sure you do not block the view of Jesus for others and don't let anyone block your view either. It can derail a person if they lack the zeal to climb up a tree like Zacchaeus to gain a view as depicted by the Bible in the book of Luke 19:4.

Dwell on the curious opportunity for a moment, if you really want to see what battles people are fighting all you have to do is look. Let proactivity control your life rather than reaction. Don't let external forces run your world, rather let your internal vision reign. This is why it is fundamental to know the vision and plans for your life so you do not settle for what the wind blows your way. You cannot blend in when you are born to stand out around people who have no interest in recognition of truth and healing. Others may have weaknesses where we may have strength, so use your strength with wisdom, a powerful essence not to be defeated by challenge. Bustle with inspirational growth hacks that will erupt questions to confirm where you stand in times of challenge rather than where you live in times of comfort.

I have travelled around the globe and dined in some of the most exotic restaurants; however, nothing beats the taste of dining in my hometown Sydney and being blessed by a woman who had so little and yet was generous enough to pay for a stranger's meal. This world needs more characters like her. Try to make these random acts of kindness part of your life. You may just change someone forever. Often these minor, seemingly insignificant gifts of courtesy and kind heartedness have a more profound impact than anything else a person could have given. Conflict and confrontation are certainly not easy, but they are an essential part of courageous leadership. An audacious leader will lead by example, so follow with discernment. A pensioner had a more profound effect on me than...

'Do not expect to be honoured in the world where your Lord was crucified.' Charles Spurgeon

In a serendipitous fashion I met Jan and our collision confirmed to me that there is always a valuable lesson in every season. No matter how difficult the season is; an amazing growth burst comes sealed with the package. I felt abandoned by my tribe, I felt used, and my generosity and grace were taken for granted. I was always giving, and no one stopped to fill my cup. Then Jan filled my cup in a way that spoke volumes to me and most importantly it reaffirmed that I should never change my primary desire to give. We are both blessed by the act of real generosity.

Photograph:
Sydney, Australia
2017

Chapter Five

A Virtuous Woman

Shaping Life Despite Invisible Pain

No one is perfect as we are all a work in progress. We all stumble and fall and, most importantly, get up and try again. As I was living in a foreign country with no family around, when I fell sick, I had no one to make me a cup of tea or just give me some basic Tender Loving Care. It was always me, myself and I. I am human and living in the big smoke, having a job that required international travel and when that was over, I was an enthusiastic globe trotter – all required precision and self-care to remain optimistic.

As with everyone else, I faced many challenges in life that I had to resolve myself. Occasionally I had someone to phone, but at the end of the call I was alone again. God made me deeply aware that when the world is moving on, I cannot stop and get off to catch my breath. I need to move as well. I do need to deliberate and rest to recover and restore. Ultimately, when I am in any turbulent situation or season of life, my real lifeline is God. When the haze and heaviness was too much to bear, this was when I said, 'Lord, I cannot do this, and I need you to carry me.'

My tomorrow and future are dependent on what I actively do today. God has already prepared the way, now I have to allow Him to prepare me. No storm lasts forever. Prepare for sunshine and expect to see God's work in your life. Expect that miracle. God knows me by name.

It is a blessing to be known by God. When we are in the eye of the storm, we all prioritise what is important. Be discerning about this and exercise wisdom. If you are trying to manage finances, then shopping for designer bags and clothes when you are trying to scrape up a deposit for a home is not top on the priority list. God has our back when we are called according to his plan and purpose. This was sealed in my heart, that I was not alone as God is always with me. I still see his interventions in my life every day.

My Journey Gleans

Feel what you want to but never be consumed by it. I discovered this first-hand while nursing a broken heart, that silence is also a response – it may not be the response I anticipated, but it spoke louder than words. I had to make peace with this enlightenment. I am buoyed by God's peace and joy and I endeavour to remain there regardless of what people do or do not do. I had to separate the past and cultivate a new norm.

What defines us are the times we choose to follow God while we are still in the tough brutal wilderness. I had to choose to serve God with a broken heart, trust Him even when my problems were not resolved. I had to discipline my desires and transform my life to cease my wants. I had to cultivate the art to listen to God so I could refrain from living by chance as I did not want to gamble with my destiny. Sometimes the best thing we can do is shed off our own desires and say, 'God, may your will be done.' When I did this, God took me from better to best. A whole new world opened up with fresh optimism and hope. God built my life into something far more beautiful than what I could have desired or prayed for.

I learned that not everyone would celebrate the transformed blessed person that God created in me. God enhanced every facet of my life to honour my destiny. However, that disappointed some people as they enjoyed seeing me chase my tail with old tribulations. God gave me new revelations to set me apart and to bear new fruit. Everything that could be shaken was shaken and everything that was meant to last did prevail.

In adversity, fear is tangible. I had to hit the ground running and learn to let my faith guide me instead of the overwhelming emotions. Faith struggles yet it prevails, while our feelings fluctuate with or without Premenstrual Syndrome (PMS). In times of trouble, I need divine insight – not the opinion of a mortal person.

'An obstacle is often a stepping stone.' Unknown

Prophetic Word

A few months after attending my newfound connect group, I received two prophetic words:

- ✓ I will bring many to God's kingdom
- ✓ I will be the first to marry in this group of females

This sequence of serendipity caught me off guard. I inquired if the prophetess was certain The Word was definitely for me as I was not dating anyone. Life had knocked the wind right out of me, and I was not actively looking for a partner. I was busy as at work and enjoyed my globetrotting with no approval form to sign off. Life was just dandy. Or was it?

I did feel a deep void when it came to real nexus with the lack of pillow talk. Travelling alone is not great when you have no one to share the amazing experience with. The void was genuine. I was not in denial of this emptiness I felt, but however I was not going to put my life on hold waiting like a puppy dog for someone to fill the space. Most importantly, I was not going to let just anyone fill the space and remedy the void. I did try online Christian Connection, which I found I needed to separate the wheat from the chaff. My work was cut out for me.

My Journey Gleans

I know connecting to the first applicant is not the answer and that will create more problems for the future. The reality of living in Sydney is evident in its male to female ratio. There is a shortage of men. Then my pond goes even smaller when I mandated it to be only Christian men. This, coupled with my age, meant that the person I was hoping to meet in this demographic is now almost non existent. If God gave me a word, He must have a plan. So the critical lesson here was to stand firm on faith and my promise from God. Do not let the reality of the situation overwhelm you. Equip yourself to accept that things will go wrong in a relationship. We all are broken vessels with baggage and sometimes we just do not find the smooth path to sail. Prepare to eradicate negative energy so you can make way for positive energy. Embrace change, as change is the only constant in this world and if we accept this then we can manage change more effectively.

Learn to live with some class and walk away from things, relationships and situations that are not meant for you. Do not jump for high grapes that are beyond your reach, and do not get disgruntled with life when you fail to reach it. With the same token, do not reach for low-hanging fruit. Know your worth and stand, kneel, pray and cry to the Lord to send you a soulmate to ensure you are evenly yoked, perfectly matched and beautifully aligned with your values, goals and love for each other.

Sometimes we cannot see the new miracles that God is doing for us because we are so consumed by the person who has left the void. We expect everyone to measure up. Newsflash! God is a God of variation and he has created each one of us as uniquely as each finger on our hand. No two humans are the same. So don't have the expectation to have the same experience with different people. Be open to new discoveries in life.

Where sin abounds, grace abounds too. So get real with God and confess your sin, ask for forgiveness, believe you are forgiven, then go live your life and sin no more. If you are caught up in a deliberate, wilful and persistent pattern of sinning, then seek help to stop and move to a new way of life. Commitment means staying loyal to what you promised to do, long after the mood and season you made it in vanishes. Remain steadfast and God will honour you in due season.

Forget what or who has hurt you but never forget what it has taught you. Learn your lesson the first time around and refrain from going around the same bush to learn the same lesson. Be specific in your approach with what lessons and informed behavioural responses you learn and store up in your data bank for future reference. It is not the strongest or most intelligent species that survives but the one that is most responsive to change. Destiny is like a picture frame and all I have to do is walk into the frame. I cannot walk into someone else's destiny. God seeks our consent to create a new purpose filled destiny. We have to allow Him permission to work with the clay to mould and shape us into a new vessel.

'Nothing will ever change if there is nothing you are prepared to change.' Unknown

Know Your Value

Ladies, know your value: people will treat you according to the tag you attach to yourself. Be discerning about the red flags. Only you have access to this intelligence or data, so use it effectively to make informed decisions for the relationship and yourself. Life is complex at the best of times – we need to cultivate the art of celebrating all the struggles and setbacks that we endure in our lives. The struggle is real and sometimes we are so focused on a destination that we forget to see the forest for the trees.

We let things slide as we value a person's company or friendship more than our self worth. Sometimes the struggles are so real that we are drowning as the situation draws the life out of us and we still paint the clown face on and prevail with the pretence that everything is okay. We all need to reach out if life seems too heavy. If you feel alone, remember that God is ever present to help in times of need. Reach out to God and pour your heart out to him.

My Journey Gleans

If a man does not value you in courtship, he never will in life. Sometimes your mind needs more time to accept what your heart already knows. As time is one of the most precious gifts we have, use it only on things that matter. The propensity to trust is dire when you want something in life so bad that you lose the focus of your true esteem. The voice of logic may seem like a cosmic killjoy. You are far better to analyse the relationship and nip things in the bud rather than hope for better days and have to untangle a more complex relationship. When people treat you like you are an option, leave them like you have a choice. Your choices dictate your value. Be resilient enough to walk away from what is dragging you south and be patiently persistent to wait for the blessings that you undeniably merit. The human mind will convince us of anything in the name of survival. Never grow attached to anything you cannot instantly separate yourself from. Until you have a healthy relationship with yourself you cannot make a healthy decision about someone else.

Absorb the variance between joining and supplementing. Joining gives you muscle, and supplementing sucks the zeal out of life. Joining of two souls and a shack up of two souls are distinctly different. Joining is in harmony when both individuals feel complete by themselves and add value to the equation by joining forces. Supplementation is when two souls collide and cling to each other out of desperation and yearning to feel complete. Supplementation is a survival tactic. Grip the strategies to thrive and seek or wait for a soul that will complement the union of joining together in harmony, so you do not have to spend the remainder of life converting your soul to the one you collided with. When you purpose to live an authentic life, then some relationships will slip into the status of jeopardy. Losing them is a risk. Your authenticity will determine if the risk is worth a real reward or not. When you make friends with your true self, then you will never be alone. Self-love is the greatest euphoric medication.

If God is the third strand in your relationship, you will see it manifest in the way you treat each other. Faith is not the destination for relationships, rather the beginning of the process. Just like vows in a marriage, it is the start of the journey. Love is a verb. It is how we treat each other, in courtship, when we are upset, when circumstances are against us, how the other person adds value and what they do or do not do when you depend on them. If you do not know your identity, then other people will seek to mould and shape you according to their beliefs. Know who God says you are and accept nothing less. Don't get swept away with squat term gains, string-pulling and associations, but rather invest in long-term significant pledges that sustain and nurture the relationship. Wait for someone to match your values and loyalties.

'Although no one can go back and make a brand new start, anyone can start from now and make a brand new ending.' Carl Bard

Defining Your Brand…Stride

From the onset of leaving my home country, South Africa, no matter how difficult circumstances got, I never lived like I was poverty stricken. I never received assistance from the government in any way. I paid my way for everything and I did not expect a handout from anyone to make life more manageable. I lived as a professional.

My female friends from my corporate, social and church circles showed struggles to find a soulmate. My male friends from the same circles spoke to me candidly, saying they did not wish to pursue a relationship with a woman who was literally waiting for a man to rescue her. A woman who is professionally employed yet lives like a student while waiting to set up a life with a man is not deemed attractive by most men as it is too much pressure on the male. Most men are looking for an independent woman who can build a life and, when she is yoked to her husband, add the same value as he does to the relationship.

I received many compliments about my ability to survive and thrive in a foreign country by myself. I had many young men think they bumped into a gravy train and asked me to marry them when I would not even give it a second thought. So ladies, what is the inner core brand, stride and profile exhibiting to the world? Are you living your true potential? You cannot attract a corporate husband when you are living like a student. Men are praying for a virtuous woman who brings something to the marriage, rather than having to become the rainmaker in the woman's life.

I did not put my life on hold to find 'the one' or feel down and out by being single. I made the most of every day that God blessed me with, living with purpose and intention while I created epic memories, laughed, networked, loved, served, travelled and mourned with those that mourned.

Prepare to take calculated risks in life. Nothing ventured, nothing gained. Increase your geographical socialising network; people all around the globe need love and encouragement. We fight too many battles that do not matter, so learn the art of being selective. Develop communication skills and remember that the method is the message. A woman who creates a full and happy life on her own is far more attractive and inviting than one who looks to a man to create it for her.

My Journey Gleans

Do not limit your exposure to just Christians and people who only tell you good things that you want to hear. Develop friendships with real sisterhood where you can have honest conversations, be totally transparent, ask about your blind spots, be real with your struggles, listen with intent and appreciate the good in others. Encourage conversations to talk about the elephant in the room, establish healthy boundaries, develop self-awareness and monitor your transformation.

Does your reputation precede you when you walk into a room? Remember that only you can create your brand and profile, so flaunt it with confidence. Do not do the same old thing and expect a different result. If you want a different result, then put in the hard yards to transform. Just like a commercial product, encourage the world to want your brand. Build your character and life in such a manner that people want a piece of it.

Faith is a core muscle that is enhanced with growth only when it is exercised and used. In the same way, we need to launch into gaining experience by exercising our faith. This will create endurance in your character and thus magnify the path of your destiny. To receive the blessings of God's Word, you need to know God's Word and let it change you. Transform to the best version of yourself. Actively work on your character, not on your reputation.

Your character is the core of who you allow yourself to be, and your reputation is what others think of you, which you have no control over. So control what you can influence and change. Strive to be whole and content rather than perfect and wanting. The core of your heart has to change to facilitate a durable transformation in your life, character and behaviour. When you personify your true authentic self, it creates concern in people who still operate from ego.

If you want to expand your horizon and soar, or develop, evolve, heal, and cure yourself, you have to relinquish the desire to be a people pleaser and wanting to be liked. Our worth does not come from how many likes we attain on social media and the world. Oh no. Our worth, confidence and self esteem come from tapping into who God created us to be. So know your worth and let it prevail in every facet of your life.

How we treat others is also fundamentally defining our brand, which ultimately shapes our reality. Our past does not define who we are, it merely reveals who we are. There is a time and place to walk down memory lane when it guides us to make better choices in the present moment. Victory comes when we choose to use the confidence and wisdom we have gleaned to write a better future. Make peace with your limitations and be rest assured that God's calling does not depend on your abilities; if He has called you, He will equip you. We are not called to be perfect but willing. Refrain from sending distress signals to your predators; instead, put on a mantle of authority, resilience, dignity and conquer those reservations.

'Right is right even if no one is doing it. Wrong is wrong even if everyone is doing it.' Saint Augustine

Mental Dexterity – HOPE

Everyday life can be overwhelming when in a storm. My feelings were real, and they needed to be validated. It was an important part of my journey and growth not to just bottle them up or shove emotions under a rug. As women we are wired for conversation. I had no listening ear pillow talk, chick banter or a sounding board.

God took me through these experiences to show me it is important to acknowledge your emotions, feel what you are feeling in the present moment and let the emotions come to the surface. Most importantly, I had a choice to choose my responses and not to react immediately. In addition, I am not controlled and consumed by emotions. I was led by God's Word.

I have attended meetings where someone thought they were in control of the situation. I know God is in charge and I have seen God orchestrate events to show that He was and always will be in charge. I have also seen God's favour in my life. These situations have created my character and given me endurance, resilience and faith. Glean and grow.

Life is rich, deep and full of blessings, yet most of them go unnoticed. To live a truly grateful life we must begin by counting our blessings both large and small. Sometimes life would feel like God was experimenting with me unceremoniously in a petri dish. I was stretched, abandoned, lied to, taken for granted, hurt, abused, used, mocked, hated and cursed. Yes, indeed this process hurt but also it empowered and galvanised me into a stronger and better person. Having charted this galvanising process, I then attended a new church with a friend for the first time on Sunday, 10 February 2019.

In the middle of the sermon the pastor pointed at me and looked me straight in the eye and said: 'The favour of the Lord has led you here. God has seen your pain and has washed you. He is smiling at you. You are a Proverbs 31 woman, and he loves and delights in you.' I had tears streaming down my face and all the strangers glaring at me in awesome wonder. It was a dash emotional to gain a direct line from God. It was a cherished blessing to be known by God.

I have read this Proverbs 31 scripture many times and spent my days trying in every endeavour to live in this shadow, and now God had confirmed that I am the real McCoy. Do what you need to do to become a real virtuous woman.

My Journey Gleans

We cannot trick God as He knows our thoughts and what we are going to do before we even contemplate them. You may be able to pull the wool over a man's eyes to dress up who you really are. God will know your heart, mind, soul and staple nature. So work on this relationship first and everything else will just click into place.

Just because I carry it well, doesn't mean it is not heavy. I had earned the nick name 'social butterfly' but I did not feel that on the inside. I lived by God's scripture and not by my emotions, do not live by your emotions but stand firm on The Word of God. For many days I felt like I was sealed shut in a cocoon. With the progression of time, conscious effort, prayer and healing, I did start to feel normal again. Being gentle and pacing myself was the fundamental art to healing and restoration.

If you can see the quality of my soul as a vivid picture, you would see that my soul was shattered into a million pieces and it's now glued together by God as a beautiful mosaic masterpiece. I gave my crumbling heart to God and He created something beautiful. I sensationally charge you to let God into your life to help heal your brokenness too. God gave me the best rebuttal and that is all the validation I need in this lifetime. I assure you that you too will have a sudden rush of magnanimity for the creator.

'The greater your storm, the brighter your rainbow.' Unknown

A House Is Not a Home

In New Zealand we had a four-level home, a sports car and we lacked no good thing. Most people who visited us were green with envy. Fellowship almost seemed orchestrated. I never felt freedom to just let my hair down and be myself. The most loved entity about a home is the person that you share the home with. I guess you bond and celebrate life within this confined sanctuary. Some details make a huge impact on the overall feel of a home. The spruce-up of customised interior and luxury designer furniture and accessorised with sentimental objects – yet the emptiness lurks within the walls of attainment. Nonetheless this house still did not feel like home – the home that I grew up in was suffused with laughter, constant flow of family and friends and a surplus of food for anyone and everyone. I loved to cook and entertain while Mr. Ex loved to be secluded and avoid people.

Furthermore, the social calendar was directed by Mr. Ex the head of the house and sadly, it set the atmosphere for his house. This air was so vastly different from when I was at high school, when at one point I had five pals from my class staying over at my home. The buzz of life was always on. I did not feel at home in this New Zealand house because Mr. Ex grew up as a recluse and he wanted to live like a hermit, which he enforced onto me too.

I have now come full circle. Almost over a decade has progressed and my key take away is that the anointing flows from the top, the head of the home. So if you set the tone to be antisocial, then people will not feel welcomed in your home. We very rarely had visitors that stayed over in this New Zealand mansion.

When I purchased my own home in Australia, the square meters measure was not the same as the New Zealand one. However the fundamental difference was this was *my* home with *my* name solely on the title deed. So I had the keys to the castle to set the tone. It was not just a cold home that I paid the mortgage to. I felt free and at home all the time.

I have sweet fellowship in my home. My doors are open to anyone who requires help or fellowship. It is a breathing ground for unity, peace and love. I entertain and nourish loved ones here, so they know without a shadow of doubt that they are authentically cherished. I have a constant flow of local and international guests. It is not the mortar and the bricks that make a home. Who we are creates the warmth and the welcome.

I know God loves me too much to have left me stagnant in a mansion in New Zealand feeling so many real abysses. He ended that season so I could transcend to the new version of myself and create a new home of my own for myself. Not just a house but a home. Have you built a home or a house? Is the equity of your heart present in your home when someone walks in? Take the steps to transform your house into a home. The home you create and the person you transcend into will cost you. It will cost you people, resources, relationships, emotions, grit, sweat, tears and cutting the cord with those that may be intertwined with you. Pray for God's wisdom and discernment to know how to navigate the path and how to prioritise yourself, your transformation and your new home. Only you can make that choice.

You cannot water a seed that has never been planted. So do not expect a blessed home when you did not plan for it. Be strategic with your home and character. Introspect your life, talk to real friends about your blind spots honestly, and weed out the parts of your character that you need to eradicate. Develop self-awareness and pray according to the promises in The Word of God. Understand your purpose and do not let turbulence derail you. When you are seasoned by vast experience, then you have the skillset to give you true perspective on the grand scheme of things. You develop thick skin and a cow hide, Teflon or built-in radar to know precisely what to ignore and when to engage.

My Journey Gleans

I needed to go on my own healing journey to heal my core and become whole again. While I struggled with my numbness and unforgiveness, I found my own level of stillness to hear what my soul yearned for. I needed time to get my mojo back. This song by Bette Midler 'The Rose' brought me both tears and liberation every time I listened to it. I knew I was a tender drowned reed and ambivalence prevailed as I persevered on knowing that 'one day when the sun shines, with love the seed within becomes a rose.'

Flourishing in every season and blooming in dramatically changed environments depends on my adaptability to change and He Who carries me. When I was living this life in New Zealand, I thought it was the best thing ever and that I had reached positively according to the top of Maslow's hierarchy of basic needs. I did not exhibit a profile of strength to deal with the real emptiness, and thus the torrid ordeal of divorce forced me down the path of real contentment. I beseech you to deal with your own barrenness before it finds you and prevails in your life. Home is wherever you feel content and truly loved!

'Hold everything earthly with a loose hand but grasp eternal things with a death-like grip.' Charles Spurgeon.

Mother With a Worthy Influence

I am not a mother biologically. However, I am a godmother to a young lass in New Zealand and a five year old lad in South Africa. The most profound example of a mother portrayed universally is in the actual example of Mother Teresa, despite the fact that she did not give birth to any children. This speaks volumes when you earn the title 'MOTHER' without giving birth to a child.

Matthew: 14:8 - So she, having been prompted by her mother, said: 'Give me John the Baptist's head here on a platter.'

What a historical eye opener this scripture is. It demonstrates how significant a mother is to a child and more fundamentally how a mother can steer a child to obtain revenge. While society may not call for a head on a platter in this day and age, they still orchestrate vengeance metaphorically. Mothers still groom their children. Hence, if they can be groomed for revenge then take heart that you can groom them to create a positive ripple effect as well. The pertinent question is: how do you groom your child?

- ✓ Always share the love of Jesus with your child – one of the greatest assets they can inherit from you.
- ✓ Instil into them wisdom and kindness – let these qualities steer the words that concern your mouth.
- ✓ Demonstrate love and patience – no matter how bad the dynamics are, always remember that you are the demonstrator.
- ✓ Prepare their hearts to make wholesome choices – a day will arrive when they will need to make hard choices.
- ✓ Fill their lives with great memories – one day death, disease and despair will arrive. Ensure that they are equipped to handle it all.
- ✓ Lead by example and cover them with prayer – children live what they see, not what they are told.

Moreover, examine the bonds that you share with your child and what you demonstrate. Does your child know of the dreams you had for your life when you were just a child yourself? Does your child know why you married his or her father/mother and what attracted you both to each other?

My Journey Gleans

In New Zealand, my good friend Jo had requested me to be a godmother to her baby. She phoned me one Monday night – she was ten days overdue and toiling on the benches of the cosmos with lack of clarity and direction. She had resolved to present to the hospital the next day and have the baby induced. She desired to have her child dedicated the first Sunday after birth and granted that I am the nominated godmother – I offered to have a post dedication party at my home. So her call was to reconfirm if I was all set for Sunday, throwing some caution to me with the finer details.

As dawn stole over the household norms on early Tuesday morning, the phone rang – my heart skipped a beat as no one usually called this early. It was my friend Jo's husband – I roared with excitement and asked if the baby was coming and he said 'Yes, she's here.' I was trying to grab something to write as I wanted the granular details of the precise time and weight as I planned to order a customised gift. I discerned a capricious silence. He then said, 'Jo passed away after giving birth.' I thought I heard wrong, so I enquired 'What do you mean?' I guess he could see the questions racing across my confused mind. He patiently repeated what he had said. My agile mind was darting like a startled deer. I was on the middle of the stairwell of my home – I fell on the stairs and the phone dropped and tumbled all the way to the bottom of the staircase. I screamed...

The peace still novel to my soul, I offered all the support I could muster. Some of Jo's family had to travel from America so her funeral was scheduled for the following Monday. Her husband still wanted to honour her desire to have baby Joycinda dedicated the first Sunday after her birth. The progression of the days from Tuesday to Sunday (the day of the dedication) and Monday (the day of the funeral) seemed prolonged. I offered crumbled fortifications as we corralled at her home and many remarked to me *'Being a godmother to a motherless child will be big shoes to fill.'* My shattered heart felt the weight. I had no expertise as a mother, and I was fresh with the shock of grappling with Jo's death. I now had to muster the strength to be a godmother and also start IVF in a few weeks.

The entourage at the church dedication was vast and my reality was sinking deep. As pastor Alex prayed for us all to raise this child in God's way, I shut my eyes and asked God to make me an able vessel. I was so far from perfect. Nonetheless God heard my prayer, and he gave me the courage and strength I needed each day. Joycinda, my goddaughter, was growing into a healthy amazing lass. When she began to speak, a few times she called me Mummy – it melted my heart. Not because I yearned to be called a mummy but because she did not get to share life with her real mum. I moved from New Zealand to Australia and felt the physical distance as a heavy weight when Joycinda was only two and a half years old. It is an advantage that God's favour, protection and hands transcend international borders. Joycinda and I still remain connected, and my prayers are still with her. She will always be a special part of my life.

During one of my visits to New Zealand, Joycinda gave me a card during our goodbyes. I slipped it into my bag and read it when I returned home to Australia. Tears filled my eyes, and the sky was so clear, I could almost see into heaven and observe what the angels were doing as her mum Jo sat on a cloud saying, 'Yes, that's my girl.' I am going to take the liberty to share this card with you. Joycinda was a twelve year old child at this stage and the abundance of her heart is startling.

I have not shared this card to gain accolades. Rather, my intention is to validate how a motherless child can go on a conquest to grasp a connection with her mother from another realm. How a child discovers what her mother stood for and what she fundamentally did not endorse. It also highlights the impact of role models on a child – a stark contrast to the scripture mentioned in this chapter with the influence that Herod's wife has.

Life in focus like Mother Teresa can stir up some sensations. However, we can all make a difference in our own tangible way when we demonstrate positivity to children at large. Our future will be built on their capabilities, which in turn depend on what you model to them. Personally escalate your roots of faith – lead by example and use words if you have to. You can make an impact even when you have not given birth to a child yourself. Just as dramatic is the impact that you make when we live in heaven and your child has your legacy as a prototype.

'When life gives you a hundred reasons to break down and cry, show life that you have a million reasons to smile, laugh and stay strong.'
Unknown

Dear Aunty Kelly By: Jacinda Abigail Paterson

Welcome back!! I missed you so much. I am glad we can make memories in the time you are here for. Thank you for everything you have got for me and the most special thing is..... giving me love and kindness. It may not seem like your giving your all, but trust me I really really feel the hard work you put in. You remind me of Mum (that I have heard in story) you never give up, you never stop showing love. you do everything with your heart and soul. ♥♥xo

Mum's verse she lives by.
"A woman full of life, loves the Lord and Loves her family, you have touched many lives" Ecc 9:10
Exactly like you. Being like her shows me a greater understanding of Mum.
Thank you for being there!
You and Mum have so much in common honestly.
"Whatever your hand finds to do, do it with all your might".
Thank you for being my Aunty Kelly! God Bless you with all your heart and soul.

Love you forever Bever: Jacinda

These words are insightful from a motherless child. It is the stark opposite of the spectrum in comparison to the referenced scripture – when Herod's stepdaughter, prompted by her mother, requested for a head on a platter: revenge. It awakens us all to the reality that we can all influence children. The captured joy of reading how a child yearns to know her mother from another realm and discern what she stood for and most importantly what she did not stand for is remarkable. We can all make impeccable additions to a child's inventory of conquests. This can be achieved by the legacy you leave behind and the example that you model even to ones that you have not given birth to. Inheritance a la Grande – what are your proud Mama moments of legacy? Are you modelling more grace and influence than a dripping bucket?

Photograph:
Sydney, Australia,
2019

Chapter Six

You Cannot Give a Shattered Heart

Divorce Stigma

I was grappling with life and the woes that divorce presented. A senior woman from church in New Zealand told me in no uncertain terms that divorce was a sin, and a divorcee was a sinner who would not go to heaven. These are heavy words to hear for a new Christian who is contending with circumstances beyond her personal control. Once again, my spirit was in turmoil.

I prayed about it and tried to resume my daily life, but the authoritative words still echoed in my mind. The church that I now attended in Brisbane, Australia, had many people in the same predicament as I. A senior pastor and almost half of my connect group members were also divorced. I sometimes had brief discussions with those who had charted these waters and shared their battle scars and encouraged me to persevere. I tried hard to not let tags, stigma, cultural beliefs or incorrect interpretation of The Word permeate my spirit.

Time marched on and I still felt daunted. One weekend, my spirit seemed tormented, and the Holy Spirit got me up in the middle of the night and led me to Google the topic. I read a bit and then I found myself searching for churches in Brisbane, even though I was happy with the church that I attended in Brisbane CBD. I landed on a church in the suburb of Kallangur. I had never been to this place before. I was new to this country and my car did not have a built-in navigation system. I had the good old hardcopy street map. I studied the map with the precision of a GIS professional and embarked on the journey to attend the evening service at this church after I had attended my normal church service in the morning.

Kallangur was over an hour from my home and this rookie did not get lost. It must have been a sign! I did not know a soul, the air felt a touch thick, I found a seat and planted myself. I was feeling rather chuffed with myself, having navigated to a new place at night using the street map in a new country and not getting lost.

The worship ended and the pastor began with the word 'divorce', intending to look at this from God's Word. I was in awe as I could not believe my ears. I trusted God to direct my life, yet I was still in shock about how he had brought me to this precise location to hear this specific topic.

The pastor's message calmed my spirit. He apologised to everyone who had endured a divorce, then apologised to everyone who had the stigma attached to them. He apologised for ignorant comments that cut an already wounded heart. By this time I was bawling my eyes out. Every word that was spoken was from God. It was the answer to all the questions I had, and my tormented spirit was at ease. Yes indeed, my God is able. He not only guided me to this place, but He also washed me and made me feel white as snow. He removed the stigma that people placed on me.

Rainfall is natural and we expect it as part of the earthly sustenance. However, quail fall is supernatural, and most people do not expect it. God fed the Israelites by quail fall. God's way is to care for his children, so take heart and do not be astonished when God works supernaturally for you. He is there for us. I was buzzing on high as I left the church and enquired about obtaining a copy of the sermon.

If God can do all this supernaturally to bring me to a place of peace and understanding, rest assured He can do it for you too. Learn to listen to Him. You will hear God if you develop the art of speaking to Him. I was in Brisbane basking in my newfound currency of healing and joy by spreading my broken wings. I decided to move to Sydney, and I had every intention to continue in this mode of peace…until I stumbled on the words of Bella and the actions of the church to encourage her behaviour.

Moreover, be careful of what you hurl out of your mouth to others and be acutely aware of what you turn a blind eye to as you may be enabling negative behaviour that impacts another person's world in an intense way. Love flows with the force of Niagara Falls, over **ALL** God's children. The operative word here is 'all', so do not choose one person over another.

My Journey Gleans

Once I received my healing, I desired to hold onto it and not be shaken by what another person may or may not do to me. I needed to stand strong in what God said about me and not be affected by what people had to say. This is easier said than done. We live in a broken world where words and attitudes do affect us. I needed to develop stronger roots to remain anchored in my healing so when any nasty words were hurled at me, I could face the storm and not be defeated by a mere mortal.

Tell yourself that no one has the power to make you feel unworthy or uneasy without your consent and that you are not willing to grant consent to anyone to inflict that pain, scar or stigma on you. Feel the emotion without the need to confront the person or the desire to shake off the tag. Master the art of not reacting to circumstances. Just as described previously when the cap blew off the man's head on the ship's deck, he was not fazed in any way, shape or form. Be steadfast despite circumstances. Bypass the blaming and shaming mentality. Relinquish the desire to understand why a person would attach negative stigmas to you.

I had to learn to stop letting the opinions of others offend me. I embraced my dark painful seasons and I understood them as a critical part of self-growth. I accepted the season for what it was and most importantly, I let the season and situation transform me. Acceptance does not ask that I be defined by my past or let others define me by an event that they have no understanding of. It simply asks that I cease the struggle and embrace how life is now. God loved me enough to forge ahead of me to prepare a healing balm in the form of a sermon. So I am determined to not permit a mortal person to rob me of my rebound healing and restoration.

Most of all, I remain astounded about how God steered me with precision to hear this sermon. When God makes you whole, do not let that peace be robbed. Hold onto it – even if you have to remove yourself from a toxic environment or friendship. Exercise your power and hold onto your healing and peace. Forgive whoever hurts you, forgiveness does not excuse their behaviour. Forgiveness only prevents their behaviour from destroying your heart. Forgiveness is processing the pain, understanding the experience and moving forward with a positive attitude towards healing. Forgiving someone to set yourself free does not mean you have to re-establish a relationship. Forgiveness is about you and not the other person. It means the incident has taught you, you are wiser from it and you can now move on living a free and restored life.

It takes courage to stand alone, and it takes courage to stand for what is right and it takes courage to commend those who strive to live by standards that are higher. Stand strong and live your truth. We all should cultivate lives to respect others and refrain from throwing stones at others, especially when we dwell in a glass house.

This quote is misattributed to the renowned Albert Einstein who defined insanity as: *'Doing the same thing over and over again, expecting a different result.'* Granted, we cannot change and control how people behave negatively. Nevertheless, we can decide how to positively respond. Noble gems can come from adversity and yet our behaviour in the core of adversity can challenge, break or ignite others. Do not let polite platitudes add salt to intense wounds. You know better but you do not do better, why? The miasma of gossip is not an accolade to frame but rather a pinch of infidelities that creates a beast that slices deep, shameful status, don't strive for it.

'Do not blame a clown for acting like a clown. Ask yourself why you keep going to the circus.' Dan Nielsen

Breaking Soul Ties

I was born into a culture and religion that had created many soul ties in my life. Soul ties can be formed unconsciously to people, places and things. To move forward in life, I needed to break the soul ties and vows that I had in my life. When a relationship is created, we share so much – milestones, birthdays, anniversaries, births, deaths, special occasions, New Year's, Christmas, traditions, family ties, fellowship and tragic times. We place emphasis on personalised wedding vows that we want to live by. But we do not live them until death. I had made vows in God's Holy presence only for the man to devalue them so lightheartedly. I now just had a piece of paper to endorse the relationship as being officially over.

There is no process to unlink two flesh that have become one. How do I undo my vows? The legal paperwork is not as emotional as the linking of two souls then having these two souls torn apart. It is literally like pasting two pieces of cardboard together with super glue to make a single piece, and then someone decides to rip apart the glued pieces.

It is almost impossible to get the cardboard pieces back as they originally were. Damage to both pieces is inevitable. So just imagine the magnitude of pain in reality when two people break apart. Position yourself to heal and to thrive. Positioning is utmost, so do all you need to do to position yourself into alignment. Calibrate to belief or unbelief, restore to hope or doubt, return to trust or mistrust; pick a side of the fence that you prefer to live on remembering that your life is mapped by these critical choices.

Refrain from being double minded. When you are double minded, you will receive nothing. If you are not trusting God whole heartedly, how can He release your portion? Strategic positioning is connected with attitude, and attitude is connected with altitude. So often we see someone perform a miracle by speaking a Word or merely raising their hand. A seemingly insignificant mere mortal person. This person is positioned and anointed by God. So get in position. Do not dwell on your conditions, start with your positioning!

My Journey Gleans

How do we unlink our hearts and vows? I needed to go on a journey to firstly identify and then break all the ungodly soul ties in my life.

The furniture we purchased together brought back memories that I was not fond of and I felt trapped. The clothes that I had worn and the compliments that I had acquired in the relationship were a constant reminder of a void. So I had to break all these soul ties and stop longing for the one that had abandoned me in the eye of the storm.

Salt creates discomfort when it is added to a wound, yet ultimately it purifies and heals. So delve into those wounds in your life, the strongholds and the soul ties. Build your confidence by releasing yourself from all contracts or soul ties. This is found in the Bible within the book of 2 Kings 2:19 -22. This shows the use of salt to cleanse. Tap into this cleansing stream.

In the Biblical days a covenant was sealed by salt. It signified loyalty and preserved a contract. 'Although salt is powerful in historical and metaphorical terms, its spiritual power often goes unnoticed. Spiritually speaking, salt is considered the great neutraliser. It can help cleanse, heal and balance energy, while repelling negative vibrations.'

Pray diligently for God to release you from all vows and soul ties by bathing in a salt bath as a tangible symbol of breaking your covenants. Read this scripture over your life:

Numbers 18:19 – Whatever is set aside from the Holy offerings the Israelites present to the Lord, I give to you and your sons and daughters as your perpetual share. It is an everlasting covenant of salt before the Lord for both you and your offspring.

Pray over the salt and ask God to cleanse and refresh you. Believe that you are healed by the stripes of Jesus and the ties that were created by your vows have released you in Jesus' name. Jesus also represents salt He preserves life, sustains life and He is faithful in every season of life. So let this salt bath wash over you and take away the past vows and let the present promise live anew in you. I had to dig deep to psychologically accept the reality of my life so I could stop wasting energy struggling with my experience, to instead conserve energy for things that I could control. This physical cleansing bath helped me heal the pain of breaking two souls apart. God is the only everpresent help we all need, but sometimes we do need something tangible to help us release what we are glued to.

I had to make each day count to live my best life by making daily choices to be grateful, show unconditional love, be authentic and live with integrity. I became so busy that I had no time to focus on those that hated me or walked away; I chose instead to zoom in on all those that loved me and wanted to share life with me. As there is no instruction manual or timeline to break soul ties, be gentle with yourself as you take small steps to process the healing. Sometimes we have to make a clean sweep, revolutionise, change tack, and renew our mind and location to propel us to a new place that we are destined to be at. Leave behind earthly contracts and plunge deeper with your spiritual contract.

'God's purpose for you is bigger than your mistakes.' Nicky Gumbel

My Boaz Prayer List

I heard a preacher ask those seeking a marriage companion to prepare a list of what they were looking for in a soul mate and take this list to God in prayer. I prepared my rather extensive list of my unsuspecting Boaz. I knew vividly without a shadow of a doubt what the deal breakers were for me.

'Love is a verb' the common phrase hit my sensors with an acute sense of discernment when I was still a teenager. I understood that if I wanted to attract certain fine qualities in a partner, then I needed to present the same impeccable qualities to the person who wanted my hand. Love is a two way equation, and it is a give and take. I needed to bring something attractive to the table as well and be an amazing catch too.

Love is not just the words we whisper into each other's ear or the butterflies we feel. It is how we relate to the other person that we love and how we respond when our carefully laid out plans go down south. How you treat someone during death, sickness, infertility and when you are in despair yourself. When I was in high school, this poem written by William Shakespeare made quite an impression on me. I clearly resolved as an unsuspecting sixteen year old that this is precisely how I wanted to love. Here is a paraphrased section of Sonnet 116...

'Love alters not with alterations. Oh no, it is an everfixed mark. If this be error and upon me proved, I never writ, nor no man ever loved.' William Shakespeare.

This is most definitely not how life panned out. Sadly, in the world that we all live in now, love is so very conditional. So I worked on myself to be the best version of myself. I am still a work in progress, but I do occasionally get the jaw dropping, head turning standing ovation in honour of the person I choose to be! The person I am at work, in the community, on vacation, with my family, at my church, with strangers, with the rich, with the poor, with those that wronged me, with those that wounded my soul and those that I love.

We can add filters on our profile pictures on social media and bring our best foot forward when dating. We can tick all the boxes on the checklist to be the best thing since sliced bread. The ultimate test is what you do when no one is watching you. How do you interact with people in your circle behind closed doors? Do you create waves of turmoil or do you bring harmony to the camp?

When God created Adam, He then created Eve as his helper. A helper's role is to enhance the person in charge with a sense of rescue. The synonyms for a 'helper' are servant or collaborator. Do you exhibit these qualities? This does not denote that we need to live in agony, feeling that one leads and the other submits. God created the Holy Spirit as a 'HELPER' so bask in the fact that as a woman your basic character matches scripture. Rise and live up to it diligently.

John 14:26 - But the helper, the Holy Spirit, whom the Father will send in My name, He will teach you all things and bring to your remembrance all that I said to you.

My Journey Gleans

This scripture shamed me to eat humble pie as an independent, corporate, successful and high achieving woman. I had to learn to let go of the reign and trust that I am the helper. The Bible says Jesus came to serve and not to be served and if Jesus can be a servant, then who am I to be on a high horse? I am delighted to be a servant and helper to my husband. We are still equal partners, and we complement each other as yin and yang. Abstain from creating metaphoric walls that stifle. When two become one, then we must realign to create a force to be reckoned with and we must reorganise, adjust, and modify to find the recurrent harmony.

I am strong and independent and had to learn to be as tough as nails. So when a situation arises and I know I've got this one in the bag, I diligently step back to let my husband lead and I help if I need to. I even have to sometimes take off the pants and let him wear them. How do you feel about being a servant or helper – reluctant? When he loves you (unconditionally) like Christ loves the church then we see the merit of a balanced equation. Create the balance. In addition, when I was single, I used my time to enhance myself so I could bring the most vibrant person to the world and all my future relationships. God's timing is not synchronised with our mortal clocks. In order to love others adequately, I needed to heal and love myself first. If you want to move on fast, find someone in the same lane – and if you want to truly find someone then FIND YOURSELF first.

'It does not matter whether you have found someone yet or not, all the work you do on yourself now will pay off in your future relationships.'
Matthew Hussey

Wolf in Sheep's Clothing

It is almost impossible to find wholesome love in today's broken world. People lie about being a Christian. One guy I met was from Iran but claimed to be Christian and presented himself so well I could hardly believe my blessings. I prayed for God to reveal to me all that was in darkness and I discovered he was an illegal refugee. I had no issue with that; however, a relationship needs to start on honest foundations with no elements of calculated evasiveness or embellishment.

When two people start a relationship, you both bring your best attributes forward. So, start with your positives, not negatives. If you start with the latter, it will surely end in a train wreck.

Another potential from Christian Connection claimed he was recently born again with the zeal to live for God. I prayed and asked God for direction. I got a vivid dream where God advised me to help him. I had no idea what was about to unfold. So once again I gleaned all this when the rubber hit the road. He was on a visitor visa and working in Australia illegally, and he would take quick weekend trips to neighbouring countries to get back in and reactivate his visitor visa. We had only known each other for a couple of months when his planned New Zealand trip culminated in his deportation. I bent over backwards to help him with legal immigration assistance, resources to live, and to land on his feet, showing him unconditional love and help. He was so broken and lost that he had no clue how to be a friend, a blessing or to simply be grateful.

My Journey Gleans

I had to let go of my heartfelt desires even when I was unsure what the future entailed or how I would navigate through life by myself in a foreign land. I created an empty space so I could find my authentic self.

When the future that I carved in my head – with a wonderful husband, intelligent kids and a playful dog – seemed to evade me, I developed the mental capacity to live in the now and enjoy the present. This did not mean I gave up on plans altogether; I still had a plan for retirement. But I choose to not put my life on hold waiting to live only when I retire. Growth and change are painful but staying stagnant and stuck where you do not belong is far more painful. Serendipity does not change your circumstances and life has no remote control. You have to get up and make change happen in this one incredible life you have. Do not wish for a change but rather instigate the change.

Get up, dress up, show up, breathe, laugh, connect, inspire, offer to help others, accept help from others, set healthy boundaries, collect strength, develop the art of resilience, cry if you have to, spend a day in your pyjamas, practise self-care, acknowledge what hurts, develop self-awareness, choose to face reality rather than live in denial and, choose your response to reality rather that reacting to it. Fall in love with the process of becoming the very best version of you. Appreciate the wrong relationships. They teach you things, revolutionise you, expand you, fortify you, refine you and prepare you for the right one. Once you reach the other end of the breakup spectrum, you will find that the experience instils character and greater discernment in you.

'Every time I thought I was being rejected from something good, I was actually being re-directed to something better.' Steve Maraboli

Chalk and Cheese

The friendship with the 'visitor visa' guy ended before it began. We only met twice before he was deported. During this time I assisted him due to the vivid message I had received in the spirit. To him I was merely an ATM. He manifested his true nature in so many shocking ways. He did not tick any boxes on my wish list for a soul mate. He was good looking and confident, still that got him nowhere as eventually people discovered exactly who he was.

Our world today is filled with choices, both wholesome and unwholesome, so be faithful by choice. Dark seasons in life define us so stay on the narrow path that brings life and hope. I went on a journey so I could experience my own enlightenments first-hand, and when I met my next suitor Dave, I could see the stark differences. It made his qualities stand out vividly in comparison. Every season is a period to learn and grow, even the painful ones.

Dave was keen as mustard and it was love at first sight for him. While chatting with my girlfriend, she asked if I was going on another date with him and I said no. 'I don't think he is my type.' Her response was: 'Come on Kels, give the guy a break as he is probably intimidated by you.'

This was such an eye-opener for me. I was accustomed to being in the driver's seat and making all the decisions that mapped my life, yet I was not so confident in my fine judgement of character. For some odd reason I had the knack of picking the rotten eggs. Dave did ask me to go out the next evening as it was coincidentally Valentine's Day, but I said no. The words of my friend just kept tugging at me. I thought, what if my radar was off and I had always dismissed the compatible prospects based on my first encounter. So then I gave Dave another chance and we went on a date the following week. With delight I quickly confirmed the condition of his real heart, what he lives for, how he treats me and most importantly his love for God. We both knew we wanted to share the rest of our lives together.

This discussion with my friend was my realisation that God had a bigger picture in store for me and it confirmed that I did not have to go by my radar. Lean on God and follow the path He has provided even though your own instincts advise the opposite. It does not matter how long we have walked with God or waited on God; He gives us time to grow to a healthy plateau. So ultimately you are in control of your growth and are empowered to create a relationship with God and others where your path is directed, and people can freely express what they feel about the situation. Be present and receptive so you can be open to another person's perception.

My Journey Gleans

Physical beauty fades. It may attract in the beginning but once the hood is lifted and the real substance is exposed, inner character and beauty come to life. Inner beauty persists for eternity if you permit it and it does not fade with time. You may look like a hot Greek god or goddess, but that won't last forever, and it does not create wholesome ties. I spent a decade by myself, looking internally and finding what made me tick. I did not seek for someone else to make me happy. I defined my path of happiness in my daily routine, the traditional norms and even when the current pulled me backwards.

Intimacy with God produces understanding, gracefulness, wisdom, discernment, mercy, empathy, compassion, respect, honour and appreciation. The way we are touched by God is reflected in the way that we relate to others. Brokenness gives off hurt and emotions that throttle. If someone has not healed from trauma, they will only dispense pain to others. Know the difference and know when to walk away.

When you are confident in God's love, it flows like a river of life from you. A healing balm with restorative powers, a gentle touch of affirmation, a quiet blessing, the willingness to give without being asked, the commitment to help a stranger, a hand to hold, a shoulder to lean on, a kiss to wipe a tear.

I allowed myself to heal from pain and trauma so I could dispense God's unconditional love; and God brought the most amazing real love to me through Dave. Be proud of what you have overcome – every single scar is a lesson to create a better and richer character. When old patterns reveal themselves and you feel like you are back where you started, then remember that healing is a process and not an instant switch. You need to deal with each layer and root cause as and when it surfaces. Trudge as slowly as you deem fit to sort out each pain or trauma and manage it appropriately, so it does not manifest in future. I had to take my foot off the gas and release the negative energy. I had to give my subconscious mind air to breathe and recover. Just like we place effort in maintaining our physical body, it is mandatory for our mental state to follow a daily healthy and healing routine too.

It is always vital to take time out to sharpen the axe so you can get the job done more effectively with a sharper blade, rather than taking forty years to do a forty days' journey. I guess the Israelites never knew how blunt their axe was! God can take you out of Egypt, but Egypt can remain transfixed in you. Transformation was the lacking key ingredient; hence the wilderness became a way of life for the Israelites – reference to a story in the Bible.

'I am not a product of my circumstances, instead a product of my decisions.' Stephen Covey.

Love
is not the only
ingredient in marriage; respect and
perseverance are key ingredients as well. I
am blessed that my soulmate comes bundled as a
great package that exhibits so much more.

To love is nothing
To be loved is something
To love and be loved is everything

It takes three to make two into one

Photograph:
Sydney, Australia
2019

Chapter Seven

Litmus Test for True Alliance

Best Friends Since Sliced Bread

I experienced some of the best belly laughs with friends and in contrast I also cried some of the most painful tears because of so called friends. I was at church in Brisbane, Australia, when I met a young lady. She was a qualified doctor but could not practise as her qualification was not recognised in Australia; besides, she had run into some personal discord with some young ladies that did not treat her fairly. I felt her plight and addressed the situation with the connect group leaders. This young lady then assumed we were best friends since sliced bread.

I will help those that need help. I have ample friends that have charted through life with me. I always give people the opportunity to rise to the occasion and reciprocate their friendship accordingly. Sadly, some people cannot discern that a healthy relationship is a two-way street of give and take.

She moved to another country and we kept in touch. I lent her my ear, I encouraged her and communicated with her on a regular basis. Many years rolled on. I would not call her my bestie; however, I did think that the relationship had transformed into a meaningful one. She expressed how she would love to see me and have a holiday together. So we planned a trip. She was in Atlanta, USA, and I was flying international to Vegas to meet her there and then we planned to visit the Grand Canyon together.

This was during Christmas and the New Year – the most expensive time to travel as most people want to spend Christmas with fine company and not alone. A few weeks before the trip she cancelled with no regard for the fact that I would be alone in a foreign country for Christmas and New Year's. Even though it hurt, I took it in my stride and understood her predicament and respected her decision. We still kept in touch as I decided not to throw out the baby with the bath water.

The following year marched on and I made plans with another friend to explore another part of USA for Christmas and New Year's. When the lady from Atlanta learned of this, she hounded me every day to visit her. Our nearest port after my Caribbean cruise would be Miami. The airline had also lost my luggage, so I wanted to stay close to my hotel to get my luggage before my departure. She phoned and abused me for not making the effort to visit her.

After the effort I had made the year before, she suddenly seemed to have developed amnesia for all the times I had chosen to show her mercy and grace for her lack of better judgement. I said my piece and asked her not to contact me again. She also assumed that she knew me well enough to offer me advice on areas of life that she had not mastered herself and had no tangible experience in. I am a firm believer of giving honour where honour is due, and also in recognising when all someone does is take and give you nothing in return.

My feelings for this one way friendship were further confirmed when she requested a copy of my resume to market herself in the corporate world. She was a qualified doctor. Yet we were on different corporate pages. Almost the same age and I had what she coveted. I am not a doctor, but my life is successful because I honour God.

My Journey Gleans

Sometimes people pretend to be our best friends because they want what we have. Keep your vertical relationship right with God and all your horizontal relationships will flow with favour. Picking up the thread of friendship should come with ease when both parties place equal priority on the relationship. I am flabbergasted how some friends pour nothing into a relationship, yet they expect so much in return.

Do not let anything stand in your way from owning your shortcomings and aiming to embrace the same calibre of friendship that you expect from others. It is magnificent to create a sisterhood where women quit seeing each other as competition. No two people on this planet share the same set of fingerprints. We are created unique, and each of us is a one-of-a-kind masterpiece. God in his infinite wisdom has designed us in this fashion. Then why do we have the urge to clone ourselves to be like a celebrity or covet what another friend has? We are all in the same boat and we create sisterhood by propelling each other forward and not by competing with each other.

All boats rise in a high tide. We need to come together and pray for that global or individual high tide. We all have different gifts and strengths, so find what your destiny is and leap forward with it. I had another 'friend' who stole my resume while she was job hunting. It was alarming but I did not confront her. I prayed for her to land a job in her field. We work in different faculties and while you may be able to fake it on paper, when the rubber hits the road that is where the challenge lies.

Sisterhood is about being your authentic self and improving as a person, helping another person reach their full potential. It most definitely is not a tall poppy syndrome where you cut someone down to make yourself look taller. You will never have a sisterhood or be confident as a person if you need to steal ideas from another to invent yourself. Celebrate the distinct differences that God has created in us. Sisterhood is not self serving, rather it is unconditional in all seasons, through every word, deed and action in both good and bad times. Sisterhood, friendship and any relationship that is an equanimous blend, forms a healthy calibre of fellowship.

'There are three constants in life: CHANGE, CHOICE AND PRINCIPLES.'
Stephen Covey

The Deed of Giving and Taking

I knew a young lass from my neighbourhood who attended the same primary school as I did in South Africa. When I was in New Zealand, I spoke on the phone to her husband who was contemplating immigrating to New Zealand by himself and then bringing his wife later as they were expecting a baby. I asked him who his wife was as I vaguely recalled her from primary school.

I advised him it was best to immigrate with his wife so they could support each other during the transition. They landed in New Zealand with their first child and the second one on the way. Life in a new country is challenging at the best of times, so I offered all the help I could rally to them. They initially stayed with me until they landed on their feet. They supported me emotionally through some of the curve balls that life threw at me during that time.

When I moved to Australia we still kept in touch. As time progressed, our friendship took deeper dives. We developed a substantial bond that transcended international borders. It is not difficult to remain present and prioritise people in the age of technological advancements today.

One day during a heart-to-heart conversation on the phone, her husband said to me with a heavy voice that it was proving immensely difficult to purchase their own home and this was heavy on their hearts. During my next visit, he asked if I would be interested in co-purchasing a home with them. I prayed about it and from all my experience I knew better than to mix money matters with friendship. The next day I gently said I did not wish to get involved as it may not logistically work. However, I blessed them with a deposit so they could purchase a home for themselves.

They were in tears as they informed their children and church family of this unexpected present and they rejoiced. I had been unemployed for six months and I was financially stretched. Yet, I did not have an element of doubt about the seed that I promised to sow. I knew God trusted me to be a wise steward with all that He had blessed me with including my financial resources. Many times I made personal sacrifices to bless others and noted that sometimes people forget the medium God used to bless them and they are very vocal to declare how prosperous they are. Take heart that we should never cease to help or bless as it is better to be a giver than a taker. Our reward comes from a far greater source than from the side of the fence that stretches their pleading hands.

My Journey Gleans

Granted that you have heard of the hormone oxytocin, you may know a little about its somewhat extraordinary reputation. Oxytocin is a hormone known to have an affirmative impact on mood and emotions. It is a powerful neurotransmitter. It plays a key role in developing emotional connection. It can also meaningfully affect the functioning of the brain and nervous system and impact our emotions day-to-day. Low levels of oxytocin in the brain are associated with several mental health conditions, including depression, anxiety, social phobia, post-traumatic stress disorder, etc. Research suggests that if you increase oxytocin, it can lead to the following benefits: reduce stress and anxiety, increase feelings of calmness and security, improve mood and increase feelings of contentment. The list goes on.

Oxytocin evidently does a lot. Due to this, some doctors have started prescribing oxytocin to their patients to help treat their mental health symptoms. However, you don't necessarily need to rush to your doctor and obtain a prescription. You can practise natural ways to increase oxytocin in the brain. There are several avenues to explore, I will let you conduct your own research. Nonetheless, I will share just one profound effect that impacts a dramatic sphere – **'Give someone a gift or simply be a blessing.'** Studies show that receiving and giving gifts or a blessing increases oxytocin levels in the brain. So imagine the ripple effect this has on society when you increase someone's oxytocin level, and they are elated with positive vibes and thus they pay the prescription forward. A natural prescription with no side effects.

Consequently the next time that you are blessed and your oxytocin level is boosted by a sheer random act of kindness, do not let the prescription die with you, rather pass it on – let your community, sphere and humanity get a whiff of it. The most precious asset we possess is not our material wealth but our word. Our word means nothing when we do not honour it as saying one thing and doing another reveals we have no integrity. It has often cost me personal sacrifice to honour my word. I would rather be a woman of integrity than a financially blessed woman with no moral or ethical code. It is better to be a giver than a taker. So position yourself to be a giver as we are blessed to be a blessing. Those who refresh others will be refreshed. The gift of generosity does not equate to your bank balance, it is simply an attitude that defines you. The heart is a chalice of love. Integrity, gratitude and kindness are also manifestations of love. The abundance of the heart is displayed in full vision when we see how these revelations rise to the surface or when negative emotions seep out instead as well.

'We do not always get to pick the parable we are living, but we get to choose who we are in the parable.' Bob Goff

Thankful Progress is Priceless

When I began a new contract role in a new office, I indulged in the normal corridor chit-chat to break the ice. A lady with South African origins, Jane, gravitated towards me. I showed her unconditional love in so many simple ways and she thought we were the new besties in town. Meanwhile, I got engaged, then the wedding plans loomed in the air. Jane asked if she could get involved in the planning as she never had a wedding ceremony herself. She had dreams of the dress and the whole shebang. She Googled wedding plans obsessively and sent me links on everything. She seemed excited to be in this space. But her emotions went down like a lead balloon when I informed her that we had decided to have a destination wedding on the Greek island of Santorini. She was crestfallen.

We were very briefly acquainted. In addition, I had many amazing friends that had walked the journey of life with me in all seasons and they were all most definitely on the list for bridesmaids. Heading to a wedding in Europe required more than change in a piggy bank. I felt Jane's disappointment acutely, especially when I considered the fact that she did not have her own wedding ceremony and had wanted to live vicariously through my experience.

I asked her to be a bridesmaid not just so she could be part of the planning of the special day but also to help her on her own journey to heal. In addition, I offered to pay for her international return airfare. Planning kicked off with full steam for this destination wedding, deciding on bridesmaids and getting wedding dresses custommade, planning excursions before and after the wedding, a hen's party and a family holiday in Italy after the Greek shindig.

Accommodation for the family group would be in Athens, Santorini and Italy. I received numerous requests from people to include them in activities and accommodation. I also had a professional job that demanded my time and attention. Very early on, I gave everyone a ballpark estimation of Airbnb accommodation costs. When the time approached for finalisation, I added service fees as we required cleaning, given the fact it was a group booking.

The theatre of life sometimes played out at work and I discovered the contents of Jane's heart. I saw her loyalty was not with me. Her social media posts confirmed she was envious of me. All she really wanted was a free holiday. She had no real love or care for me. Our love needs to focus on love for people and use material resources however often individuals use people and love physical things rather than cherishing and valuing human connection and richness – society ends up chasing material wealth with no filter for human emotions. This is a tragic way to live. No matter how little you have, treat people with dignity, love and respect as people are far more important than money.

I was at church praying for a relative who was in intensive care after a tragic accident. My phone vibrated a few times in silent mode. I got a message from Jane where she accused me of having my own side business and charging different accommodation costs for the destination wedding. She made me feel like I was stealing $180 from her when I had instead given her $2,000 for her return flights. I could not find logic in her accusation.

I was perplexed. I had blessed this woman with a couple thousand dollars for her flight to Europe and now she was penny pinching about a few hundred. I sent her the screen capture of precise Airbnb costs and the fact that I had rounded down and undercharged everyone. In addition, we had paid in euros for all the other excursions and absorbed all the international conversion charges. But her vitriolic accusations kept erupting like wildfire.

Lack of growth and absenteeism in times of need can fray the bonds of friendship. Pretence is dead weight and eventually we all have to purge our circles. You get on the purge list by the things you do and most importantly DON'T DO as a friend; when you take a friendship for granted or just don't show up in the circle of trust. Plastering the same rehearsed smile with superficial intentions is not friendship, it is mateship – know the difference! Corral the dead weight and cut them loose.

In times of need, real friends are priceless. Their value is far greater than a mountain of money as money is inanimate, breathless, cannot wipe away a tear and provide confidence when you need it. Money lacks the ability to empathise when you need it most. So when God sends you a real treasure of a friend who listens and offers a helping hand, be grateful. Honour is tested in how we treat each other – especially the hand that feeds us when we are hungry!

Jane went into a frenzy and decided to not attend the wedding. She returned the bridesmaid dress and sent a text to inform me that she had cancelled the flights and would pass on the refunded amount to me. Money is a resource to me and I am not consumed by it, as I have the capacity to give it so freely, even to strangers that I deem are in need. A relationship is as real and strong as the moment it is tested, so if you want honey do not kick the beehive.

My Journey Gleans

I had felt Jane's plight and acted with kindness, yet how quickly she forgot the blessing that was so freely given to her. It was so easy for Jane to pull the plug as she invested minimally in the equation, both financially and emotionally. It was better to have this surface now rather than at our wedding. I noticed how she did not care about losing the cancellation fees on the flight because she did not pay for it ($700), yet she could get into a penny-pinching fit for a few hundred when service fees were included to the accommodation ($180). The shocking wakeup call was the fact that she did not care about losing $700 because it was not her money - $180 was her money, so she had to demand a price variation report from me. Sometimes we help but we end up being the victims.

If you value someone, do not let money come between you. Most importantly learn the art of taking responsibility for your part in the experience and be aware of the negative energy that is introduced when money is a high priority. Remember to be grateful when you are blessed, you may have received the answer to your prayer on a platter but perhaps someone had to make a great sacrifice to present that blessing to you.

There are three reasons why we do not trust people:

1. We do not know them
2. We do know them
3. We treat them well but only notice their true actions when we need a friend to depend on

Get to know them before you add them to your circle of trust. Be comfortable with the knowledge that the most painful moments in our life can also be the most purposeful. I established a new norm in my life by escorting people out of the VIP section of my life and into the regular section where they rightfully belonged. This created positive energy to focus on the people who truly mattered and to enhance my relationships with them.

I may not be able to control someone's negative behaviour, but I can certainly control with what magnitude it affects me. I have the power to defuse a negative situation. If I let the negative situation prevail, eventually it will become my natural habitat and impact me adversely. I cannot reach new vistas without expanding my circle and calibre of affiliations. The true test of friendship is how we respond when we are chastised. A real friend weathers the storm but a superficial one runs for the hills.

Even though I was a real friend, I knew Jane offered nothing for me to maintain the friendship. A little yeast leavens all the dough. I could not overlook these issues as I knew it would have caused a negative ripple effect on all my guests. A tree is known by the fruit it bears as a good tree will bear good fruit. The noticeable fruit harvested from this work acquaintance revealed the calibre of her heart. It was not my job to take her on a gratitude journey and I was grateful that she decided not to attend our wedding.

Although Jane did not return all my resources, I still had peace and joy. Many things broke my heart, but I had a restored vision. This encounter gave me clarity and the spirit to maintain healthier boundaries. The way I was treated in the office after I showed her so much unconditional love confirmed to me that Judas still exists in everyday life and I needed to sift the chaff from the wheat. A friendship should not drain you.

When a relationship matters to you and you value it more than money, then it is better to be quiet and thought of as a fool rather than speak and remove all doubt. When you speak, the true intentions of the heart are revealed. It is a sad day when you value your $180 much more than the $2,000 that was freely given to you. It reveals where your heart is. It is strong for money and rather weak for people. I learned to extend care, kindness, understanding and love to each person no matter how trivial the contact.

I have done this with no thought of a reward. When the person has an ungrateful attitude and expects me to do much more than I already have, then rest assured I will step away and that will be the end of the gravy train relationship. Do not let people milk you just because they now know the nature of your heart. 'We are what we repeatedly do. Excellence then is not an act but a habit. Sow a habit and reap a character, sow a character and reap a destiny. Habits are powerful factors in our lives because they are consistent and often form unconscious patterns.' Unknown

Our actions express our character and produce our effectiveness or ineffectiveness. There can be no friendship without confidence and no confidence without integrity. You cannot be successful with other people if you have not paid the price of success for yourself. You cannot talk your way out of problems that your own behaviours have created. The most important ingredient we put into a relationship is not what we do or say but what we are. When someone shows you their true colours, don't try to paint a different picture.

We may be able to paint on a façade about our character, but we are naked and transparent to God, so always behave knowing that God is watching. Do not be a charismatic taker on earth. The greatest lesson I got out of this situation was that I do not have to set myself on fire to keep someone else warm. Realise the talent of loyalty and foster the practice to say thank you especially when it is merited. Hints of hope twinkle when we learn the skill of practising gratitude rather than just wearing the aroma or hire the attitude of gratitude for an hour. I release money with joy, and it returns to me multiplied without any hard sweat. Relational equity is priceless so discover how to add and maintain that in your life. When you disregard a person's effort, you also wound the estimate of the friendship and no goodwill flows out of that.

'Some cause happiness wherever they go while others whenever they go.' Oscar Wilde

Bonds That Beckon, Forty Years and Counting

My bestie Elaine and I have been friends for over forty years. We live in two different countries, but we know each other's genuine hearts. We talk almost every day. Even in text messages we can sense if something is wrong in each other's world.

One day at work, I got a text message from Elaine saying 'Can I call you? I need to speak to you.' My heart sank as I knew immediately that something was wrong. I feared the worst and texted back 'yes sure' as I dashed out of my office for some privacy. I learned that her mum was diagnosed with terminal brain cancer. Elaine cried and I heard the anguish in her voice. Tears rolled down my cheeks and I asked her if she wanted me to get on a flight to be with her. She negated, saying she just needed to talk to me.

We talked almost every day despite being in different time zones – where there is a will there is most definitely a way. Elaine still juggled her corporate job while providing medical care for her mum. She was surrounded on all fronts by challenges that demanded her attention. Her mum reached palliative care and the emotional toll was extremely apparent on Elaine. I had a trip planned to South Africa to attend my cousin's wedding, and I decided to spend some time with both Elaine and her Mum.

Elaine was excited about the visit. I was all packed and ready to soar the skies. I got to the check-in counter and the airline staff informed me I could not board as I did not have a visa. Even though I was born in South Africa, I had a New Zealand passport. No visa had been required in the past. The travel rules had changed, and I did not get that memo.

I called my travel agent and he rather arrogantly told me to inform my family that I would not be attending the wedding as South Africa does not grant electronic visas and it would take ten business days to process a visa application. The South African High Commission in Canberra was approximately 300 kilometres away. Most importantly, I could not just turn up at the South African High Commission without a prearranged appointment. It was Saturday and the office would be closed. My travel agent's suggestion was I go home and travel at another time as I would never get my visa in time.

Tell me it cannot be done, and I will show you how many different ways I can get it done. I was in a cab on my way home from the airport. I called Elaine and told her that I could not board the flight. She thought it was a joke. I told her about the visa saga. She said, 'I cannot believe the universe right now, I am on the brink of despair and just waiting to see you.'

I called my friend from church, Gab, a prayer warrior, and I explained my predicament and told him I needed a miracle and to pray for me. I stayed up all night researching visa requirements. Gab called me and said, 'I prayed, and you got your miracle and you will get your visa, you do not need a plan B.' I was not feeling so confident, but I had faith that God is able and faith without works is nothing and I need to do the work to execute this for a positive result.

I spent Sunday getting all my visa items checked. I waited anxiously for the South African High Commission office to open on Monday morning. I called as a zealous trooper and explained my situation. The lady gave me an appointment for 9 a.m. on Tuesday. I was excited about the appointment, but I had not slept since Friday night and I most definitely could not drive 600 kilometres sleep deprived. Even if I flew to Canberra, I would not get back to Sydney in time to board an international flight. I called my regular cab driver, Sasha, and he offered to drive me to Canberra and back. The taxi bill was larger than my international flight cost. Desperate times call for desperate measures.

My Journey Gleans

I knew that this was the last time I would see Elaine's mum. I knew how much my friend yearned to see me in her greatest season of need. I wanted to see her mum while she was still alive, talk to her, spend time with her and say goodbye in person.

Sometimes life cannot equate to a monetary value. I knew assuredly that money is not and never will be my focus. What was important was jumping through every obstacle to offer the little comfort that I could to both Elaine and her mum. I obtained my visa, drove back to Sydney, dashed home, fetched my luggage and headed to the international airport to catch my flight all in the same day.

Upon reaching South Africa, most did not care about the effort I had put in to attend the wedding. No big deal, as I had made all that effort for my friend. Friendship is about so many things. There is no friendship like the one when someone you love is in need. Do you look at the money it costs to be a friend or the choice to be a friend despite the cost? A compelling portrait of a blessed friend is found in the threads of sacrifice we all make to maintain the friendship.

When I was at this crossroads, I chose to put my friendship above finances. The pull of our friendship strengthened to another level. We both promoted our bestie level to a new dimension of friendship. We are placed in awkward situations to grow and to glean what we mean to each other. Harness your strength strategically for what really matters, it is the legacy and bonds we create, not the inheritance that we leave behind!

I purposely live my life to never fear failure but to be terrified of regret. Affirmative life is epic when you have an authentic friend that travels to you in well appointed time to hold your hand when you have to bury a loved one. Nothing in life can trump this bond. Rest assured that your destination is in focus if you have just one such friend. Be a real friend first and real bonds will beckon with the progression of time. Regret has the mouth of a crocodile, it bites hard. Do not leave undone what you can do. With God, there are no failures, only learning curves – don't let it be a steep one. Therefore, what the world labels as failure is essentially: process, development, enlargement, refinement and enhancement. So rise up and see how and where you are transforming and developing, what negative traits are dwindling off and how faith is built. When you show up rather than run when it gets rough, then you are different from the average. This is why you have the ability to do remarkable things and be valued.

At high school, Elaine and I had sung this song with the rest of our class at a school social – *That's What Friends Are For* by Dionne Warwick. Disclaimer – we both cannot sing for peanuts. When I sent out invitations to my Santorini wedding, Elaine took a long time to RSVP. She responded long after the stipulated date as she had to choose to either attend my wedding or travel to celebrate her twentieth wedding anniversary later that year. She could not afford both trips in one year. After much deliberation she decided to attend my wedding in Santorini. This meant that she and her husband would not celebrate their wedding anniversary as they had originally planned. I was in the car driving one day and the above mentioned song blared flamboyantly from the radio. This reminded me of the horrific school singing and yet it was more profound than that. I knew every lyric and I could sing it from my heart, and I knew that Elaine felt the same way too. I turned up the volume and sang…

'Keep smiling, keep shining. Knowing you can always count on me, for sure. That's what friends are for. For good times and bad times. I'll be by your side forever more. That's what friends are for.'

…Tears gushed down my cheeks. We have been friends for more than forty years and we had navigated some seasons that we never dreamt of. However, our friendship is now far beyond sisterhood. We have reached a new level of distinct camaraderie. It is evident that we are connected by visceral and grounding love that beckons unconditional hearts. She values the friendship just as much as I do and has made efforts and sacrifices as I did to maintain and take our friendship to the next level as well. The element of sadness that taints this sweet walk down memory lane: The fact that I so freely and instantly blessed Jane with free return tickets to my wedding and she had no regard for me or the occasion.

On the other hand, Elaine made every effort to be present at the milestone event because she loved me. Some people wonder why they never experience real friendships that withstand the test of time. Well, that's because we all reap what we sow. If you invest in a friendship, rest assured you will reap the rewards as well. I was deathly sorry that I chose to buy a ticket for Jane instead of Elaine. We should not throw pearls to swine as they do not know the value of pearls and they will not appreciate it. A genuine friendship will offer both parties unharnessed rhythmic energy to nurture and reap the eternal legacy of the friendship.

'Friendship is not how you forget but how you forgive. Not how you listen but how you understand. Not how you see but how you feel. Not how you let go but how you take care.' Unknown

Only you can define and value true friendship! As Newton once wrote, 'If I have seen further, it is by standing on the shoulders of giants.' For me these shoulders begin with impressive humans in my life… one is my bestie. Elaine, thanks for making the journey of my life so much sweeter.

Photograph:
Sydney, Australia
2018

No One Is Invincible

When I was at school in South Africa, my brother and I lived away from our parents to have an easy commute to school. During weekends we often visited our parents. One time our dad asked us to wait in the vicinity of a relative's home so he could fetch us after he finished work. It was Friday night. The sun set and darkness crept in and there was no sign of our dad. When our relative arrived from work, he was distressed to see us still in his yard and called our dad.

Eventually when Dad arrived, my relative's mother-in-law greeted him with affectionate revulsion. Waxing lyrical at him, she asked him not to leave his kids in her yard again. Dad responded, 'I just needed a favour and one day you will need a favour too.' She scorned and mocked saying they would never ever require a favour from him. We had waited about five hours after our school bus dropped us off in our school uniform with nothing to eat, drink and nowhere to sit - just standing outside. My heart experienced something that day that I did not understand and did not care to understand, but I knew that I did not want to be like that when I grew up. I had no clue what I wanted to be; however, I was certain I wanted to be a giver and help others.

Fate does come around even if you do not believe in it. This same lady that mocked us and yelled with absolute confidence that they would never need our help, nonetheless, years later required our assistance when their business experienced financial difficulty. Circumstances do not make you who you are, but they reveal who you are. Accept that your expectations will not always be met and strive to leave a better example to the world. Do not let your pain and brokenness dominate the positives of your life. Use your experience and resilience as a tool to help others. Be thankful that people have given you exposure to life changing lessons that enhanced your character. This is what creates courage in your core.

My Journey Gleans

We cannot choose the family or situation we are born into, so do not act privileged or treat those who are less fortunate than you with disdain. We all reap what we sow, so be discerning about what you sow. The next generation may need to reap your harvest. Learn to transform like water taking the shape of the vessel it is poured into. Be ready to take any form or shape to help in any way you can. Soften your hard edges by being more tolerant and understanding.

If mercy is a song, then let it be saturated from your lips, let your thoughts, words, deeds and actions be soaked in mercy. This experience in life afforded me the takeaway that has moulded me into an adult who holds nothing in the clench of my palms. I have lived and experienced what the circle of life does and how it humbles those that deem themselves to be mighty. Be kind, merciful and gracious. Remember, gestures of kindness can be infectious and can carry hope from one person to another across all international borders. How can you be salt to the earth when you never leave the saltshaker! We are not defined by our worst or our best. We are defined by our God, perfectly in process. Pay attention to the process and be very intentional about the calibre of character you wish to subject the world to. Acknowledge every life that you cross paths with, regardless of how insignificant you may consider it to be and dispense elegant grace.

Just because the past generations behaved this way, you do not need to continue. You have the potential to break the generational curse. When someone says: 'It runs in the family' you tell them: 'This is where the buck stops.' The best self assessment and care is identifying old patterns of behaviour and harmful traits and analysing why you arrived at this space. Who conditioned you to think and act this way and why? The key to growth and change is choosing to break old corrupt patterns.

'Those who live passionately teach us how to love. Those who love passionately teach us how to live.' Paramahansa Yogananda

Chapter Eight

The Rollercoaster Extravaganza

Killing the Bird With Broken Wings

David, Samson, Noah, Abraham, Moses, Sarah, Jacob, Joseph, Samuel, Job and Joshua, characters from the Bible – all had their fair share of afflictions in life. None that went down in history were immune to problems. Problems are a part of life. Life meets no one halfway and the onus is upon us to make the trek to the destination. So we need to plan and prepare for the trip in accordance. Go into combat mode, learn how to excel in alien territory, learn how to manage a health issue, how to live when your world is shattered, how to sleep when you have no future assurance, how to manage in a worldwide pandemic, how to be a social butterfly when you have no family in the country and how to trade your sorrows for joy.

True joy and contentment are wonderful to experience. It is a blessed destination and requires work. Unfortunately there is no genie lamp to rub and no magic carpet. We need a plan, cognitive realignment of our mind and active steps to implement the plan. Fresh after my divorce I embarked on a trip to New Zealand. My wounds were still tender and remiss of closure, I was sinking in an ocean of unanswered questions. A bunch of ladies from my former church arranged a night of fellowship. I thought it would be wonderful to be with familiar sisters and have sweet fellowship. Perhaps it was just the prescription I required. The lady that hosted the social had gone through a divorce herself and was still on the road to recovery.

As the night progressed, she started hurling words at me just out of the blue in a high pitched roaring voice. Constantly yelling the name of my ex and saying, *'so and so used you and discarded you like a dirty piece of rag.'* I was baffled by her remarks as she did not really know either of us. I wondered if she was speaking from her own pain, so I reserved the right to react, but she just continued with the same line as the night progressed.

The appalling aspect of it all was that the rest of the ladies just laughed as if it were a night at the rodeo. The distinct difference here: I was a victim of the bull and the pain was real. I walked out of that home perplexed and wondering why Christians would shoot the wounded. Why did they invite me to a night out to expose me to this? Miserably, not one of these women asked me if I was okay after that fiasco or contacted me to talk or offered any support.

My Journey Gleans

I know what Jesus did on the cross for me. I have received his gift and I am whole. I felt no void or brokenness as my day of restoration had arrived. I was at the destination of joy and contentment. I had walked right into the picture frame of my destiny. The best days arrived, and I was living them at last. Sometimes God's grooming and preparation is packaged as pain, so stay strong and do not give up even when the pain is too intense. Complete the training to receive your reward. He has better things for you at the other side of this training.

We all have an archetypal dark side: The 'nicer' we purport to be, the darker the shadow we cast. Our darkness is comprised of unveiled parts that can leak out in vicious power plays or as malice toward other women. Essentially, there are a few reasons why women are nasty to other women:

- ✓ They conceal their unwanted parts from other women, especially their distress, spite, jealousy, resentment, lack of self esteem and confidence
- ✓ They presume that they can get away with it because of the lack of tolerance of differences or the inability to handle another woman's success
- ✓ They lack interpersonal and communication skills to recognise and alter their behaviour
- ✓ Hurting people conjures up rhetoric with the extreme intent to influence peers and hurt the receiver for no apparent reason
- ✓ They live as if their heyday never arrived because they do not value what they have within themselves
- ✓ Authenticity is a rare commodity, and it becomes a competition rather than a trademark

On numerous occasions both at work and socially, I have been told that I seem calm, cool and collected even in stressful situations. Rest assured I do feel the weight of the burden; however, I choose to live by higher authority rather than my emotions at the time. My wounds of divorce were still fresh, and I did not understand most of the unprocessed pain; it was sheer bewilderment how another woman could channel up a PhD thesis on my pain and reasons for divorce.

I had to turn the other cheek and walk away with all my dignity intact. Over a decade has progressed and the same woman that abused me so senselessly decided to stalk my LinkedIn profile. Ah the penny finally dropped! She was obviously checking out where my life was at. I had gleaned her true intentions a decade ago and I was now filled with peace that I chose to not react that night but rather respond despite my own pain. My greatest lessons from this are ones we hear so often yet we need to practice them more:

- ✓ If you do not have anything good to say, then do not say anything at all.
- ✓ When you sit in company to laugh at others and foster bad behaviour, then you are just as bad.
- ✓ We all endorse what we accept. Be cautious with how we endorse other people's behaviour that impacts others negatively.
- ✓ Never ever shrink your character to fit people and places that you have outgrown.
- ✓ You find a real friend in the person who holds your hand and stands with you in the storm. Circumstances reveal to us who our real friends are.
- ✓ Implement the Kon-Mari methodology to tidy compartments of your life.
- ✓ Command to be an efficacious example.
- ✓ Sisterhood is not forged by drive of façade.

People may irritate, annoy and perplex us but how we treat them is a reflection of our own character. Sadly, many who seem to covet my life but are clueless about my battles, scars and victories. I am content with who I am and what I have, I want to be the best version of myself. I do not desire what another woman has. I am not a cheap carbon copy; I am a one of a kind masterpiece, and I most definitely will not destroy my authenticity by being envious of another person.

The way you speak to yourself and the way we let others speak over us matter. The enemy loves to use this voice to embellish bilious qualities. Catch yourself when this happens and nip it in the bud, then replace it with what is true. I use positive talk, scripture: *'I know who I am in Christ, If God is for me no man can be against me and I can do all things through Christ who strengthens me.'* Be flagrantly you and afford others the same pleasure. When you know the true calibre of a heart, you can then make better choices with the level of affiliation that you choose to commit to.

Boorish characters will not consume your energy, but rather dowdy and guileless circles ought to bring out the best effulgent woman in us all.

Realise that sometimes your personal growth and perceived finesse with catastrophe is a major threat to others. Every bit of friction may be due to the fact that your life holds up a mirror to reflect what is not working in their own life. When you compare your vocation, you grab vulnerability that may drown you rather than propel you to your true calling.

'We are simply passing through this earth. We should bless it in our transit but never yoke ourselves to its affairs.' Charles Spurgeon

Craft Your Own Lifeline

I took for granted that one day I would be a mother and when reality presented me with my medical diagnosis, it was a hard pill to swallow. It was the classic step of the cha cha, two steps forward and one step back. I was feeling overwhelmed by infertility and angry with God for handing me the unfair state of affairs and my mind was full of 'why me' questions. Some days I would get up ready to tackle life and other days I felt like crawling under a rock. Carrying a heavy and invisible burden all alone is beyond draining. More than a decade progressed yet the pain was ever present.

I read a few books on infertility and there was no 101 guide to fix it all. How do I let go of a desire that I so deeply beseeched God to fulfil? Lamenting for something that I would never experience? The emotional rollercoaster was literally sucking the life out of me as I still had to be a competent professional, wife, church leader, sister, daughter, friend, daughter-in-law and sister-in-law. Life did not stop to offer me a respite. I had to dig deep within myself to make peace in my heart to let the desires of my heart go. I cried bitterly to reach this point. I needed to assess the reality and prepare to make the rest of my life the best of my life. A new season is intimidating and unsettling, but rest assured if God brought you to it, He will not just equip you to survive it but enable you to thrive despite it. Sometimes the process is traumatic, but keep going. Wipe the tears and march on.

Sadly, society does put a time limit on grief. Sympathy and understanding expire with the progression of time. It almost feels like selective amnesia sets in when no one recalls the IVF treatments, the positive pregnancy, the miscarriage and pain of losing an unborn child, when Mother's Day rolls on and the world is celebrating while your heart is shattered into a million pieces and a vast unspoken numbness fills your insides.

Unequivocal grief...infertility + miscarriage! The pain is real, yet it is invisible, and people have expectations of you to show up and deliver the walk that you talk. The world does not care about what you have survived and how deep your scars are. Everyone is busy dealing with their own catastrophes. I gleaned for myself that most people are not truly interested in having deep and meaningful connections with you, to hold your hand as you navigate the pain. Most people do not want to get their hands dirty. They want a happy, superficial connection to escape from their own reality. You need to keep your real pain at bay.

I could not find a morsel of peace to let go of the punctuated dream of motherhood. Pleasure had left me without the promise to return. I somersaulted intensely into my cubbyhole of distress. But I still had to be a professional who showed up to work and to the world at large. Admittedly I staggered under the weight of this pronounced but undetected trauma, but none could see it painted on my face or cared to look beneath the surface! Desperate with poignant desire to accelerate to a better season, I put on my big girl panties and lived my best.

I could not continue life with this model as I needed to find my equilibrium. I developed my own hero program and the art of active listening. I chose to respond to a person's pain in the way I would like others to respond to my communicated pain. This brought its own challenges; many saw me as a soft touch to get what they wanted. The help I offer is offered unto the kingdom of God and if mankind abuses that, then that is their business with the Lord. I have learned to establish better boundaries but still show empathy and unconditional love. Empathy is a vulnerable choice when all you feel is emptiness. I had to dig deep to connect to those who were crying from a scratch but had no clue of my copious bleeding.

In addition, I had to process the invisible pain of miscarriage. I had to take steps for closure, mourning, letting go, respecting the circumstance, naming my baby, praying release over Mr. Ex and releasing myself. Having the dreams of impending motherhood shattered is traumatic. Sorrow grips your heart in a deep and intense way as you trudge along with daily life. How can you let such deep angst of pain just disappear without actually processing it? It is a fact that busyness does not drive out pain. I tried it and it did not work.

I developed my own hero program to rescue myself. God helps those that help themselves. He did not pour the manna into the mouths of the Israelites. They had to get up each morning and gather the manna. They had to work for it. So I got up and worked on my healing. I noted that my whole experience of losing a baby was drowned in the noise of grappling with the death of a friend, relocating to a new country, divorce and Mr. Ex not acknowledging the negative energy he brought by mandating we only fertilise one egg. I introspected my pain and sought a resolution.

This took me to New Zealand where I had a ceremony for my unborn child. I named her, I prayed for her, I asked for forgiveness and I released myself from the pain. Other ladies shared their journey with me. My friend made me the cutest keepsake to remember this milestone. I look at this now and I am not overcome by grief as I have processed the pain. It is still heavy, but I feel lighter than before. I lack the words to describe the magnitude of anguish I feel as a person who is unable to conceive yet the rest of the world takes this simple but intense biology for granted. The global resolution to condone abortion is a heavy debate. I am not a theologian so I will make no attempt to address abortion in correlation to religious beliefs.

Abortion is a controversial subject and includes the complete gamut of sentiments. I sympathise with rape victims and understand human plight and I do empathise with all women who have found themselves in situations beyond their control. This focus is a zoom into consensual unplanned pregnancies. My outlook is simply from my universal exposure. Pro-life versus pro-choice is the classic debate and it dissipates into the shades of grey in human rights discussions, making the issue far from simple. Society harps on 'Pro-choice' and as a woman I understand the fundamentals of the woman having a choice – there is much power in exercising your choice with informed discernment and insightful knowledge. Pro-choice is a longitude equation and most definitely not a fundamental right to be enforced as a solo human in the equation. Let's explore where the longitudinal equation begins and ends:

- ✓ Pro-Choice begins with the fact that your mother exercised her legislative right to choose, and she chose to give birth to you. You would be a statistic if she chose otherwise. Granted, her circumstances may have been different but ultimately your circumstances are created by your choices – period.

- ✓ Pro-Choice starts before you remove your knickers and hop into bed. You need to consider your choice, your rights, the risks and the mitigation plan before the deed and preferably not after. As a woman, celebrate the fact that you are uniquely capable and liberated to actually make your OWN CHOICE, so you do not need the government to introduce legislation to mandate behaviour. Your behaviour patterns should be set and driven by you and not the government.

- Pro-Choice most definitely includes all humans in the equation: The one that gave birth to you + YOU + the one that procreated with you + lastly but not least the unborn foetus. The foetus has a right to Pro-Choice as well and if you beg to differ then the equation is unbalanced when we remove your mother who gave birth to her foetus.

Whatever you are, be a good one. The simple mantra of life is: live your truth as long as you do not hurt another. Live your choice and afford everyone that same choice. Place the precinct of your heart where it yields profits that truly matter. Do not let your heart be served by a status of self rights at a brutal price of others in the equation. A mercurial heart is not a choice attribute to proudly wear on your sleeve, as it undoubtedly creates molten tears.

Injustice to the voiceless is inexorable and it brings to life this simple speech from the Empire Strikes Back:

'Do, or do not. There is no try.' Yoda

My Journey Gleans

Uncertainty and unanswered prayers get the best of us all. Take time to connect to God and seek to obtain his perspective. Then eradicate the irrelevant wants in the equation and concentrate on the path to reach your destination. Be gentle with yourself and others. Refrain from taking things personally as not all wounds are visible – we are often unaware of the issues others are facing.

No matter how intense the magnitude of pain is, God's grace is always there and is sufficient. Just a conversation between God and I, even when I did not use words, God got me through my darkest days. He knew which balm to dispense and who to align my path with. Pain does not disappear because it is invisible. I needed to acknowledge the pain, refrain from shelving it, embrace it, dissect it, get to the root cause and actively work on a solution. This was a mammoth task requiring small steps towards my end goal. Granted I had walked this path, so I possessed the experience to help someone else walk this path with gained compassion. I learned that victory is in attuning my walk with God and not in God granting answers to my prayers. My faith took a deeper significance when I was in the fire, broken and on my knees. God used circumstances to draw me to his bosom so I could change the tone of my narrative.

I recall activists for animal rights having a prop of an artificially roasted dog on a spit – making a strategic and acute argument about why we should not kill animals to eat them. With the stark reality of the grilled dog making onlookers churn inside while driving home the core message that we should all adopt vegan diets. I have no qualms with anyone's personal preference. Each to their own. However, I am bewildered that in Australia and the world we can be outraged about animal rights in such a profound way, yet the world's approach to value human life (aka the unborn foetus) is tagged 'Pro-Choice.' As a nation if we deem life is precious and worth saving then let the decorum of emotions launch with human life.

Hebrews 11:1 – Faith is confidence in what we hope for and assurance about what we do not see.

The trough of sorrow is a gruelling path to travel. This scripture gave me hope that God will restore all that the locust has eaten. I walked a long road to recovery, and I learned to constantly stop the pity party mindset and hold on to the promised hope I had. **H.O.P.E** = **H**old **O**n, **P**ain **E**nds. Outlined are some helpful turn arounds from my pity party journey to the Promised Land:

Hopeful – Optimist (New Thinking *with* God)	Hopeless – Pessimist (Old way of Thinking *without* God)
Active hard work, sweet fellowship and positive creative thinking. I pushed through no matter how difficult the situation was.	I have no future – Pessimism, the situation will never get better.
I spoke positive words over my life and future and continued with business as usual.	It is too late to dream and pray for a better life – Accepting defeat, doom and gloom.
I accepted what I could not change. I changed things that brought negative energy to my life.	Constantly feeling distress and emotional captivity.

'Some people could be given an entire field of roses and only see the thorns in it. Others could be given a single weed and only see the wildflower in it. Perception is a key component to gratitude and gratitude is a key component to joy.' Amy Weatherly

One Day or DAY ONE – Your Resolve

While I was living in Sydney, my mum and aunt visited from South Africa. I enjoyed taking them on the intrepid Australian shenanigans. One day I pulled into a service station to refuel my car. While doing this my aunt grabbed her camera and hopped out of the car to take a photo. I enquired what she had seen. She replied, 'Nothing, we are fascinated to see you filling petrol in your car.' A quizzical smile spread across her face. This is obviously a rare sight in South Africa, where underprivileged young men earn a living by offering to refuel cars and the driver just tips them without leaving the vehicle.

Her fascination took me down memory lane, to over twenty years ago, when I was heading to my all important practical exam and Mr. Macho left me on the curb in a car with an empty petrol tank. I am no longer terrified about driving to a service station and filling up my car. Quite frankly, I am terrified about nothing now. I have experienced so much in the last two decades that I know who gives the strength to face every predicament and curve ball that comes my way. I am anchored, so bring it on!

I am the youngest of five and I grew up predominantly with hand me downs. That's just how life was, and I did not know any different. Now I can travel to any destination in the world and walk into any store my heart desires and shop for what I want. Growing up with hand me downs did not make me who I am. A peach is not its fuzz, a toad is not its warts, and a person is not what society thinks. I am who God says I am.

When I was in South Africa on the day of my dad's funeral, someone said, *'What a shame he died without having any grandchildren.'* Boy oh boy, some people just know how to exhibit sensitivity to every damn element – not! We were all brimming with emotional grief and I understand the stark truth of this statement however it did stir up some emotions. All my siblings and I are flesh, blood, bone, brain, heart and so much more than a baby machine. We have blessed this world and our parents with so much more.

Why does society find the dire need to focus on what's absent rather than what is present? God created the ability to procreate. He alone gives and takes life. I understand that having a child is a gift from God, and we all should be honoured **if and when** we are blessed with that natural science. It is demeaning when you boast about having a child like it is a skillset derived from university that gets headlined in your LinkedIn profile. God exclusively controls your ability to conceive, and in addition, He also controls the next woman's inability to conceive.

My Journey Gleans

No one can ignite in me what I do not have. Decades have progressed and I own the grit that comes signed, sealed and delivered with this package. Have you discovered your grit? Be steadfast in your ways and God will lift you up. God's timing is not synchronised with our mortal clocks, so take heart and trust his plan. I made peace with the fact that I am not the main character in everyone's story. Sometimes people don't even include me in their story, sometimes people paint me as the villain in their story, but I know otherwise. I do not get to dictate to any human how to narrate their experience and their reality of what transpired. We all have freedom of choice and expression. I have made peace to align my world with the variations that exist out there.

Choice is a gift, so strive to use it as a blessing despite your circumstances. There is a silver lining to every experience, even the darkest ones, so take heart. I personally escalated the roots of my faith and the statements of others on this funeral day to God's hand – He is better equipped, as His infinite wisdom can deal with it. Sadly even at a funeral it was evident that people would enlarge your voids to make their own shortcomings look irrelevant. Giving birth to a child is not a choice like obtaining a university qualification. It is an exceptional gift from God, period. We should learn the modest lesson and develop the grace to be grateful if we are blessed with that gift. Refrain from using it as a marketing tool to elevate and compare yourself with others. The power of archetypes and narratives are startling in life, so ensure you have the right role models to polish up your inner being as it all starts from the heart.

'Fear is a reaction; courage is a decision.' Winston Churchill

A Golden State of Mind in a Pandemic

During this unprecedented unique situation of the coronavirus (COVID-19) pandemic, a work colleague posted on social media his superannuation was losing money at a reckless rate and another commented she was scared to log into her account to take a look. I remembered the scripture about not storing treasures in a place where moth and rust can destroy them. While many people were losing money, everyday life was shaken and rattled but not taken for granted anymore. It is a stark mortality dripping with reality.

We all had to reprioritise what was important to us. Sadly, money cannot really help anyone in a pandemic. Hopefully the world will learn to be kinder and store up greater treasures than superannuation. I am normally extremely busy living this one life to the fullest and I barely have the time to scratch myself. But the lockdown during COVID-19 presented me with the opportunity to sit and write down parts of my life journey. I wrote this book in ten days. God propelled me to use my story to help others.

My life has not been a walk in the park. Life is a journey and when I graduated from one tribulation, another one arrived packaged with care and garnished with enriching lessons. I own the battle scars and I now bleed less during training. I can get into combat with the experience God granted me. Most importantly, I can now help, inspire and motivate others with compassion, experience and grace. The same elements and measure that God used on me, I can now dispense onto others because I have already received them myself. The year 2020 has wrecked so many curated plans around the globe. However, despite the circumstances, how did you grow? What are the highlights of your year? We will always have more royal failures than successes in life. So get strategic about how you handle failure and most importantly how you develop from it.

My Journey Gleans

Faith lives on the edge of disbelief. I lived my life by daring to step out in faith and trust that God had me in the palm of His hand, He is sovereign, and He alone will reign. Our greatest fear should not be lack of success but rather succeeding at things that really do not matter. Sadly, we prioritise success and wealth. No one is immune from the cosmos at play. The same wind blows on us all irrespective of our geographical location. Disaster, change, opportunity and uncertainty affect us all. I learned to be discerning during this pandemic as even the smallest decision I make can impact many people around me. We all have the prerogative to live as we please, but we also need to consider how our boundaries or lack of boundaries affect others in the equation. Boundaries are also to develop awareness of what the other party requires so you can act in accordance. We have all witnessed this during the pandemic.

Give yourself a moment to acknowledge the impact and heal, so you are ready for the next chapter. When you are in utter despair, take heed that you are still breathing and the sun still rises and sets, the earth is still revolving. In essence, life is moving on. Nothing stops to wait for our emotions to catch up. Next week or next month, your emotional tank may register differently, so do not use your emotions to carve out your life. Focus on what is constant, a true fundamental that does not change.

Use God's blueprint that stands the test of time, along with your IQ – Intelligence Quotient, AQ – Adversity Quotient, and EQ – Emotional Quotient, to make informed decisions. We need to develop the art of building all the components to work together in a symbiotic way to harness life at its optimum best. Let it work in your favour and synthesise complexities in a rational but effective manner. Never do the right thing for the wrong reasons. Live a calculated life with direction from God rather than leaving it to arbitrary chance.

'If you are going through hell, keep going.'
Winston Churchill

Chapter Nine

Highlight Your Core Beauty

Sweet Life of a Giver

When I lost my home in New Zealand, I was saddled with the shipping bill to move our assets from New Zealand to Australia. Still grappling with infertility and a miscarriage, I was now in a new country struggling through the perils of divorce alone. I was financially stretched, and no kind soul offered a helping hand. I did not expect a handout either. If I earn it, I eat it and I am a firm exhibitor of building my own dreams and paying my own debts.

I prayed for guidance and read ample literature on being a wise steward with my finance. These pearls of wisdom stood out to me: 'God is my Jehovah Jireh' which translates to, 'The Lord will provide.' In real adversity a phrase from the Bible may seem like weightless and inanimate words. However, I knew that The Word is a living double-edged sword and a force to be reckoned with. I changed my personal email address to incorporate this word JIREH so it would be a constant reminder that God will provide all my needs.

I left my needs in God's hands and also made a covenant with Him to use all resources that he blessed me with for the glory of his kingdom. God took my professional career from strength to greater strength. Shutting and opening doors that no man could, as he blessed me by design with a corporate remuneration that most people only dream of. I remained steadfast in using that money for his kingdom, including blessing those that God placed in my path even though some were wolves in sheep's clothing.

My Journey Gleans

God has given us his blueprint to live by. Not all of us live by every word. I am no paragon of ideal perfection and at best I am a work in progress. When I had a need, I read the Bible and put it into action. In the book of Deuteronomy it clearly states in no uncertain terms 'Blessings for Obedience' and I tapped into this. I made every effort to obey God's commands, and some days my endeavours failed, and other days God helped me up again. I was blessed in the city and country I was living in and I could truly shout this from the mountain top. Amen!

Go forward no matter what the circumstances are. The only time we need to look back is to gain and glean from the past, never to live there. The Word states 'we are more than conquerors' Romans 8:31 – let this Word be etched in your heart – you are more than any circumstance that is thrown at you. Let it be your modus operandi for life. When you live with a 'more than conqueror' lifestyle, then your life is transformed in a noticeable way.

In every predicament ask yourself what God is trying to teach you, what areas of your life he wants you to grow in, what he desires to reveal to you in this season. What is your blessing in this situation? There is always a blessing, sometimes it is under a rock and you have to look for it. Rest assured a lesson and a blessing always come hand in hand. Do not learn the hard lesson and forfeit the blessing.

'Do not judge me by my successes but judge me by how many times I fell down and got back up again.' Nelson Mandela

Forgotten Seed That Still Thrives

While living in Sydney, a pastor that I knew from New Zealand tracked me down. He and his family were now living in Sydney as well. It was over a decade since I had last seen them. His in-laws were visiting from India and his wife Annie introduced me to her parents by explaining who I was and elaborating that when she gave birth to her first child, they had planned a trip to India so her parents could see her baby. They had no money to purchase milk for the child, so they fed the baby sugar water. She was fasting and praying all week and trusted God for provision as they had no money for the international trip to India from New Zealand.

One Friday night, it was almost 10 p.m. and her flight was at the crack of dawn on Saturday morning. She still trusted for a miracle. I had just finished connect group, and made a quick dash to her home to grab a cuddle with her new baby and wish her bon voyage. As I hugged her goodbye, I gave her some cash and told her to enjoy her trip and buy something for the baby as I had no time to go shopping. She explained how, after I had left, she fell to her knees and thanked God for answering her prayers. Her husband dashed out and purchased milk to feed the baby, and later they bought clothes and had money for their trip to India. She told her parents God used me to answer her prayers as they purchased travel tickets via a credit card and had no other money for the international trip and essentials for the baby. She got the last minute miracle that she prayed for.

I did not even recall the seed that I had planted and the profound effects it had had. The seed was not only growing but was thriving. What a joy to see good blessings paid forward. So refreshingly different than serving a roast chicken to someone and then having them throw the bones back at you. I spent Christmas with all of them at their friend's house. After our Christmas lunch feast, their friend Carol brought out the Bible and began to read. She then began a feet washing ceremony as we all sat around the table.

Carol and her husband own a very lucrative business and are much older than me. To have her wash my feet was an experience beyond humbling. It showed me her staple heart of servanthood and confirmed to me that money, status and age are not the ingredients for a true heartfelt connection. Humility expressed in such a philosophical way stunned me, especially when my mind drifted to people who had treated me with no regard, respect or kindness, and now Jesus, you do this for me. Tears streamed down my face.

As Carol dried my feet, she prophesied a word over me: *'God is taking me into a season of restoration and redemption.'* I had just met Carol for the first time and was experiencing a unique covenant friendship just like the one that David and Johnathan were blessed with in The Word. Do not judge each day by the harvest you reap but by the seeds that you plant – this was now real to me as I was living it.

My Journey Gleans

Whatever is built by faith can be passed onto future generations. I was blessed to hear the faith that this pastor's wife had and how she detailed this to me, her children and her parents. What a superb testimony of faith and Jehovah Jireh in action at HIS best. Sometimes the little acts of kindness we render are a profound answer to another person's prayer. I always pay attention to the prompting when God drops in my spirit to help someone, visit someone, bless someone, call someone or simply be a ray of sunshine in the room. People are the heart and soul of the world, so strive to do something profound for another human who cannot pay you back. I can attest there is no greater joy than to be a blessing.

This act of humble servanthood (washing of my feet) was so powerful that the allure of this sophistication caused me to transfix my gaze on Jesus. People may not say 'I love you' but sometimes the abundance of their heart is revealed in thoughtful acts like washing your feet, sending flowers, cooking a meal or simply sitting with you when you have no answers. In addition, praying for friends is vitally important as sometimes they fight and endure battles that we are unaware of.

Pronounced gratitude, relief and pluck are found when one remembers the same sun rises every day but the day that rises is rarely the same. I have experienced unemployment, downtime in between contracts, even postsurgery recovery without pay, and not once did I have to beg for bread. I have never ever obtained money from either country's government. I gave my tithes and offerings. The Word says the righteous never beg for bread. I lived this word and I continue to live it. I am not just a believer; I am a doer and I fail but still strive to follow the blueprint. Bounty is when you always give as if it costs you nothing, yet it makes the supreme alteration to the receiver.

'Gratitude is born in the hearts that take time to count up past mercies.'
Charles E Jefferson

Shine the Light

While residing in New Zealand, my mum visited me. Before her arrival I prayed for her to have a real experience and touch from God. I took her to a production at church called 'Heaven's gates and Hell's flame.' It is a play that portrays life after death. At the conclusion, the pastor had an altar call for people to make a decision to be born again. My mum responded and prayed the sinner's prayer. I had my reservations about her Christian walk as she was a staunch Hindu, rooted in that culture since birth with a room full of idols.

In God's kingdom, old dogs can learn new tricks. I gave her some great books to read while she was with me in New Zealand. She was deeply engrossed, and I could see God transforming her. One day I returned home from work and I could see her transformation was noticeable as she emotionally explained what she was reading in the book, *'Foxes book of Martyrs: a great English classic. Interesting as fiction, because it is written with both passion and tenderness, it tells the dramatic story of some of the most thrilling periods in Christian history.'*

It gave her the precipice of hope to live life with a newfound zeal. It was an opulent moment to watch my mum transform her mind, to think beyond what she was born into and had lived by her whole life. The world is populated with a diversity of people, mindsets, cultures and traditions, and I had deemed my mum was far too old to foster change in her life or have the mental acumen to think outside the traditions of her birth. She had more than just a mind transformation all those years ago – she still has the capacity to live by her choice of decision to date. She is truly capable of investigating the perils and truths of her existence on her own accord.

As we prepared for the end of her holiday and goodbyes, I asked her what she was going to do with her 'Diya' *(a lamp that is lit daily and prayed to, symbolizing the Hindu god)*. She did not respond, and I thought that it may be a sensitive subject. We said our goodbyes at the airport, and she departed.

My Journey Gleans

Months later I discovered that when she returned home, she removed all her idols and her lamp. She got water baptised and attended church regularly. She has now been a Christian for over a decade. She is over eighty and she still reads the Bible and attends church regularly. Transformation at its finest and it is a choice. Choice begins with us all despite our age.

As long as you have breath, you can discover, grow and glow.

'Don't worry about failures, worry about the chances you miss when you don't even try.' Jack Canfield

My mum has taken the believer's mantle and she lives by it as a fine example that is amplified in so many profound ways without waiting for society to affirm her. She is a symbol of resilience and transformation. She will forever be my inspiration.

Photograph:
Durban, South Africa
2012

Ethics Are Not Limited Edition

Lady in the Park

During my tertiary studies in Durban, South Africa, I spent my free time in between classes at the park near a student hangout called the Workshop. I would head for a quiet spot on the lawn in the sun daily. An older Caucasian lady came out to smoke on a regular basis in the vicinity. With the progression of time I reached out and spoke to her. Just normal random banter. I gleaned she was a checkout operator at the local supermarket, and she seemed rather wound up by her general character as if life owed her something.

The real reason I raced to the park was to complete my mounting studies, so I really did not want to adopt a park buddy. On the contrary, she seemed to love the chit chats. Eventually I informed her I would not be back as I had completed my studies and would be returning to my hometown. I saw the colour drain from her face. Then she began to cry…

Awkward, especially when we did not know each other too well. I enquired why she was crying, and she said that she really enjoyed talking to me and would prefer to continue. No harm, I thought, and I pencilled my number and handed it to her as I walked off.

A few weeks later I received a phone call and she told me how no human at school or work had ever spoken to her or made her feel visible. She cried and said: 'Everyone treats me like I am invisible just because I am fat. You are the first person to talk to me and be so kind to me, I love you…I really love you; I also just told my family that I am a lesbian and I wanted to tell you too.' I really did not see that coming. Nonetheless, I listened to her and then gracefully told her I was not inclined that way. She never called again.

Young Lad at Checkers

During month ends, the local supermarket Checkers would be a frenzy in South Africa, literally a mob. My aunt needed to return a malfunctioning electrical appliance. My acumen set in and I bravely told her that she was on her own. I waited out at the front of the store while she conducted her business. The front end of the supermarket had smaller vendor stalls. I was waiting for her next to the cobbler stall. A young indigenous lad was working there, and he offered to polish my shoes. I politely declined. He was tenacious and then added: 'I need the money for my school.' I asked him what he was studying at school and he blurted: 'Mathematics, physical science, biology and chemistry. It is really hard to work for so little money to help my family plus pay for my studies.'

I had sandals on, which did not need any polishing, but I asked him for his address, and I informed him that I would post him all my books and study guides as I had completed school and studied the same subjects. He did not have an address to give me. He probably did not have a home either. I thought maybe he was living in a shack and so I did not continue with the idea. He then said: 'I would love to get the books from you. Can I get your address? I will write to you and let you know where to post them.'

I was only nineteen but had my inbuilt radar of security, so I gave him my postal address. Few weeks later I got a letter. He was professing love and asking for my hand in marriage and elaborated how I was the first non-indigenous person to speak to him and treat him like a human. He said no one had ever offered to ever help him or his family before. He was in awe that I had offered to give him my books.

My Journey Gleans

The lady in the park and the lad in the supermarket merit attention as they reveal the unfortunate truth that we make others feel invisible and devalued by what we do and organically by what we do not do. It echoes a culture and brings fruitfulness to our well toned palettes. Well toned to what is the ultimate question? Humans have the absence of empathy and compassion nonetheless to hand out stigma so intensely just by the fate of someone's existence. Society's unchecked behaviour fosters this stigma. How is it possible for humans to exist but be invisible? We are too busy guided by our own brand of optimism. The norm is to create wealth and zoom in with blinkers to our own personal best interest. Life is full of quixotic quests and colourful characters that bring so much depth per diem. Remember, context exists even if you do not know it. Do we need to live by a healthier example? – Determination is a choice!

I learned to stand up and help someone be a light to someone, show them a better day or way. I broke out of self inflicted captivity and ceased to dispatch signals of fear – you can too. Put on a mantle of dignity and authority and conquer all that life has for you. I learned that there is no Plan B as Plan A prevails.

Our non-verbal communication can reveal our true feelings and intentions. Inspect your principles before you reinforce someone's world with emotional inventories. I beseech you to not overlook how you impact other lives daily. Life avenues are opaque because we create that potential backdrop by our protracted behaviour. We tend to act on our innate creativity when so few of our organised behaviours work for us. Sequentially this creates a wild untamed divide. Self growth, critical thinking and compassion are the tools to use and reuse!

'To live is the rarest thing in the world. Most people exist, that is all.'
Oscar Wilde

Be a Voice Not An Echo

In Sydney I had a colleague from Iran, and we became work besties. Zoey was drawn to me or perhaps what lived in me. I gave her some books to read to help her with a few challenges in life. She kept them for a while and then returned them, telling me she had better stuff to read. Not everyone in life has been blessed to seek quest and revelation. Some people believe what they are born into to be the absolute truth and they never question it. Sadly, they have no conviction to delve deeper to seek answers as they are content with what has been served to them. As I did not want to rock our friendship, I respected her choice. I could discern she wanted to tap into my stream of life. There was something in the water that I drank. Or was there?

Eventually I invited her to church one weekend, and she attended. She also responded to the altar call and prayed the sinner's prayer. I did not break out the champagne as I knew it would be a hard road ahead. I prayed for her and I gave her a Bible. We have both changed jobs since, but the bond that we created was real and it did stand the test of time. We still keep in touch, and when time permits, we catch up. During our last catchup, she shared that she is an active and regular member of church, her son attends Sunday school and she invited me to her church. I met her church family, and they were excited to update me that she attended Bible study regularly.

My Journey Gleans

I am called to plant a seed and not fret about what happens next. God is bigger than the universe and He will bring the labourers to water and harvest the seed that I have planted. I learned that no outreach is insignificant. I understand what the great commission is, and I don't live a life that lets each day slip away with no purpose or real value to relationships or encounters that have been entrusted to me. I found my authentic and highest values and carved my own happiness by living up to those values. I found an exquisite version of myself in heartbreak. We are temporary visitors to this planet so leave it in a better state than we find it. Discover your value and improve the world with gained wisdom. Train your life conclusion on precise actions before your heartbeat runs out.

Do not let anything hinder your metamorphosis. With the progression of time, caterpillars turn to butterflies. We all can change to something better. Do not stay stuck where you are or do not change for the worse. Transform your character to be less of the old self. Despite how broken I was; I learned to get up, show up and complete my designer dressing with an authentic smile. There is beauty in a broken vessel, it is your faithful heart. Strive to live authentically, marshalling your personal strength and aspiring to advanced ideals so your behaviour does not impede the progress of humanity.

'You can never cross the ocean until you have the courage to lose sight of the shore.' Christopher Columbus

Zoey my friend was inspired by my example to delve deeper into her own life to become a better version of herself. We are painting Sydney with our vibrant smiles as we enjoy real honest friendship captured in this picture. Friendship is not a social media status but a culmination of values that speaks of your bond even when you are not present.
We are all blessed if we can find the rare person who can value us in every season.

Photograph:
Sydney, Australia
2017

Eradicate the Green-Eyed Monster

Popcorn is prepared in the same pot at the same temperature, in the same oil and yet the kernels do not pop at the same time. Do not compare yourself to others, as we all pop at different times. The grim reality is that people compare themselves with others as if life is a competition. I have experienced this in every facet of life – from those in the corporate world who were ranked higher than me yet felt inadequate, from relatives that have the classic tall poppy syndrome, from acquaintances that really did not know me well and even from the kingdom sisterhood.

Undoubtedly the most excruciating experience of this is having people change behaviours and affiliations like a chameleon overnight. My world as I knew it erupted, once I changed the title by deed poll from Mrs to Ms, people who lay cousin close to my heart vanished. For some of the friendships that remained, the fellowship seemed orchestrated and inorganic, almost like I was a threat. Strangely when I relocated as my nomadic life unravelled, women from a brand new sphere exhibited the same traits. It was impossible to actually get real authentic fellowship in a circle. No matter where in the world I found a disturbing undercurrent at play at the best of times.

My spirit always smelt the aroma of envy, the green-eyed monster, which made others keep me at arm's length. In the story of Cain and Abel, we see the classic green-eyed monster. This story happened in the Biblical days and serves as history, a story that we all ought to learn from. Yet we choose not to take heed, instead we reject people because we are envious, and we feel threatened by their presence.

Cain was brimming with envy all because God accepted his brother's offering and not his. He felt rejected. The rejection was not true, as God was not rejecting him but reprimanding him – the initial step to progressively discipline him to bring the right sacrifice. Reprimand is distinctly different from rejection. He lacked the emotional acumen to glean how to enhance himself and step up. Instead he let the green eyed monster prevail and it ended in murder. Such a powerful lesson from history, but people still let the green eyed monster in to taint and distort them from sweet fellowship.

Proverbs: 14:30 - A tranquil heart gives life to the flesh, but envy makes the bones rot.

My Journey Gleans

We are called to not live by bread alone but by every Word of God. This scripture is a beautiful reminder to sear into our hearts to live by. Envy does make the bones rot and it also hurts in so many disparaging ways. I am in a foreign land living away from my family and in every situation, I am merely seeking fellowship, to be part of a new family. I have my own life predicaments and I am not seeking to add more by threatening others in any way, shape or form. If we all lived by The Word and did not let the green-eyed monster in, then people like me would not have to feel left out!

When life is harsh then we all gain perspective as to who our real tribe is. Take heart that I discovered the same lessons to sift the chaff from the wheat. The winnowing is a painful but mandatory process if we want to grow old with a tribe of friends that spells fine distinction. The calibre of authentic friendships makes all the difference. Deeds are formed out of the abundance of the heart, so ensure that your heart has no trace of green envy that leads to murder. I am blessed that God directed my path to the most amazing friends; for those that chose to be controlled by the green-eyed monster, I pray and hope they have fulfilled and enriched circles that they can depend on. We all grow and glow when we reject the urge to compare timing, ideas, blessings, talents, dreams, to do lists, mistakes and lessons.

It is vital to know who you are, so you recognise exactly who you are not. Be strategic about not conforming to the stereotype. Do not treat a person like a statistic, with disdain or insecurity, rather connect with each person by embracing diversity and providing unyielding support. Embracing diversity is a condition of the heart and an artful force of optimism to master. You must get real about who you are if you want to progress in this world and leave it in a better state than you found it.

The rendition of life is not defined by the Good Samaritan who helps those that sync in with personal affiliation. Cease the stereotype.

Help others unconditionally, especially those from a diverse post code, culture, race, country, status and colour. Revolution starts with you. Dignity has nothing to do with status or materialism and everything to do with how you think, live and treat others. We react to others in a fashion that is motivated by our psychological disposition. In retrospect, do you think this is fair and does it give the correct atmosphere to the scene?

'When you finally learn your self worth, you stop giving others discounts.' Karen Salmansohn

How to Wake Up Pretty

Beauty is not limited to the aesthetic pleasures of the senses. It runs into deeper calibres of the heartstrings. It is the quotient of how we connect to ourselves and others. How do you treat others when life is not going so well for you? Do you still find ways to connect and bless others? Do you strengthen bonds and community in every season of your life? How do you respond to someone's crisis? Is your life filled with random acts of kindness towards others?

When we get up in the morning, we are not all ready to snap a selfie picture to post on social media. We need to brush our teeth and hair, get out of our sleepwear before we are ready to present to the world. This is an important part of our daily routine. Just as equally important is the need to get up with a pretty heart, not just an outward appearance! How do you prepare your heart before you step out into the world? In The Word, Solomon tells his son *'Above all else guard your heart, for out of it are the issues of life.'* – Proverbs 24:3.

This confirms the fact that what you think controls the rest of your life. What you think is what you are. Your thoughts – good or bad, positive or negative – control your attitude. Your attitude is the sum of your total thoughts. Your attitude determines your actions.

My life came packaged with a great share of trials and tribulations, a fraction of which you have just read in this book. I had to get out of bed each morning and make a choice. A choice to be bitter or better: this was my CHOICE THERAPY. I would get dressed after a shower ready to brace the world – that was the easy aspect. The difficult but mandatory component was to get my heart and mind to align with the pretty woman in the mirror.

I did not want an unbalanced life and I wanted to be heard by my herd. No person has the capacity to make me happy or unhappy, no human has that much power over me, I had to crawl around the mulberry bush to learn this, and rest assured my cognitive mind has grasped this now. It was MY CHOICE THERAPY. My mind was the key that unlocked how I walked out of the door each morning and how I added salt and light to the world despite my circumstances and emotions.

I chose to believe God's word about me rather than what my emotions said. I would literally and audibly say: I can do all things through Christ who strengthens me. The operative word here is I. Faith without action is meaningless. So often we have faith, and we sit like a puppy dog expecting a treat, when it is faith coupled with work that gets the result.

My Journey Gleans

I am now victorious on the other side of all these catastrophic and redefining life experiences without any prescription medication, holistic therapy or psychological help. I am most certainly not advocating that you follow the same path as mine. You do what works best for you. I am simply sharing my journey. My mind was at this state, I found the capacity to bounce back and so I did, period!

The Greek word AGAPE in accordance with the thesaurus means 'the highest form of love, charity.' When I got out of bed every morning, I got ready as we all do, but my heart was already in this pretty state of AGAPE love, this was the designer outfit and smile that gave me the confidence to conquer whatever curve ball came my way. If true love conquers all then self-love gave me the fortitude to thrive, and AGAPE love gave me the zeal to help others and make a positive difference in their world. Life is not about having good cards, but sometimes playing the poor hand well and receiving all the benefits that come with it. It was never easy. Some days I had to dig deeper than others to find that optimistic zeal.

I had to learn to not live in perpetual hope but to live in reality. I had to make a conscious choice daily to live my utmost best with what I had at that time. I did not focus on what I lost and who hurt me, and I was not dreaming of what pleasures the future would bring. Choice is your therapy. Choose to live your best life now. How pretty is your heart when you wake up? Transform your mind to be an overcomer: govern your speech, guard your sight and guide your steps. If you want to know what is in your heart, then just listen to what escapes from your mouth. Wake up pretty inside and out and go add your pretty flavour to this world. Aesthetic scene of beauty spills from inside.

'Make up your mind that no matter what comes your way, no matter how difficult, no matter how unfair, you will do more than simply survive, you will thrive in spite of it.' Joel Osteen

Chapter Ten

We All Have CHOICES

Chronicles That Ignite Choice

Death Is Not My Portion

It is a rollercoaster of emotions to experience the death of a loved one: I was just sixteen when my granny perished of a sudden heart attack. We were all grappling with the loss as we followed cultural Hindu ceremonies and traditions. It was the tenth day ceremony to appease her parted soul. As accustomed, a Hindu priest was performing all the rituals and I was part of it along with all my cousins. The priest stopped midway unceremoniously and began reading the palms of my cousins.

Palm reading is heavily etched in Hinduism. It is perceived to reveal your personality, marriage compatibility with the unsuspecting other, character traits, important life milestones even in predicting death. The extended family seemed to welcome the punctuated interruption to the mourning process. Maybe they saw it as a breath of fresh air during mourning or simply they all revered the priest as god and had no spine to tell him to get back in line. I personally have no desire for astrology or palm reading and had no intention to uncover the apparent future of my life. (Turns out it was pretty damn great anyway – He did not predict that, did he?)

I was reluctant to volunteer. Astonishingly the priest did not read the palms of the young lads, it was only the young ladies, who were all blushing with excitement about their future that was signed, sealed and delivered. He then called for me and I said no, he insisted, and my obliging aunt pushed me forth. He rambled a few things that I paid no attention to, and then loudly exclaimed, 'You only have two more years to live! You're going to die.' Everyone went into a hush…

Medical Diagnosis Does Not Navigate My Life

During a routine medical assessment in primary school, I was apparently diagnosed with a heart condition. I was dragged to several different hospitals for assessments all my childhood years. I was exposed to:

- A head up tilt table test: no food for twenty four hours then strapped to a table and turned upside down for several hours with an electrocardiogram (ECG) equipment connected to my heart.
- Numerous X-rays
- Tons of ECG tests
- A Holter monitor: a device strapped to me for twenty four hours monitoring my heart rhythm

Despite the series of tests, I was not diagnosed with a clinical condition, but it was just labelled as 'a heart condition' and under clinical advice I was instructed to avoid all sporting activities. With my height, I reckon I could have shown the lasses on the netball court a thing or two but that was not my portion in life.

Perplexed Tance Lady

With the progression of time but unfortunately not of mindsets, I was now in secondary school enduring more heart assessments. I had a scheduled hospital appointment and my mum in her infinite wisdom (not) decided to take me to a local temple lady for prayer. My neighbour accompanied us, and my mum asked the temple lady to pray for me. I personally think that my mum was a tad worried about the death sentence that the priest had pronounced over me years earlier.

The lady broke out in trance *(a state where humans enter a deep subconscious mind, and this enlightened person can now let God speak via them)*. She proceeded to communicate in very bad sign language, and I just looked shocked at the caricature face and general shenanigans that were approved as god's presence. Granted that the priest told me I only had two years to live and now it was almost the end of the two year period, but I still had no expectations of dying – sorry to disappoint the priest who could apparently read my palm.

I was taking it all in with a grain of salt. She then started speaking to my neighbour who was translating for us. The temple lady prattled on not even noticing that I was detached from her shenanigans. It was reminiscent of a Trevor Noah comedy. She was warning my mum to exercise caution with me as my future was now repainted with more precise predictions: *'she is going to get pregnant and run away from home'* oh I was so sensationally charged…I really wanted to punch this woman. She made the assumption to stereotype me as a wayward child and that is the only reason why my mum had brought me here for divine prayers.

Living Undiagnosed

With the trickle of time, I began tertiary education. One day on campus in South Africa I had such excruciating pain, I literally could not walk into my next class a few steps away. The last moment I recalled was reaching for a fire hydrant to hold onto before I blacked out. I was taken to a hospital via ambulance and woke up in the emergency department. After a series of tests, I was discharged with no diagnosis. I was on my monthly menstrual cycle, so the pain and loss of consciousness were attributed to that. People mocked and laughed at me ending up in hospital due to just having my periods.

With time, my monthly cycles got more severe, and I resisted the urge to discuss painful periods with a clinical practitioner. I relocated to New Zealand and a few years later I was on my lunch break reading a random magazine when I came across an article on women living with undiagnosed endometriosis. I read all the symptoms and identified with the writer as I had all the same symptoms. I did more comprehensive research and knew without a shadow of a doubt that this was the cause of my pain. The magnitude of pain did not feel normal. I scheduled an appointment with my general practitioner and explained my symptoms and asked her to order tests to confirm it.

She was dismissive and refused to accept I had that condition, despite having lived with labour like intense pains all these years. I then went to another doctor and got the exact same response.

I was now working as a professional in a pharmacy. My manager was the pharmacist who owned the business, and his wife Judy was a qualified nurse. I alerted them of my undiagnosed condition. Few months later I was knocked out cold from pain at work. My manager carried me to the car and his wife Judy drove me to the medical centre next door to the pharmacy. I gained enough composure to explain to the doctor that this was endometriosis, and I needed an ultrasound to confirm it. She also treated me as if I had no idea and I dare not tell her how to do her job. She almost concluded I was trying to pull a sickie. She prescribed painkillers and dismissed me.

Given the fact that Judy had clinical experience as well and the medical centre had a professional relationship with their pharmacy next door, Judy insisted that she schedule an ultrasound test for me. The doctor rang me immediately upon receiving the report, informing me I needed surgery immediately. She also informed me that she had already contacted the hospital to fast track my admittance. My operating specialist said she had never seen such a radical state of the disease before.

My hope was abbreviated when I unfortunately discovered that scar tissue reoccurs post operation, so the condition is perpetual. I fell unconscious again later at a post office and was taken to the nearest emergency department via ambulance once more. I woke up in a hospital bed in a ward with a clinician telling me *'Do you understand your condition! You will never have children.'*

Deceptive Astrology

My mum was in the final trimester of her pregnancy with me when she found herself at the funeral of her bother. He perished in a sudden heart attack with no previous medical diagnosis. He was still in the prime of his life, so the shock was enormous. My mum was pregnant and the due date was some weeks away, yet she suffered complications at the funeral and was admitted to hospital. I made my debut. Beating the odds in and out of the womb…

My late uncle had officially answered to the name Kalichurran, but all his loved ones would affectionately call him Kelly. My mum was still unwell and recovering so she could not perform the normal cultural traditions of presenting me to the priest to pray for me and give me the very important name that would define me and my destiny in accordance with astrology. I had to be named according to the planetary alignment at the precise time of my birth. My aunt stepped up and took me to the priest and my official name in harmony to astrology is 'Dhanika' with reference to Vedic Astrology. It means wealthy young woman – able to overcome any kind of hurdle with ease and extraordinary leadership qualities. However…

My aunt had a daughter in May that same year and she presented her to the same priest and bingo, my first cousin was named according to the positioning of the stars at the time of her birth. She was given the name 'Dhanika.' I was born months later in August and how can the cosmos be duplicated with precision to afford me the same name? It is shabby and creepy, and my life will not be dictated by these standards. Granted that my cousin was born first, so I felt she was entitled to the name.

Dhanika is my official name given to me by a priest who clearly had no command on astrology. My dad gave me the preferred name 'Kelly' that resonates with me. Even with something as deep and meaningful as my fundamental identity, I had a choice on what was handed to me. It was my resolve that determined what could confine me and what could liberate me. I have no desire to change my official name as I do not live by the limitations, dictations, prescriptions and descriptions of astrology. I am who I decide to be. My choice and solely mine.

Decision Flow Between a Victim Mindset Versus the Choice to Transform Your Mind

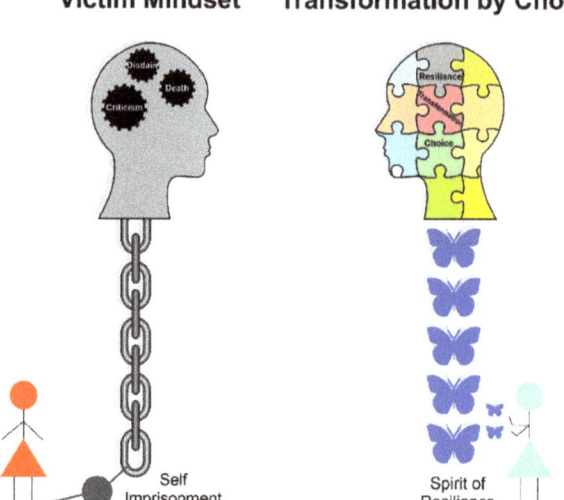

The diagram above depicts how we choose to let our mind influence us and thus define our life. If you decide to make an arbitrary move, you still have to pick which way to go.

- ✓ Victim Mindset: Victim mentality is a psychological term that refers to a type of **dysfunctional mindset** which seeks to feel persecuted in order to gain attention or avoid self responsibility.

- ✓ Mind Crafted by Choice: Every day we are confronted with a bombardment of choices. We make choices about the shoes we wear, the place we live, the friends we make, the things we say no to, the integrity we display with time and the promises we make…the list goes on. Living an abundant and satisfying life means making good choices and maintaining that momentum.

You have the power to make a good choice. Worthy choices are decisions that keep you heading in the direction which you want your life to head in. A victim mindset is an adverse choice, which impacts your life in a negative way. The table overleaf depicts some reactive and proactive choices we can make:

Victim Mindset – Reactive	Crafted by Choice – Proactive
Sticking with the tag that the world throws at you	Constantly renewing your mind
Continuing to nurse battle scars	Developing resilience in your character
Placing limits on yourself	Setting transformation as the default option in your mind
Never tapping into your full potential	Enabling the freedom to reach your full potential
Outlook that creates a ball and chain to anchor you	Live by Gods truth and not what others say
In denial	Ability to shake off negative vibrations
Lacking the ability to make wiser choices	Grasping you are not the circumstances
Refusing to outgrow low expectations from others	Actively learning from setbacks and accelerating.
Accepting contempt from others	Personally committed to becoming a better version of yourself
Accepting a negative medical diagnosis	Performing constant character introspection and ways to overcome.
Permitting others to speak death over you	Taking responsibility
Accommodating undesirable labels placed on you	Making better choices
Compliant with harmful and negative words spoken over you	Indulging in cognitive assessments of your life
Destroyed by setbacks	Conduct routine transformation health checks to establish how you need to change and grow

If you so desire, you can find a billion reasons to hate life and be bitter with the world. Or you can find a billion reasons to love life. That is the power of CHOICE – your choice – to define your world and status of contentment. When life gets unpleasant and emotional distress boils up, getting stressed and chasing our tail may feel like the correct reaction, but this cultivates the wrong results. Consequently, this makes a challenging situation even tougher. Self awareness and psychological acceptance help us to grapple with the discomfort in a strategic and meaningful manner, thereby bringing the desired positive result.

Analyse the discomfort without letting it consume you. Do not spend all your energy resisting it. Instead preserve your energy to create value by directing your energy towards an action that you can control and master. You can resolve to choose where you channel your energy – reconditioning your mind is a basic therapy that presents a healthy natural enhancement to constantly feed your mind.

The Charisma of Choice and Courage

With reference to the dictionary, the meaning of courage is 'strength in the face of pain' and charisma is 'a divinely conferred power.' When the perils of life are thrust upon you, do you let the status quo lead you or do you let wisdom and discernment drive you to a directed path? We all have CHOICES when facing our predicaments. You can permit an undesirable situation to overshadow your life and linger in your mind forever, or you can scrape up the courage to transform yourself – the conferred power is yours to unravel. No one is born feeling self empowered. Confidence is learned, the first step is choice.

Everyone has fears and insecurities. However, we can ALL empower ourselves with perseverance, determination and better choices. If you take a tiny step towards becoming a better version of the person you were yesterday, then you are moving in the correct direction for positive transformation. I am certain there is a wealth of wisdom out there on making great choices, but when I was young and faced with challenges; I had no access to any greater wisdom. All I could do was understand enough about the dynamics to choose better rather than accept what was served up.

The most fundamental consideration with choice making is to ensure that the choices you make are congruent with your all important values.

Even as a child I had the ability to discern and choose better. We are ALL messiahs of change; some know how to tap into it, while others choose to resist or deny it and avoid doing the hard yards that come with change management. Nothing is worse than the profound absence of hope. Despite ALL the negative reports handed to me, the choice was mine to create hope and chase after it and now thirty years later, I am still alive and full of hope for the future, which I carved with my sheer determination despite predictions to the contrary. If you let the world set expectations for you, they will start low and remain there just like those that spoke doom about my future and life.

It is your future and your life, so YOU need to take charge! We can bury our injuries but still have a victim mindset. Don't let the victim mindset pollute your mind with negative thinking and self disparaging talk, but rather attempt for the hallmark of growth: dollops of tangible self transformation. What is the most defining decision that shaped your destiny? For me it was my ability to make wise choices despite my circumstances – some conscripted in this book. Life may be thin with enthusiasm at times, but never see a catastrophe as a pit, see it as a ladder. Get your destiny in Kodak focus and shake it like a Polaroid picture. Continuously lease positive psychology to lead from every incident.

The perquisite of self awareness is recognition of the visceral emotions in your own body then resolving how you want to channel these emotions to align your mind to conquer the goal with confidence. Design your own emotional alignment. The act of living by finer choices is both cognitive and emotional – a towering achievement to master when you tackle your default distractions head on. I have challenged my own dysfunctions to make better choices. The art of making an impact with your personal choice is profound and the best tool you have to conquer life. It is a choice we make every day; all day, to protect our hearts and be careful with our thinking. To make sure our affections and energies are focused on the right things, to concentrate on the desires that push us along a wise path. Refrain from habitually making poor choices and then using up all your resources and energy to defend your culture of choices. You cannot undo the past, but you most definitely can make the next step better. The right choices are not easy adoptions, but they are enriching. If you are going to be brave, start with your weaknesses, your life depends on it. If the challenge is daunting, get your joyful spirit on and realign.

An abundant life is making choices that impact your life so dramatically that you do not have to constantly plan to escape the reality you created. Life offers us chance after chance to hone our choices. For every emotional quandary there is always a remedy - a behaviour to be changed or a talent to be acquired. My life attests to the choices I make – both good and bad. I have experienced numerous setbacks and each experience has left me transformed. Don't allow anyone to take you to a level that you have graduated from.

Procedural knowledge is not the ultimate but rather the key is to put this knowledge into action. Learn how to do what you know as standard operating procedure – put your choices into actions daily. I often hear the phrase 'I need closure.' Even I felt this, but discovered that closure is a choice too. Closure is not an apology, or justice, or answers. It is not waiting on another person to have revelations about the situation. Closure is your choice to move on. Find your own answers or create a new list of questions. Choices, celestial favour and hard work have anchored me. Conquering obstacles is a practice not an achievement. Do not wait for people to validate your confidence – step out and build it.

You are not going to have an obedient life without first having an obedient thought life. Proverbs 3:27 *'As a man thinks so he becomes.'* You have the power to choose your own thoughts and drive your life in a direction of favour. We all render a powerful verdict of our future in the courthouse of our mind. Affirm the finer things and the mediocre will vanish. Get acquainted with the inexhaustible store house within your mind. Do not live in a mental atmosphere of lack and limitations. Practice and enter the mood of opulence and all things that are necessary for an abundant life will come to pass.

Behind every strong person is a story that gives us a choice. Life is impacted by choice, commitment, elbow grease, tolerance, fortitude and simple will power. We all reap what we sow! Take your cue from the creative principle within you. Your thought is the path, and a new path produces a new effect. An average mind is ruled by the power of inaction. Don't let your life be ranked by the community culture either – navigate from the driver seat yourself. A mediocre mind is ruled by external forces. Don't let your life unravel by the value or attitude of your community.

You have the key to victory in mastering your mind. Change your thought and keep it changed. Adorn your choice, exalt your desire in your mind and create a vivid mental picture jacked up by faith; this display will manifest in your subconscious mind and ultimately in your life. Your thought concept governs and masters you. Do not authorise your emotions to unify with an image of restriction as you will harness the consequences of your unsavoury adoption. Develop the mechanism to transform your trial into triumph. Gain confidence in the application of your mind as all tangible assets are fleeting. Channel your emotions effectively – the secret power of declaring God's Word over you and whatever is bothering or vexing you. Don't carve your life out of experience but rather out of potential. Align your mind and life to your true capacity. Don't expect to go anywhere noticeable without organising your mental facilities with structure. Your mind is the creative medium that defines your life. Select your thoughts the same way you select your clothes and cultivate your future.

'It is our choices, Harry, that show what we truly are, far more than our abilities.' JK Rowling.

My Journey Gleans

My life has encompassed tribulations and betrayals that were acutely painful. However, they were an essential part of my destiny. They gave me zeal and fortitude and spelt out what honour is in every facet of my life. Misery will find you even if you try to hide from it; hence be strategically purposeful to live the days of ecstasy with no abandonments. The shaken, rattled and victorious encounters changed who I want out of life. It showed me it takes courage to forgive and charisma reigns when FORGIVENESS became my best character trait – that is the character I want out of this life! Forgiveness is accepting what has happened and still propelling to new dimensions of life. It takes a fortitude of strength to forgive rather than remaining hurt and angry, but forgiveness is the reward you bestow onto yourself because you are the most important focal point in the equation: a choice that only you can make.

I had a traditional name thrust upon me by custom, my official name on all my official documents. It was my choice to connect to my primary identity, to accept the limitations of astrology as a child and adult. I chose to resonate with the preferred name that my dad selected for me. We are all responsible for the life and happiness we sculpt out. You generate it, you invite it, you manifest it, and you live it. You are the architect of your reality. You choose your thoughts, your behaviour patterns, your perceptions and your reactions. You are the power. Create the mind and life you deserve.

Present your graduated character to the world. Our heart is the window to the world. Refrain from creating a profile to market your brand – be the brand! Let your core persona speak without words. Let your gait, actions, choices and deeds align to the ideals that truly matter. Whether by providence or an innate harmony, I often found myself on the precipice of moments that shifted the axis in a proverbial direction. Nonetheless a resolve that I constructed by choice; that reshaped the world in my wake and empowered me to a renewed me, myself and I by the choices I created and not just made. CREATE WISE CHOICES! *It is not the mountain we conquer but ourselves.'* Edmund Hillary.

Be patient with the process. Don't get discouraged. Steadily and surely your vision will be fulfilled. Even the snail reached the ark by persevering. TRANSFORMATION is the best progress – do you have the courage to make that choice? It can hurt to shed layers of yourself to reach refinement; we simply cannot nurture new dimensions without the discomfort of change. The result is not just the splendour of the new you, but also the shaping of this outcome: You and the magnificence of transformation!

Courage, choice and fear are a compendium deal. It comes packed with mastering the art of succeeding personal dreams, shaking off tainted limitations that others set, acutely tolerant of the lack of assurances and the natural threats – this mix creates a hornet's nest of resistance to live the abundant life. We assume a constant in life that advocates the sun must be shining and we must be happy. The rain is vital, and we also grow when we are sad. Develop the art of making choices in a way that ignites growth in you. Even when you cannot see how to accomplish your goal, create a new path one decision at a time through the valley. Make invaluable choices in every season understanding that progress is not a solid formula. Expect to stumble but most significantly, you will develop.

Society will always stereotype others and offer obscure banter based on their level of evolution, limited knowledge and profound finite wisdom. It was my choice whether to believe the priest or not. Well, it's now thirty years later and I am still not only alive but have lived my life with no abandonments. I did not shake in my boots for one day or even an hour thinking my life was doomed. The masses will throw all kinds of curve balls at you but the fundamental elements that propel or sink you is your attitude in life, the choices you make and the actions you take. I had numerous clinical reports saying I had a heart condition with no conclusive diagnosis. As an adult I paid for the best medical assessments with several different specialists and actively engaged in due diligence only to arrive at the conclusion that

I have no heart condition. Let me draw you to the fact that even as a child who was used as a pin cushion and had medical devices strapped to my heart, I did not wear the label and believe the prognosis given to me.

My mindset was where I won the battle. Our mind is a powerful tool. I am not advocating that you ignore medical intervention, my parents did not either. However, I chose the best outcome for my life in my mind. I knew I had a future and a hope. Life is not about what people, or the medical report says, it is what you believe in and most importantly what actions you take to achieve that. You can have a victim mindset, or you can craft your own life by fine decree and choices. Do not let jeopardies seize any territory of your life. The quality of your life is directly related to the quality of your mindset. Go within and reassess who you are and what you want. Your personal values will change and evolve as you do. Stay tuned to these changes and don't get caught off guard wondering why life does not align. Calibrate your internal compass with fine precision.

Every fibre in my body yearned to be a mother, but despite exploring the options of IVF I remained barren. Barrenness is painful but I had to choose not to be bitter. I was not going to live like a victim. I am so much more than my unanswered prayers and dashed dreams. I have so much to offer the world, so I had to dig deep into my well of resilience and live my best life despite the voids. My prayers remained unanswered, and I know that plight all too well, so when you call on me as a friend, daughter, wife, sister and human, rest assured that I will answer in every way I can.

When your phone rings at any time – during dinner, in the middle of your favourite program or in a meeting – you can choose whether to let it ring, check who is calling, let it default to voice mail or simply answer it. You control the outcome by your behaviour, aka your CHOICE. You make basic and complex choices every day. Simply reach a state where you enhance the choices you make. Be acutely aware of the cascading flow on effects of each of your choices. You are responsible for your life and choices, just like Bill Gates was for giving us insight into the advancements of the technological world. Success is not about excellence. It is about sustained efforts, the ability to implement and maintain your effort every day, week, month and year, ultimately influencing and reshaping your life. Transformation begins with little steps but can have a great impact. Refrain from playing victim to circumstances that you created. Today is THE DAY you can transcend your circumstances.

Become a mirror that reflects personal growth and transformation. Humans can spill so much to taint our world, but they can never break or taint our spirit or mind unless we let them. Be a vessel that facilitates healing. None of us have freedom without responsibility. Bloom with the seeds that you planted and refuse to let all the weeds thrown around you dictate your survival. You may experience calamity and victory on the same day. Both will elapse with the progression of time, so use something constant to reflect your true north. Your most obnoxious experience is your best teacher. Some of us have not yet experienced the contours of perils, so take heart to build the grit to handle the unknown future.

There is a fine line between fear and courage. The art is to balance hesitations of the unknown with the tug of innovation. Fear reminds us of jeopardy. Courage reminds us of probability. Important axioms for life: your heart is planted where your mind lives, so make a material difference however soft, vocal or tangible. Don't drift through life without making a significant mark. Reconstruct your mind even if you have to start with fragments – it is a vital part of growth. I am so glad I have navigated through all that has come my way so I can guide you to empowerment rather than victimisation. Every inch of me bespeaks valour - choose what dignity looks like for you, only you can make that fine choice to include hope into your remit. Our hard choices are not a liability but rather a key to unlock a greater path.

In the book **The Power** of the SUBCONSCIOUS **MIND** author Joseph Murphy writes 'The dictionary says that a suggestion is the act or instance of putting something into one's mind, the mental process by which the thought or idea suggested is entertained, accepted, *or put into effect. You must remember that a suggestion cannot impose something on the subconscious mind against the will of the conscious mind. In other words, your conscious mind has the power to reject the suggestion given.'* We do not need to live by what circumstances or others suggest to brand us with. We all have the power to create an impeccable brand regardless of what others say. *'The tremendous power of suggestion. You must realise by now that your mind is the 'watchman at the gate,' and its chief function is to protect your subconscious mind from false impressions.'*

We are not victims of our past but rather a product of our CHOICES. No one can alter your mind, so live there with what you allow in and out. The point of self discovery can be a bridge to thrive if you let it. Reaffirm where your mind dwells every day! Once we mire our lives with external control then we need to spend precious time to untangle from the consequences. Develop a gallant reminder to make choices that eradicate the external forces. Even if you feel like a victim, make a conscious choice to channel those emotions towards a sense of victory instead of victimhood.

Society will always offer their free opinion, it's a common commodity – anything with real value is rare and has a greater value to it. Furthermore, use these free opinions for your personal growth. Life is about the fine choices we make with poor circumstances. Return to a flexible transcend as you dabble with finding your focus. Curate choices and habits that nourish you; don't just fill an empty space. Turn your obstacles into opportunities by cancelling your subscription to issues and signing up for solutions. Your choices echo and impact eternity. Swap the microscope for the telescope.

'Values are rooted in basic optimism about life and a faith in free will – a confidence that through pluck and sweat and smarts each of us can rise above the circumstances of our birth.' Barack Obama

The Choice to Cultivate Prayer Patterns

During my holiday to Las Vegas, I visited the titanic exhibition museum. It was sad to see the documented tragedy. This ship was designed, built and marketed as unsinkable. Yet it sank. The forces of nature brought it down. It was reduced to nothing. Innocent lives were lost. The culprit – an iceberg. A force to be reckoned with. One of the reasons why these icebergs were certainly not seen as a threat is because most of the time approximately twenty percent of the iceberg is above the water surface and the other eighty percent that is below the surface goes unnoticed. It lies with the façade of unsuspecting and dormant characteristics that echo I am beautiful and harmless. Thus, there was no mitigation plan to contend with these forces of natural wonderment. The same parallels can be seen in our daily lives. We have forces that come against us, yet we choose not to look below the surface.

Philippians 4:6 – Do not be anxious about anything, but in everything by prayer and supplication with thanksgiving let your requests be made known to God.

This scripture is our true north to guide us in every facet of life. When we are dealing with so many perils that are seen and unseen, the only weapon we have is the power of prayer. It is our real and direct link to God. Have you cultivated your direct link to God? Enlisted are some of my personal cultivated links to prayer:

- ✓ In New Zealand I was part of the board members of church and it was mandatory for the senior executive team to meet in the office every Sunday before church to pray.
- ✓ The senior executive team then went up to church and prayed with the church congregation in the preservice prayer meetings. Preservice prayer meetings were scheduled at both the morning and evening services.
- ✓ After the service there was an alter call and those that responded required prayer and I was part of the team to meet these needs.

- ✓ I facilitated a connect group at my home and I prayed for my group members.
- ✓ Thursday evening was the church designated prayer meeting and as a leader my attendance was mandatory.
- ✓ Another couple from church joined forces with us to establish a prayer partner group so we could pray together before sunrise once a week.
- ✓ I maintained my personal prayer time.
- ✓ We prayed together as a couple – family.

If prayer is a direct link to God, why do we still have such a casual attitude about it? Positive energy creates a positive change. From my above mentioned prayer habits be acutely aware that they all came packaged with confrontations that I did not invite. Challenges that I had to consciously navigate daily. Some battles that presented:

I was born a Hindu and immersed in my culture and religion. As a Hindu I prayed with my eyes shut and I recited my prayer in my mind. After a few minutes my mind could wander to 'what's for dinner' or a million other things. I was still at ease as I quietened my mind to focus on the task. No one could hear my deviating thoughts out loud. I controlled the think tank and I felt regulated.

When I converted to Christianity the model for prayer was rather different. It is out loud verbalisation, and everyone around can hear the abundance of my heart. I only just landed on this side of the fence and with board members – required to pray out loud. Pastor Bill was born a Christian – He was a seasoned ninety five year old who knew the Bible from every angle. The senior team consisted of most members that were born Christians with a wealth of experience under their belt. I was summoned to this table with no experience as a Christian and I had not even read the Bible cover to cover. Both God and the church leadership saw something in me. Yes, indeed the experience was daunting, but it fortified me for life. Staying in the vine is about encouraging growth – I am so glad that my chosen tribe at this point in time did not regulate me to stay put in my comfort zone.

After the prayer with my fellow board members and two preservice prayer meetings then two alter call prayer sessions – Five sessions for a Sunday (I was pouring out but felt depleted myself). I sometimes felt like I was burning the candle from both ends. I worked all week. Saturday was housekeeping and life logistics and most of Sunday at church. I sometimes felt like life was passing me by. Hindsight confirmed to me that I was exactly where I was positioned for a significant reason. I was building my character; traits that I did not know I would need or even wanted. Sometimes I got home after a hectic day at work, and I just wanted to lie on my bed and not move. But I had to find the zeal to get to the evening prayer meeting.

Having prayer partners and meeting before sunrise was not a walk in the park either. I had to crawl out of bed and get dressed in my corporate attire and drive to church. Pray for the world, New Zealand as a country, the church and the remaining agenda then drive to work. This included the peak winter mornings that my South African bones were not accustomed to. I would arrive at work bright eyed and bushy tailed ready to contend with my day.

My Journey Gleans

Prayer is a direct link to God, so we get out what we put into the connection. When we lack the ability to be strategic, then catastrophe strikes just like the titanic. They deemed the ship to be unsinkable, moreover they did not plan effectively. Instead they reduced the number of lifeboats to increase the deck space. Thus, when the iceberg struck many lives were lost. As humans we do almost the same thing. We make choices to improve our own personal deck space and lack the foresight to plan for what may be lurking. I have noted that people have different degrees of connection with prayer:

- ✓ A person who expects someone else to pray for them when they are hatched, matched and dispatched. They have no real connection to God but because a pastor prayed for them during their baby dedication, marriage and planned funeral they assume a connection to God.
- ✓ The ad hoc prayer – who prays only when the need arises. When they need God to move that mountain.
- ✓ Cultivated prayer trooper – every tear and every joy are shared with God. You are in constant conversation with God. You have developed the art to hear his voice. You establish, build and maintain a direct connection and relationship with God.

Despite my cultivated prayer life, I still had more questions than answers. My prayer partners – she ended up dead and he was left to care for a new baby by himself. My life ended up in disarray. I was perplexed and confused with many situations. Yes, indeed I even felt that my prayers were unanswered. God answers our prayers in his time and in his way. Rest assured that he has heard all your prayers and in his time the season will present. The possibilities are endless with the power of prayer, tap into it. Every single time you draw yourself to pray and deepen the connection the narrative changes.

In 2020 a global pandemic surfaced. The global economy drastically drooped down south. Worldwide financial tension prevailed. Yet I had the capacity to purchase another home. Despite the harsh conditions

I added another asset to my portfolio. I bought another home in the middle of a pandemic – cash. Not by my might. I have favour bestowed on me because I established, built and maintained a relationship with God decades ago. The harsh COVID-19 circumstances do not dictate my reality. My connection to the living God does. The 2020 iceberg did not sink me because I planned for what was unseen.

I work in Medical Health Technology. I am currently working on a project to set up a new hospital. My office is based at the heart of the old fully operational hospital. Parramatta the suburb is a COVID-19 hot spot. I still need to liaise with clinical staff that are exposed to patients. I am exposed to patients myself. Many models of care require reassessment to operate at optimum through a global pandemic lens. It is a complex task to set up a hospital at the best of times and added demands create a cocktail of scenarios. Long before the 2020 COVID-19 pandemic hit – I established, built and maintained my direct connection with God. I am working on eight different deliverables within my project simultaneously. Even in this predicament I saw the favour of God go before me and prepared a way in the wilderness. He cleared my path daily. I did not have to look for a weapon to combat this season of plight. My cultivated prayer habit decades ago, has paved my way. No heavy lifting required!

In Sydney I joined every connect group, so I was out fellowshipping and praying every day of the week. In one group I noticed an Australian guy who was shy to pray. I encouraged him a few times to pray and one day he said, 'Ok I will pray today.' When the group concluded and the usual attendees prayed, it was his turn. He prayed 'Lord thank you for bringing us here and thank you for Rick Astley' and he played Rick Astley's song – 'Never gonna give you up' We all burst out laughing. This highlights the fact that praying out loud is daunting for others as well. He persevered and he is now an eager prayer beaver. I had the capacity to recognise this because I went through the same thing. Let's develop awareness of our surroundings and help others reach a place that seems so natural for the rest of us. It pays dividends not to be like the cold Benguela water current

– an ecosystem that is unpalatable. Be warm and caring instead – a current that forms greater tides.

God knows me by name because I have introduced myself; I have given Him a familiar handshake. Sometimes I have rocked up with tear jerking shake ups at God's collar. God knows me because I made myself known via a direct link of prayer. Guaranteed that this link is far better than 5G Wi-Fi, so do not be fazed when people do not hit *like* on your status. The only status that matters is the status that you cultivate with God. Eagles love to soar; the sentiment is definitely wrong when you have the eagle DNA but refuse to SOAR. Cultivate a daily discipline that brings favour and eternal fruit. Establish a line to hear from GOD. We are all products of our daily habits. Plan your patterns and work that plan for your greater advantage.

'When the well is dry, we know the worth of water.' Benjamin Franklin

Chapter Eleven

The Unconscious Bias

Inherent Prejudice

Labelled With Assumptions

When I first moved to New Zealand I was in my twenties: young, unsuspecting, full of life and enthusiastic with big dreams. One weekend I decided to investigate the local open homes in the real estate market as a new immigrant to a foreign country does. It was a gorgeous new home with all the modern lavish designs. I was composed and acted nonchalant when I asked the real estate lady the cost of the home. *'This home is $300k for those who earn at least $100k and I don't think you qualify,'* and she shifted her focus off me. What rich hues of assumption she had of what I could afford. I did feel annoyed with her biased attitude.

Just as well I was not in the market to purchase a home. Over two decades later, I had purchased several homes and was now domiciled in Sydney. It was late at night and I had just hopped into bed when I heard an email arrive in my inbox. It was a real estate agent updating me on a property for sale. I was looking to purchase, so I emailed back asking when I can view this. He replied immediately *'How about tomorrow?'* I drove to the site after work, looked at the details and signed the offer of purchase on the spot. I was happy with it. It was Sydney real estate, and I did not deem I had too much room to negotiate so I did not want to engage in pointless banter.

This property was significantly more than $300k and my income more than serviced the purchase. The real estate agent was somewhat taken aback that I did not bargain and could purchase this on a single income. I did not plan to prove a point to the universe but more fundamentally I did not live my life believing the label that the real estate lady in New Zealand had inflicted on me. I did not let her condescension get to me. My mindset did not live there with the limitations she placed on me.

Colour Dictates Affordability

As a young professional working in Auckland, New Zealand, at the trendy Parnell corporate hub, one day during my lunch break I was taking a walk to decompress. I found myself in an elite art gallery, though I was most definitely not looking to purchase art. I was dressed in corporate attire so not too shabby, hence I was surprised when a gentleman came out and rudely expressed, *'This place sells expensive art that you cannot afford so why are you here?'* I was stunned that people behaved in such a poor fashion, especially in the developed world.

Fast forward to twenty five years later: I was on a sojourn in San Francisco undertaking the tourist browse and found myself in a space of awe-inspiring contemporary modern art grandeur. It was an art gallery where famous artists sold their masterpieces. I instantly fell in love with two pieces and felt compelled to purchase them. While embarking on the process of completing international shipping and insurance forms, the manager started probing me about my profession and how he would love to add me into their gallery network should I wish to purchase any art in the future?

Upon completion of all the forms, the manager then informed me that he had made dinner reservations for me at the best Italian restaurant that serves a delectable roasted crab. One of his staff took me to the restaurant, where the line for entry was literally hundred deep. My chaperone made a call, and the manager of the restaurant came out and personally escorted me to my table.

I have travelled the globe and dined at many fine dining restaurants, but this by far guaranteed the results of the advertised delicacies. When I was finished, I asked for the bill and the manager came out once again and informed me the bill was already paid by the gallery and asked if I needed anything else, and then arranged a cab for me to get back to my hotel. Such a distinct juxtaposition in the way I was treated at both art galleries.

Too Colour Blind to Uphold Legislation

I was driving in Auckland once in peak hour traffic and halted at a red traffic light. I needed to turn left, and I was in the right lane, so I had my indicator on to change lane. The signal at the traffic light changed and the driver in the left lane flicked his lights and I still looked to confirm if all was clear before I proceeded to change my lane.

Out of nowhere a motorbike rider came speeding in between the cars in no designated lane and collided into my car. We exchanged details, even though he looked perfectly well with all his leather gear intact. He informed me that he had no insurance. Days later he contacted my insurance and put a spin on the facts. He claimed I had crashed into him. He was filtering lanes, overtaking me from the left and was speeding. I informed my insurance that was not what happened, and I preferred to state the facts in court. I was in my twenties, spring in my step, as I presented at court, while the biker looked to be in his mid thirties and had brought his dad, who represented him, and his brother for moral support.

My insurance representative was present. I stood out in the room not only for my gender – I was the only female – but also for my skin colour. I used the chalk board to explain precisely what had happened, while the biker's father explained how his son could not work for eight weeks due to injuries and all his biking gear had been damaged and he was seeking compensation for all of this. Why anyone who knows these risks of personal and property injury does not have insurance stuns me!

The judge said he could not make a decision that day and explained how we needed to adjourn to discuss further – it was really not rocket science but rather a classic case of filibuster and selective perception. Logically there was nothing else either party could present to this case. A wasted day off work, I thought, proceeding to leave when my insurance broker asked me in the presence of everyone, *'You do know *that all bikes drive in between cars?'* I was perplexed at his statement and did not dignify him with a response, so he repeated himself much louder almost yelling at me. I wanted to erupt with outrage but exercised my best judgement despite my youth.

None of the men present seemed to care about what the road rules echoed. For the first time an insurance organisation proved to me they were willing to settle on a claim where the case was fabricated. He then screamed, *'Which country are you from?'* I did not take another day off work to watch the kangaroo court circus in action. My insurance settled the claim and must have bought the biker lunch too.

This occurred over twenty years ago in New Zealand: motorcycle lane filtering was illegal but none of the men in the room could uphold or enforce the law. A New Zealand bike magazine got a letter from the police outlining; 'the rules around lane splitting – it's legal to do, but you can only overtake on the right.' New South Wales, Australia, only changed the motorcycle lane filtering legislation in 2014 to permit some lane filtering in specific conditions. So why did all these men treat me so unfairly especially when they were natives to the land and had a better knowledge on the laws of the country? How can someone who breaks the law get away with it and then get compensated as well? The unjust rule and reign in peculiar ways, and it's an embarrassment indeed.

Was I surprised at the highly polarised response from the judge? No, not at all, I was born and raised in South Africa and I left as soon as I could for a better life. The perks of residing in the capitalised world did not afford all that the immigration poster echoed. Discrimination has no international borders. Stable world citizens offer their patronage to their country and they love the laws of the land, yet they failed miserably to uphold it - even the judge did not do the right thing. The matrix behind life is to transform to a better state to enhance our habitat, community and world in equal proportions.

We have scrambled, scraped and intellectualised our way to the top of the apex. Then why do we not vibrate higher and deeper? Be impeccable with your word, deeds and actions. What chance do any of us have even when civil servants break the law to quench their bias? Seek first to understand, then be understood, then ALWAYS DO THE RIGHT THING especially when it is dictated by law. Apparently, I had to prove that I could speak, read, comprehend and had attended an

English medium school to facilitate my citizenship process. Mandated to meet the criteria for basic elements to reside in this country, the system seems inconsistent when those within appear to not comprehend the laws of their OWN land written in simple English. Serial inconsistency!

A Black Person Can Dispense Your Medication but Cannot Serve You

My corporate portfolio took my career to Northshore, New Zealand, working in a community pharmacy. It was lunchtime and I was the only resource in the pharmacy when Mrs. Donahue walked in. She had dropped off her prescription with the shop assistant earlier, so I had dispensed the prescription: packaged and ready for pick up. I grabbed the cocktail of medications and went down to the shop counter as the Kiwi shop assistant was on her lunch break along with everyone else.

I advanced to provide Mrs. Donahue mandatory medication management advice and she literally screamed at the top of her lungs, *'I do not want to be served by a black person.'* She grabbed the medications and flung them at me, everything went flying and glass bottles were shattered. Everyone from the lunchroom scurried out. My manager, the owner of the pharmacy, was just as astonished as I was. He grabbed me by the hand and asked me if I was ok and then told me to go to lunch while he managed the situation.

Everyone in the lunchroom was trying to comfort me. I was born and raised in South Africa, a country where apartheid reigned. However, due to segregation law, I was never exposed to this level of abuse. The systemic racial divides ensured each race lived in areas allocated to that race. My school was not multiracial. It was an Indian school with equals, and I was not treated with disdain. I am a by product of apartheid.

I witnessed South Africa becoming a democracy in 1994 – what an enormous leap for mankind. Or was it? I recall relocating to New Zealand and Australia then for the first time as an adult exposed to such a cosmopolitan diversity that presented its own challenges. Sadly, the first time I experienced real active racism was outside South Africa, in the developed world by people who perceived to be so evolved. People have cried, lost lives and endured imprisonment to taste democracy, yet injustice still prevails in murky hearts all around the globe.

Disdain With No Restrain

I was working as a professional in clinical information technology for an organisation that managed all the branded pharmacies. My role was predominantly linked to the dispensing software used in the dispensary by the pharmacists. The model of community pharmacy has two different software applications: a) Dispensing software used in the dispensary b) Point of Sale software used to sell over the counter products in the shop area and process payment of prescriptions dispensed by the clinical system.

One fine day I received a call from a rather irate pharmacist explaining issues with the point of sale system used in his pharmacy. I very politely informed him my influence and role were with the clinical dispensing system only. I asked him to speak to the point of sale software vendor directly. He began yelling about how he hated to call the POS vendor. *'Every time I call them, they have a bloody Indian answer the phone. I hate speaking to those Indians.'* Heavy breathing on the other end and I was silent. He said, *'Are you there.'* I replied, 'I am unsure how I can help because I am Indian myself.' He then said, *'Oh ok bye.'*

A few weeks later we had a company conference, and I had the opportunity to meet this pharmacist face to face: the memory was still unshaken. He just looked at me sheepishly and made no apologies but then proceeded to narrate the incident to the group hoping to inform me how the whole gang hated calling that vendor: a business that had nothing to do with me, but he purely did not want to follow the standard operating processes because they had Indians responding to his issue. I walked away towards better vibes at the conference.

Newsflash: every substantial organisation has an information technology department. The complex bandwidth, enhancements, programmed logic, and technology innovation most people take for granted have predominantly Indian gurus behind the works. There are pronounced reasons why so much of information technology work is outsourced to India or major IT vendors have set up shop in India. Everyone wants to be part of the technological advancement.

However, get a grip: it is not unlocked by colour, creed or race. It's sad when people tarnish innovation with personal bias. Dehumanisation is a challenge and not progress. We all should have the same zeal to advance in our culture and not just limit it to advancement in technology. You are a sad human when you love the innovation of a race but hate the race itself. Time to wake up and smell the conscious divide.

Bias Bites but Beckons Nothing

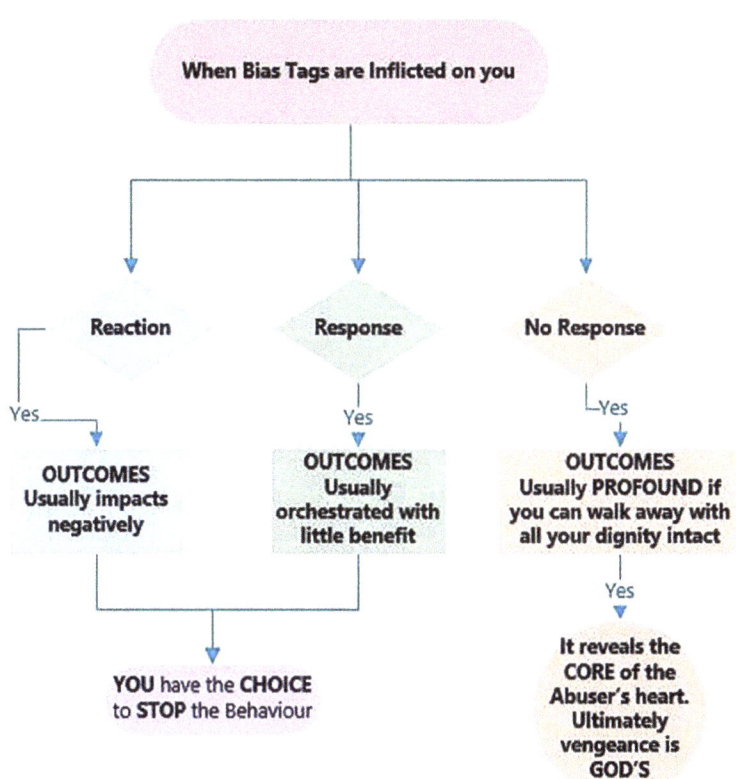

From my tangible life experience, I have learned that no matter which part of the globe I live in, people are flawed. I have experienced so much more than I care to write about, but the fashion in which I process these bias tags that are so freely inflicted upon me is the operative part of this process flow equation depicted overleaf. No one wants to be a victim, and in an ideal world there should be no victims. Sadly, humans are conditioned in so many negative ways that they manifest in unsatisfactory ways as well.

The relinquishing behaviour I chose, and you can adopt this too is to just walk away. Having a reaction when treated negatively will magnify the issue. Indulging in a response may be sweet but do you really want to drop to a level of a human being who is already exhibiting flaws in such a profound way? Harbouring implicit bias towards a particular social group determines how you treat an individual from that group. Although explicit forms of workplace discrimination are banned in most developed countries, humans have not developed at the same pace as the law.

My Journey Gleans

Discrimination is rife in the developed world and corporate legislation has not eradicated it. I have lived through numerous other situations where senior management and organisations have displayed bias and racial prejudice. We all have the choice to become self aware, actively resisting harmful behaviour. How we behave is a benchmark to the next generation. The racial beast is like a seven headed dragon that will just not die because the behaviour that we model today is internalised by the next generation and they add another layer of hate to it before dishing it out.

The cycle can stop with you, if you choose to stop propagating detrimental racist stereotypes, biases and prejudices. Live by example and leave a legacy that you can be proud of, a legacy of love and hope, not of trauma and destruction. Sadly, Mrs. Donahue from the pharmacy saga died a week after that altercation in a fatal car crash. The high priest of political correctness is only pertinent when you are receiving bad behaviour as a privileged race, colour or gender and it has no considerable clout when you dish it out to others. Indeed, a sad scale and blindfold to live with when you treat others in a fashion that you would never accept for yourself.

I left South Africa on a quest for a better life. The developed world does offer me better opportunities, but they are sometimes no different to the *'knee on the neck'* that the world witnessed in America in 2020. I have worked in numerous organisations and while they advertise respect and collaboration as their core key values, the reality is so far from it. It is vastly advertised that unprofessional conduct will not be tolerated and must be reported. The perpetrators are mainly senior managers, so no action is ever taken in reality. A norm has developed to ignore racism, discrimination, victimisation and bullying. This is a whole new book and just one paragraph will not suffice.

Progress is sometimes as rare as a ship at an airport. This adds to the perpetrators' authority to live by their utopian fanfare with their assumed authority both in the room and the world. The most basic element for life is oxygen. Oxygen is free, it is not bottled up and sold as per status or race. God in His wisdom granted us all free rights to breathe, to live, to bleed, to cry and to sing, so how did disdain get into your equation? Why do humans find the need to shred an innocent heart into pieces just because they can? Refrain from judging my skin before you see my humanity, the colour of my heart and the actual size of my purse. Even if you move as slow as a glacier, strive to move to a better state of mind.

Your perceptions, life and conduct are your window to the world. They create a legacy for others to follow and express our character and produce our effectiveness and our ineffectiveness. Valour, strength, peace, harmony and love are not conjured from an exclusive tribe. God created variation in many species for a philosophical reason. The essence of synergy is to value differences. Everyone should be granted the freedom to enjoy this world, we are all just travelling through for a finite period so bring your best version to the party and enjoy the happy hour. Be patient with the process. Don't get discouraged and allow others the same token of measure to mess up and find the way back.

It's a rare commodity for a tainted society but if you give yourself the latitude to grow, then you present all of mankind a galvanised hope for the future. Let the record show that I am a regular blood donor – this sustains life in a profound way and to date absolutely no recipient has ever refused my blood due to the colour of my skin. I am also a listed organ donor, and I am certain the same is applicable here. Why are humans not so calculating and shrewd when it comes to saving their own life? Then the racial divide is miraculously eradicated. The pertinent question is what are you giving to the world? Apart from your flawed mind!

If you do not speak up for justice and realign the default bias, then perverse forces will take over the narrative. A sad place indeed, for us all to live in. Fact – thousands of artists have painted Christ not as the dark Middle Easterner that he was but as a fair skinned man of the picture in their heads. Perception paints a beautiful picture, but the beauty may be deceptive and cuts deep. Most people who deem to love Jesus may have difficulties reconciling with a God that is dark skinned. If your perception of Jesus is distorted, give credence to the fact that knowledge conquers ignorance and equip yourself with vital knowledge before you create perceptions. Prejudice is an emotional dedication to ignorance, especially when perceptions are distorted. New behaviours are usually simple and individually almost inconsequential, but added together over a period of time, they shape and reshape the way we deal with the world: they become our personalities. I beseech you to make the Holy shift of your mindset and the simple shift of your behaviour to generate a better world – humanity.

Racism is a jarring experience, so please be aware of the impacts that your unfairness can ignite. We are all born with love, but we learn to hate…so we can most definitely learn to unhate too. If you ignore the whispers of your world and circle you build a concrete wall of false emotions and rest assured, you keep the poison pot stirred for future generations. Incur enlightened protégés for humanity and your purpose as an instrument game changer – the smallest step in the direction of harmony makes a great difference. Thorns give birth to thorns; the garden of your heart can become seamless, weaving a bountiful harvest when the thorns are purged. Have you zoomed in to identify your thorns? Think in some kink or crevice of your mind and heart to dispel all lurking thorns before they take over the universal garden. Look to humanity's visage rather than your own crooked countenance, change the channel your brain – the real saddening aspect is when good people remain silent and look away. Love ought to transcend all creeds, why is it not so evident to reign supreme on earth?

'Loyalty to a petrified opinion never yet broke

a chain or freed a human soul.' Mark Twain

When I donate blood, I do not specify the preferred colour and creed of the recipient. I simply give my blood to all those that may need it. How can society never question the colour of my skin when I am literally pumping life into them, and yet they get scales of injustice to their eyes when they metaphorically suck the life right out of me with intrinsic racial chauvinism? My blood donor key ring breathes no contempt and discrimination, neither does my heart. Love is the recipe for a society to eradicate systemic discrimination. Cohesion healing is a task for all. No man is an island, and we all need to work in concert to bring effective, lasting and positive affirmation of change.

Photograph:
Sydney, Australia
2020

Developing With Apartheid

I lived in a trifling town called Tugela in South Africa. During the holidays my extended family often congregated at our home. Once we decided to embark on a road trip to Richards Bay: a bustling holiday destination approximately two hundred kilometres away. Some of my uncles, aunties and cousins could qualify for a small army, and we all jostled off with oodles of picnic food to have a beach bash. We reached our destination with amplified eagerness. We began to unpack and stretch our legs while all the locals looked at us as if we were from outer space.

Eventually one of the adults broke our hearts by pointing to a sign on the beach. It read: *'No dogs and Indians allowed.'* I was just a teenager and was faced with the taste of unfairness as if it was a specific distasteful cuisine. My younger cousin probed, *'Who owns the beach, have they bought it?'* All the beaches in Richards Bay as well as the parks had the same sign, so we eventually gave up and started heading back home. Pulling the food apart while we travelled in our respective vehicles with a slayed spirit.

Back then, without the benefit of a Google search and international travel, I had no clue what the rest of the world looked like apart from the over sensationalised depictions on the television in our living room. However, I categorically knew that I did not want to contribute or be part of a society, culture or country that enforced humans to live like they were born with imperfections and deemed some people second class by mandated laws that only serviced the advantaged. I dreamed of a better future.

I did not feel a compulsion to build or contribute to this economy as it was clearly flawed. I was proud to vote in the very first democratic election in 1994 even though my grandfather had just died, and his funeral plans were up on the priority list. Other priorities deemed attention as well. The policy that governed relations between South Africa's white minority and sanctioned racial segregation, political and economic discrimination against non-whites had to be prioritised.

The implementation of apartheid, often called 'separate development' since the 1960s, was made possible through the Population Registration Act of 1950, which classified all South Africans as either Bantu (all black

Africans), Coloured (those of mixed race), or white. A fourth category — Asian (Indian and Pakistani) — was later added. Group Areas Act of 1950 established residential and business sections in urban areas for each race, and members of other races were barred from living, operating businesses, or owning land in them. In practice this Act and two others (1954, 1955), which became known collectively as the Land Acts, completed a process that had begun with similar Land Acts adopted in 1913 and 1936; the end result was to set aside more than 80 percent of South Africa's land for the white minority.

The first time my Australian husband saw this sign he was in shock. He asked me, 'Do you really want to include this?' My response was yes because this is what I grew up with. This was the reality inflicted on many humans. Eventually the elite decided to take their pet dogs to these locations, and they merely scratched out the words on the sign 'no dogs' and created a new law for themselves to take their pet dogs with them. The law was not changed but broken for a pet; however, if a human outside the elite group broke the law, then punitive action was taken in court.

Photograph:
Richards Bay, South Africa,
1986

Strategically, other races were permitted to work in these segregated developments to boost the economy to keep the place in ship shape, but the fauna, flora and places of recreation had signs displayed to prevent the use of these reserved areas. The privileged were able to live, dress and dine with eloquence and clarity and thus were capable of engaging in the civic life of their communities and persuading others to unscrupulous and reckless standards. This entertained accomplishment through suppression and discrimination of the masses so a few elites could have the butler service as birth rights.

The jury is still out on the disputed fact to establish whether the dominating elect was really born with the butler bell attached to their correctly coordinated hip or was it simply inherited from the past generations. Ludicrous to even jot this down but I cannot grasp how people actually passed it as mandated legislation and lived it out loud. Most revolting was to enforce it on those that actually and truly owned the land.

The law is defined by the government in authority, but have you really studied the jurisprudence of your own heart – does it consist of any internal logic? Life is not about living in the confines of misguided laws; it is about deciding what you are going to do about the erroneous reality. Shutting your eyes to dehumanization is a choice that many make daily – it is deliberate tunnel vision. Rise up and live to higher ideals with passion, conviction and purpose for healthier advancement. Taking no action is a reaction too; an insightful one.

'The people who sheltered Anne Frank were breaking the law. The people who killed her were obeying the law.' Unknown

Have you pondered to introspect your heart with deliberation to examine and uncover where and why you harbour indifference and injustice? The herd mentality does not help, regardless of who or what models apathy to you: first hand, passed on as inheritance or contrived as an undercurrent. In your indulgence, do not grow indifferent. Don't let your heart and hands be filled with blood. Don't bask in formality but rather live a life that is in concert to real compassion. It denotes dysfunction when: personal decadence reigns, inequality sways the path, lack of empathy rules and injustice influences the future. You cannot live genuinely by your values until you define them and align them with the core of your heart. Give credence to the fact that you may need to renew and recalibrate your heart to fit a new purpose and vision. *'If you don't stand for something, you'll fall for anything.'* Ron Chernow.

We are now living in the twenty first century. Pet animals are now implanted with microchips so that they can be traced by their owners if they ever get lost. The Holy Grail for the pet industry. My grandparents and parents were treated no differently to these pets! To help enforce the segregation of the races and prevent non-whites from encroaching on white areas, the government strengthened the existing 'pass' laws, which required non-whites to carry documents authorizing their presence in restricted areas and mandated them to carry an identification document constantly. Citizens were punished by law and imprisoned if they did not present 'their papers' similar to microchipping. Nevertheless, those with pets could break the law without any consequences.

Other laws forbade most social contacts between the races, authorised segregated public facilities, established separate educational standards, restricted each race to certain types of jobs, curtailed non-white labour unions, and denied non-white participation (through white representatives) in the national government.

On the night of June 7, 1893, Mohandas Karamchand Gandhi, a young lawyer then, was thrown off the train's first class 'whites only' compartment at Pietermaritzburg station in South Africa for refusing to give up his seat. A white man had objected to Gandhi travelling in the first class coach in spite of the latter possessing a valid ticket. When Gandhi refused to move to the rear end of the train, he was thrown out. Gandhi had gone to South Africa with a one year contract to practice law from India. But when his contract ended, this incident was instrumental in his decision to stay back and defend the rights of the discriminated citizens. He had stayed at the station that night shivering in cold and the bitter incident had played a major role in Gandhi's decision to stay on in South Africa and change the country.

During his time in South Africa, Gandhi went on peaceful marches and presented himself for arrest against unjust laws. This became one of the great political tools of the 20th century and even influenced civil rights movement in the United States of America. Mahatma Gandhi was sentenced to four terms' imprisonment in South Africa during his

Satyagraha campaigns. An important event in the Satyagraha movement took place on August 16, 1908, when Gandhi encouraged people to burn their identity documents. More than 2,000 documents were burned outside the Hamidia Mosque in Jennings Street, Fordsburg. Another pivotal campaign in South Africa was initiated in 1913 to protest a £3 tax imposed on ex-indentured Indians as the state had declared Hindu and Muslim marriages invalid. When Gandhi was leaving South Africa in 1914, he described Satyagraha as "perhaps the mightiest instrument on earth."

For decades, the country's black majority was controlled by racist laws enshrining white supremacy. From 1948 through the 1990s, a single word dominated life in South Africa. Apartheid – Afrikaans for 'apartness ' – kept the country's majority black population under the thumb of a small white minority. It would take decades of struggle to stop the policy, which affected every facet of life in a country locked in centuries old patterns of discrimination and racism.

The South African government's focus was to educate only the white children. No funding was available for the other races. The Indian community joined together to build and fund schools in the most basic form so their children could get some education. They created a model that worked well and financed it out of their own humble pockets. So the immediate obligation was education. There were no funds for extracurricular activities.

These established blooming schools were eventually taken over by the government and provided little funding, which did not even come close to the spectrum of funding that was afforded to white schools. Basic sporting events were included in the curriculum. Most Indian children could not swim in pools as these facilities were only for the elite in segregated white areas. The majority of the indigenous children did not attend school as the segregated laws prevailed and no schools were available in the townships that they domiciled in.

Now that the Indian school had some funding from the government, they mandated the protocols. It was enforced upon every student to learn Afrikaans – a language that was foreign to us. Passing English and Afrikaans required a score of fifty percent or more, if not, the student failed the entire year. These Indian children passed both these languages with flying colours. It did place a strain on our mother tongue – Hindi, Tamil and Urdu – which took a back seat as kids grappled with excelling at what was enforced on them. I can speak, read and write in Afrikaans better than I can in Hindi.

I have been away from the savanna of Africa and lived and worked in four different countries. I have never ever used the Afrikaans language once, not even by coincidence, yet we were mandated to learn and pass it. The indigenous have several dialects in their language and have more mouths per capita of land, yet the desire to communicate effectively by learning their language was shunned and ignored.

On the other end of the spectrum, when the realism of the country was portrayed in a song 'Gimme Hope Jo'anna,' **This song was banned by the Apartheid regime in South Africa. The first chorus refers to Jo'anna as the regime that at the time implemented and enforced racist laws to "run" South Africa.** 'Gimme Hope Jo'anna' is an anti-apartheid song written and originally released by Eddy Grant in 1988, during the apartheid era in South Africa. Even though this song was banned by the South African government when it was released, it was still widely played in South Africa nonetheless. It reached number seven on the UK Singles Chart, becoming Grant's first top 10 hit in more than five years.

Gimme Hope Jo'anna by Eddy Grant

Well, Jo'anna she runs a country
She runs in Durban and the Transvaal
She makes a few of her people happy, oh
She don't care about the rest at all
She's got a system they call apartheid
It keeps a brother in a subjection
But maybe pressure can make Jo'anna see
How everybody could a live as one

Gimme hope, Jo'anna
Hope, Jo'anna
Gimme hope, Jo'anna
'Fore the morning come
Gimme hope, Jo'anna
Hope, Jo'anna
Hope before the morning come

I hear she make all the golden money
To buy new weapons, any shape of guns
While every mother in black Soweto fears
The killing of another son
Sneakin' across all the neighbours' borders
Now and again having little fun
She doesn't care if the fun and games she play
Is dangerous to everyone
She's got supporters in high up places
Who turn their heads to the city sun

Jo'anna give them the fancy money
Oh to tempt anyone who'd come
She even knows how to swing opinion
In every magazine and the journals
For every bad move that this Jo'anna makes
They got a good explanation
Even the preacher who works for Jesus
The Archbishop who's a peaceful man

Together say that the freedom fighters
Will overcome the very strong
I want to know if you're blind Jo'anna
If you want to hear the sound of drums
Can't you see that the tide is turning
Oh don't make me wait till the morning come

The system was rooted in the country's history of colonisation and slavery. White settlers had historically viewed black South Africans as a natural resource to be used to turn the country from a rural society to an industrialised one. Starting in the 17th century, Dutch settlers relied on slaves to build up South Africa. Around the time that slavery was abolished in the country in 1863, gold and diamonds were discovered in South Africa. That discovery represented a lucrative opportunity for white owned mining companies that employed — and exploited — black workers.

Those companies' all but enslaved black miners while enjoying massive wealth from the diamonds and gold they mined. Like Dutch slave holders, they relied on intimidation and discrimination to rule over their black workers. Though apartheid was supposedly designed to allow different races to develop on their own, it forced black South Africans into poverty and hopelessness. 'Grand' apartheid laws focused on keeping black people in their own designated 'homelands.' And 'petty' apartheid laws focused on daily life restricted almost every facet of black life in South Africa.

The definition of the Equity Theory, popularly known as Adam's equity theory, aims to strike a balance between an employee's input and output in the workplace. This theory and so many other realities did not reach the round table discussion ethics in South Africa during this era. The pertinent question now is – does the world remain STUCK there with preconceived perceptions, mindsets, bias, actions and lack of actions?

Apartheid also received international censure. South Africa was forced to withdraw from the Commonwealth in 1961 when it became apparent that other member countries would not accept its racial policies. In 1985 both the United Kingdom and United States imposed selective economic sanctions on South Africa. In response to these and other pressures, the South African government abolished the 'pass' laws in 1986, although blacks were still prohibited from living in designated white areas and the police were granted broad emergency powers.

In a more fundamental shift of policy, however, the government of South African president F.W. de Klerk in 1990 – 91 repealed most of the social legislation that provided the legal basis for apartheid, including the Population Registration Act. Systematic racial segregation remained deeply entrenched in South African society, though, and continued on a de facto basis. A new constitution that enfranchised blacks and other racial groups was adopted in 1993 and took effect in 1994. All race national elections, also in 1994, produced a coalition government with a black majority led by anti-apartheid activist Nelson Mandela, the country's first black president. These developments marked the end of legislated apartheid, though not of its entrenched social and economic effects.

Our blood is the same colour, yet our skin differences reigned to create a gamut of these signs that mandated legislation. Signs that ruined the simple pleasure of a family trip to the beach. Even basic simple natural resources were earmarked for those who had a default right simply by their skin colour. The Word of God says in the book of Acts 10:34, *'God is not a respecter of persons.'* Newsbreak – it's not the colour of your skin that matters, it's the colour of your heart that counts and that makes all the difference.

Photograph:
Durban, South Africa,
circa 1980

My Journey Gleans

In this vein of my heritage, I am convinced that if we can initiate prejudices then we can most definitely also surpass those biases. Or are we simply stuck because no one can teach an old dog new tricks? Our ability to change is an important facet of our humanity! How racist are you? Racism often operates beneath our conscious awareness. Even people who outwardly detest xenophobia can make stereotyped or unfair assessments of people, exercising prejudices of which they are not even aware. As a species we seem to be equipped and conscious of the upsides in life and thus we have mastered the art of handling the perks in life. Often ignored but equally important is our ability and skill of the unconscious mind and behaviour patterns. We need to train our intuition to bring equilibrium to the equation, so we can govern and control the perceptions and behaviour of both our conscious and unconscious selves.

A life of opulence and accomplishments means zip when you cannot treat another human as a human and lack tolerance for diversity in creation. Rudimentary may be the default mode for you. Why are you configured this way and what are you going to do about it? It's unnatural to scorn others just because they don't fit your idea of normal; look beyond your limited horizon. Step outside your psychological box and dare to create a new perception. Conversely, we do not think about how our conditioning and behaviour bottlenecks the world in an adverse manner.

Do you ask yourself what you can eliminate or streamline to make this a better world for everyone? We are all history makers; the chronicle is yours to pick. The tree of liberation must be refreshed and paved with new colours: the rainbow nation. No one owns a black and white television set in this era. We all crave colour for a reason, so let the colours of the rainbow reign in your soul and not just on your television. 'We are the world' is a powerful song with philosophical lyrics, we are still singing this song, now let's live it, what a liberating idea! Go confidently in a new direction. Paul wrote in The Word 'when I became a man, *I put away childish things.'* Take your place in the circle of life even if you are shaken and rattled to ensure that you are heard.

Now is the time! The mountain is waiting...what we do and fail to do in life echoes for eternity. Think strategically and awaken your genius. An overture of love needs to gestate in your heart before you can paint the world with colours. Conceptualise better escarpments for the world with tiny but profound decisions if the ladder has twenty rungs, climb but a few – make a small difference in our big world, together the ladder is much easier to climb. Foster a JUST culture, not an elite one. Stand back and look at the terrain. Discern nuances and the active or passive role you play. Let your emotional barriers corrode, dig up your confidence in spades and live the new you out loud.

Live a life that leaves goose bumps on the skin and warmth in hearts. You will be trapped in an unfulfilling moral force if you do not empower yourself to do better when you know better. A great idea can hook the world. But ideas are cheap. It's the execution that matters, your execution decides how this world will be for future generations.

Life in South Africa and the rest of the world has not yet reached the utopian goal standard. Change in legislation is a small step in the accurate direction. Transformation of the mindset that is passed from generation to generation is the biggest trait of the real rainbow nation that Nelson Mandela, our Madiba dreamed of. The biggest asset in the world is our MINDSET. The vital question is, are you in this equation to shrink this gap or not? Your valiant labours and enthusiasm for liberty can get us all closer to the finish line. Is your general outlook highly polarised or even minded?

What are your tides of contentment and waves of mystique for this life? If you are more fortunate than others, then build a longer table and not a higher fence. When death takes us, the essence of the soul escapes but the aura remains. You can define precisely what remains...the manuscript of change is in your hands. Building a house of wellness is great but building a world of equity is much more profound. The power of archetypes and narratives is startling when you strive to build a quintessentially profound legacy that's beyond your own gene pool. You are only as fair as you treat humanity! Stereotyping is another pillar of many generations and tags as pitiful. Bent attention to someone's group affiliation for no apparent reason invokes a negative stereotype to the wider landscape that is exposed directly and indirectly. Group stereotypes brings emotional imbalances that affects humanity on a mass scale. This impacts the community, economy and the resilience of a soul.

Prejudice is emotionally virile and disastrous for the workplace and the world at large. The human heart default state is love, so love without prejudice. When you see abominations causing desolations then do something about it. Professional curiosity is when you foster the symbol of resilience; it is a resounding victory for more than just the organization that employs you. Let personal epiphany arrive – do what you need to chase it down, hats off to the way makers who stood up for what matters and to those who will stand up with conviction. We need conviction in our hearts to change the world. Character is not showing up with your average strut. Dig deep for real persuasion and exceptional character.

Go forward with a heart coated in reverence and hope. Hope for a better world. The most expensive liquid in the world is tears – it consists of a very low percentage of water and higher proportion of actual emotions therefore deliberate before you hurt others by cultivating a psychological internal vector. Dispense your love louder than your hate. Get your own ship to face true north then others will be inclined to follow your direction. Our most valuable currency is the example we pose – step forward and make your mark.

Our behaviour is a style that continues to change as we perpetually add creativity in modest, and sometimes prominent, portions. If you analyse your behaviour, you can easily become aware of your creativity. For instance, when I cook a curry, I conjure it up with ease without real deliberation. However, sometimes I may run out of a key ingredient like coconut cream, and I think on my feet and substitute normal fresh cream and lime juice instead. This innovative fusion is minor. Nonetheless, the new creation is sensational, and I have often gained revered compliments. This illustration demonstrates that I can behave creatively and rack up a positive accolade. Then so can the rest of the universe and we can do this with issues that are more dramatic than culinary delights. Creativity sparks in so many profound ways. We wear hair, apparel and smiles defined by exclusive market brands. Yet our heart and character are the most vital branding tools. The dawn of a new humanity depends on your awakening to create a better and renewed universe.

'You must be the change you wish to see in the world.' Arleen Lorrance

Chapter Twelve

The Best Has Come, and It Prevails

Living My Truth

I am now embarking on the fifth decade of this amazing life. Some of the lessons I have learned literally came with blood, sweat and tears. Some of these gems are:

- ✓ The most powerful trait in life is resilience.
- ✓ Walk your own path no matter how difficult it is. It is much easier than discovering that those you bank on just don't care.
- ✓ Create your own vision; otherwise, you will be influenced by other people's dreams and aspirations.
- ✓ Experience what you have learned. Theory is great but true experience is wiser and stays with you for life. Gain leverage from past experiences by remembering how you were propelled, led and ushered through the snares. Use these experiences to break the cycle and move to a new season.
- ✓ Become acutely aware of 'the power of free will.' We are all blessed with free will. God's will does prevail but sometimes our free will derails God's plan. Be wise and know when to exercise your free will and when to utilise God's will.
- ✓ The greatest test is how you manage people who botch up your life.
- ✓ Establish an energy maintenance check list – know what depletes you and what fills your cup.

My Journey Gleans

This world does not care about your professional portfolio and success. This world is craving for you and me to make peace, stand in the gap, fend for someone when they cannot, help when they cannot help themselves, love the unlovable and forgive even those who wrong you. Leave behind a legacy that will live long after you perish. Obtaining qualifications and titles do not make a great leader. The ability to lead by example makes a leader. Love leaves a memory that no one can steal. You are made of the same cosmic stuff that galaxies are made of. The same energy that spins planets around the stars, style electrons to dance and rhythms with meticulousness in your heart – everything that makes the world go round. This substance is in you. It is the focal point of your beautiful essence. Light up your heart, the room and the world; trust in your grand design and calibration and leap forward. Let every molecule be moved when you enter the room.

'If there is one lesson I've learned from failure and success, it's this: I am not the outcome. I am never the result. I am only the effort.' Kamal Rayikant

Let Your Success be the Noise

I work in medical information technology and it is an industry that permits almost no room for error. Clinical systems used by clinical practitioners must offer the best and safest patient care. If the software is wrong, a patient could die, or it can translate to a lawsuit. Precision and competence are necessary at every stage of software development, lifecycle and implementation.

I started a new job at an organization that produced Electronic Medical Record systems for hospitals. The next version of this software was piloted at the emergency department on the Gold Coast, Australia. Things came to a grinding halt as a showstopper bug was found and clinicians could not risk using this version of the software. The hospital had to revert to the older version of the system.

Weeks later, the company's chief executive officer and lead developer were having a meeting and discussing the pain that this bug was causing and its impact on future roll outs. As they scratched their heads, I overheard the conversation. I enquired what the issue was. They both looked at me in surprise and said they had assessed this and could not find a fix or recreate the issue for the last two weeks. I read between the lines and the consensus was that they were the gurus and if they could not fix it, then a rookie like me had no chance. I asked them to email me the details and I would take a look. I was on my way to the bathroom when I lifted up my hands and prayed. I asked God to give me wisdom and discernment to look at this showstopper bug.

I got back to my desk and, I kid you not, in less than two minutes I found the cause of the bug. It was not rocket science as it was a really simple issue. I thought this cannot be it. I played with the software for a while and then I said to the lead developer, 'I think I found the issue.' He came to my desk and I demonstrated the issue to him. He let out a sigh of relief. The chief executive officer was now at my desk and the lead developer was checking the code and he found the bug in the code. They both looked at me and said they should have asked for my help sooner.

My Journey Gleans

Every time I felt the gush of emotional pain from my realities of woes when I was at work, I went to the bathroom. I spoke to God and told Him the pain was too much and I need his help. I spoke specific scriptures over myself. My favourite was *'I can do all things through Christ who strengthens me.'* I would come out feeling lighter. I did the same when I needed help to review this bug that was affecting so many hospitals.

With the progression of time, I understood that God gives me understanding, grows my wisdom, provides discernment, showers deep revelations, creates perfect vision and blesses me with favour every time I reach out to Him. In my weakest times, I run to God. He is the beacon of light and He uses me as a willing vessel to accomplish His purpose. I do not look for my worth in the world or in others as I know my worth in God. Live bravely and meaningfully with energy that really matters. Cut off the noise so you can focus and zoom in on the positive vibes.

'Try not to be a person of success but rather a person of value.' Albert Einstein

Sisterhood That Anchors Strength

A healthy support system has its obvious benefits. Studies have repeatedly linked healthy relationships to better physical, mental and spiritual health. Traditionally plants obtain their nutrients from the soil in the same fashion humans need a source of nourishment as well. Authentic sisterhood is craved by many and enjoyed by those that are gifted enough to invest in its strong towers. Sisterhood is loving and accepting your friend as she is however dependably stimulating her to reach her next level. Some women excel in disparagement and pain and want nothing but to see you fail, some will pretend that they are for you. I am not addressing that calibre here, that's another book! This is about the fine discovery of a real sister and maintaining a sisterhood (same as the brotherhood for the men reading this).

When you find that friend with inherent warmth, charm, values and traditions: it is a recipe for successful memories, abundant laughter and growing old with finesse. You acquire a mental prescription to hop skip and jump. When I relocated from New Zealand to Australia a friend from New Zealand passed on the details of a lady, informing me to contact her if I ever needed a friend or help to transition. A few months after my relocation I called the number and I explained who I was and my relocation transition – quest for a church. The woman showed no interest or zeal – she did not even invite me to come check out the church. Nonetheless I rocked up to this church in Brisbane and I sat next to the most amazing woman – she had a friendly disposition and we exchanged numbers. With a progression of over a decade we have not yet lost touch.

Penny is the big sister that I needed in Australia. I am humbled by the impeccable example she displayed, unconditional love and remaining loyal despite state borders. Authentic sisterhood tells the tale every time! I recall going through a harrowing event and I felt emotionally and physically depleted, I phoned Penny and narrated the saga and she said 'Kels I got your back – all you need to do is just breathe, breathe to stay alive and I will cover you in prayer and my mum is praying for you as well.' Regardless of all my courage and strength sometimes I need the human tender loving care, as we all do. We both bring different gems and value to this sisterhood. Sanctified sisterhood dictates that we move in a different realm where we build each other up and never tear down. I can sincerely attest to the fact that we graduate as formidable friends with true fellowship of agape hearts. We cannot choose our family however we can make fine choices with getting the cream of the crop in a true friend.

Penny and I are blessed to graduate with stellar rating distinctions as our friendship has now transitioned to real family. We are sisters from another mother and have bonds that bind us deeper than genetic data. Go make some friends and some changes to your current circle if you have to. Choose fellowship that will help you with every facet of your transition in a positive direction. When you find those special souls who resonate with your positive values then keep them close and add to the string of bows as well; they are your tribe – cherish them just as much as they cherish you. If there was no change then there would be no butterflies – do not resist the change. Find the butterflies, find your tribe. You will then feel a palatable sense of fellowship akin to family.

Penny and I are connected by agape love that is a living symbol and we are well practiced at maintaining it. Where insights are born and clarity comes to visit. Sisterhood ignites when you show up authentically, period.

Photograph:
Brisbane, Australia
2019

Another church in Brisbane and we spent our Saturday completing the 'Belong' course together. I struck up a conversation with a woman and before we left, we exchanged phone numbers. Katrina and I have remained friends to date – more than a decade has progressed. Our friendship found tons of luxe that served up sophistication and glamour in equal measure. Sharing exquisite culinary delights that matched our notoriously robust appetites, no coaxing required with the simple pleasures synonymous with sisterhood. We radiate integrity, good cheer and purpose amid any curve ball hurled our way.

I amplify these sisterhoods because the inventory of life calls us all to have the skill in defining our circle of friends and who we let in and how they influence us and how much they influence us also. It is a futile exercise to invest in yourself to transform to a better version then find that your circle of friends are on a different page. It consumes energy and effort to convince someone who does not want to be convinced to reach latitude with life. So be wise with how you create your support system, they can only inspire you as much as they are enlightened.

No one wins when we have masked values that don't align. All parties need to be real with who and what they bring to the circle of friendship. We remove transformation from the equation when we become tone deaf or lack the ability to self inspect all the layers of our growth both complex and accomplished. Our greatest asset in life is not our bank balance but the richness of our relationships. Personal, social and professional relations that are emotionally stable – built on trust and integrity, network and relationship is distinctly different. One takes and the latter gives – adding value. Know what your friends bring and what you give in the friendship as well. Mentioned below are typical sorts of friendships, ultimately your personal values will define the calibre of circle you wish to foster:

- ✓ Friendship of convenience – when the element of suitability ends then the friendship also vanishes.
- ✓ Friendship of usefulness – when the helpfulness ends the juncture of friendship disappears.
- ✓ Friendships with a common enemy – when the enemy is eliminated then the stage of friendship also evaporates.

- ✓ Friendship established and built on mutual respect – trust is the key ingredient and tolerance is **not** the foundation to these heart strings.

Immense historical growth in deep enriching friendship engulfed both Katrina and I as we kept each other accountable and most importantly we are real and can talk about everything. A superficial connection will take you nowhere noticeable. A beneficial relationship is mutually satisfying and unorchestrated; it rests in knowledge of knowing that both friends have each other's best interest at heart constantly, regardless of the season of life. It cultivates the reassurance to trust even more.

Katrina and I are propelled
by the spirit of jubilance that coaxed
resilience and warmth in every season that has
thoroughly jacked us with anchored hearts to the future
in a blessed sisterhood. Life is always better when you can feel
warmth. Sisterhood is created with reliable purpose and genuine
dependability.

Photograph:
Sydney, Australia
2016

My Journey Gleans

Helping each other is a duty of a friend and never the purpose of friendship. If it becomes the purpose then the friendship ends, and aid begins. Helping is always incidental to any healthy relationship with no ledger book to keep tabs. To build a lasting and fulfilling sisterhood we must add value to the equation of friendship. This is built and maintained not obtained by a click of a button on social media. When we know our values, we can remain loyal to our attuned self and know precisely when and who to part with. Some friends value your generosity more than they value friendship.

Don't waste your time investing in those who love your money more than they love you. Heart and soul, laughter and tears are the fabric of fine friendship. Everyone wants the truth but very few can navigate a friendship with undressed honesty. We can all discover friends tomorrow who have improved intentions for us than somebody that we have acknowledged constantly. Time means zilch, character speaks louder. We acquire more from a person's actions rather than their words, so let the litmus test guide you.

When a pickpocket meets a saint all he sees is pockets. Our motives shape how we see the world, all attention is selective and what matters to us the most is what we automatically scan for. That's why it is vital to establish your true north values so it will rule and reinforce in auto mode. Let your revolution grow deeper and allow it to light up the dimmest facets of your life. Harness growth from all the data you obtain, let the force bubble up your most salient values and then align your emotions, motivations and circle to that. Do not let any earthly bond veto or tone down your authentic values and self worth. Don't just fly, SOAR higher and deeper.

Do not be lackadaisical about who influences you in both noticeable and subtle ways. Continued patronage is not the goal of a stale and unedifying friendship, but rather a zoom in on fortifying your own personal values that align you to a tribe that flows in your rhythm. A single friend who knows your tears is much more valuable that a host of friends that only know your smiles.

Emotional competence requires the ability to pilot through the emotional undercurrents always at play rather than being swept under by them. A toxic well will poison everything so be discerning with the friendship well that you drink from. Emotions are a hyper efficient mode of communication to ourselves and the world moreover – use these alerts strategically and be purposeful. I will not do anything that will render those that really love me to feel uncomfortable. Ebullient Superficial connection enthusiasms creates a strong sense of drama – develop the art to filter the drama that you wish to harness in your circle of real friendship. Drama with real friends do not suck up your energy instead you use up every ounce of energy to make a tangible difference and you are ever willing to go the extra mile.

The most consistent display of accurate friendship is endurance, an unwelcomed alias of the 'unpolished warts.' Bonds that are most likely to prevail exhibit capacious consideration and patience for each other's inadequacies. Instead of excluding each other friends agree to take a journey of life with each other.

When you reach a challenge then talk about it, it reveals the calibre of the friendship if you have that skill set. May your favourite people never turn into strangers and if they do, then therein rests a deeper message. Vulnerability is tested when you place your heart on a chopping board and your friends have the butcher knife in hands trusting that they will never use it.

When you need to address a tie and it burns down with arrogance on the forefront then that is not what you need to invest in. Invest in friendships that have character, respect, experience and the willingness to hear you. A healthy relation will radiate comfort, inspiration and be void of tone deafness, most importantly you will not be taken for granted and your friend will not condone others disparaging you. It is not a worthy bond when a comrade becomes comfortable disrespecting you and fosters the same behaviour of others on the platform. Friendship is relational not transactional – life changes we lose friends and with the progression of time healthier friends come along and your circle gets sturdier and prudent causing you to soar higher than before.

There is a litany of facts about friendship. Get familiar with the vital deceptions and simple truths. Grab a few gems and purposely put them into action in your current circle of friendship. Charm, status and social polish are not the vitals for a rewarding friendship. The core of it is fostering open communication – receptive to both good and bad seasons in a friend's life, modelling effective give and take emotional registers and it is mandatory to deal with difficult issues in an effective and straightforward manner.

The tone and trust of one friend in your circle ripples down with remarkable precision – the mood and disdain flows with the same current as well. Being able to read the human currents and act accordingly is a skill. Proficiency in reading human context and acutely aware of its play is vital to the health of a fantastic friendship. Choose not to be blind to these dynamics. When you feel your own boundaries are dissolving then cultivate trust and rapport and build it with friends that matter. Zoom in on symbiotic friendships. Birds of a feather flock together. Life is graced when the authentic journey is the only thrall that empowers.

'At the end of life, what really matters is not what we bought but what we built; not what we got but what we shared; not our competence but our character; and not our success, but our significance. Live a life that matters. Live a life of love.' Unknown

Tap Into a Deeper Well

When Joshua was in the heart of combat fighting an army, he was doing God's will and he felt overwhelmed as night was setting in. He needed more daylight to conquer the enemy, so he prayed out of desperation for God to stop the sun. The scripture is entitled 'The Sun Stands Still' in my Bible.

Joshua: 10:12-13 – On the day the Lord gave the Amorites over to Israel Joshua said to the Lord in the presence of Israel: 'Sun stand still over Gibeon and moon over the Valley of Aijalon.'

The sun stood still, and the moon stopped until the nation avenged itself of its enemies. God stopped the sun in orbit in answer to Joshua's prayer. Take heart for He will answer your prayers too. Rise up and pray as a habit, then miracles will become your supernatural ally. Live by quail fall – the unexpected – and not by rain fall – the expected. Your walk with God must harness you to introspect all aspects of your life to achieve the best version of your God-ordained destiny.

We are constantly bombarded with the hash tag #TheBestIsYetToCome. The best has come, He is Jesus. He offers us a better way and that way prevails. I was born not knowing Jesus, yet when He found me, my heart was open to receive him. He changed my life and that has made all the difference. The heart of life is God and I challenge you to sensationally live this out loud.

My Journey Gleans

Do not pray for an easy life as everyone's life has obstacles. Pray to develop the skillset, emotional intelligence and empathy to be an overcomer. Do not let any situation derail you, no matter how much it rocks your world. Pray for steadfast strength in every season of life. Each predicament in life transformed me to reach my full potential and destiny, just as metamorphosis transforms a caterpillar into a butterfly. I am now transformed to not just fly but to soar.

One of the greatest lessons I have learned is that kindness is loaning someone your strength instead of reminding them of their weakness. I will strive to live by this for the rest of my finite days. Some of the kindest, most attractive deeds and offerings of love are the ones that need not be recognised on any platform but are rather recognised in the heart of the giver and the recipient. The best example of persecution in our time is Nelson Mandela. He was in prison for 27 years. He had no Netflix, no social media, and no refrigerator of food. When he was released from prison, he had to cognitively renew his mind to leave the bitterness behind.

He said if he did not leave the bitterness behind, he would remain in prison. He also used the 27 years wisely by exercising and reading. When he was released, he was ready to be president. He did not have to spend years in therapy, and he did not walk around wounded. Use your time in the valley to launch into your next season. Step out as a better version of yourself and not a bitter one.

Disruption breeds innovation and resilience. So, what are your levels of positive change so far? Are you stagnant living each day with no real target? Sometimes God does take us through suffering, but He never leaves us there. So come out a victor and not a victim. We do not go into a Holy temple to seek God's presence as His presence is always with us. His presence has never left me. So He will walk with you too if you let Him. Get real with God and He will protect you. Live your life and let go of other people's expectations and judgments and focus on living your truth.

Do not grapple with the 'why' question as the world does. The Word of God says that we will suffer in this world. God did not promise us sunshine without rain. Instead pray, plan and visualise your dream. Cultivate a path to the highest ideals you have for your life. Perish the thought of expectations of others in your equation. Your plan is fundamentally for you and other elements should not throw you off track (what others do or do not do is irrelevant). Rather than allowing them the power to feed your doubts, deprive them and watch them diminish. Never restrict yourself to a timeline.

Metamorphosis occurs in the right season. Prepare for the season. Accept your past with no regrets as you cannot change it. Handle your present with confidence, authority, assuredness and zeal. Look forward to your future fearlessly, dauntlessly, with childlike enthusiasm and intrepid exuberance. A gamut of adventure awaits you.

In The Word Isaiah 59:19 reports that when the enemy comes in like a flood, the spirit of God will raise a standard against him.

When the enemy comes in like a flood, have your plan of action ready

- ✓ Understand the spiritual nature of the attack or the problem you face. Harness the power of spiritual weapons against the issue.
- ✓ Do not give up before the battle is over.
- ✓ Understand that the battle will cost you. What are you willing to pay to reach your goal? List the plan of action that costs you the least and the one that costs you the most. When change presents itself be prepared for it. Do not be surprised and hit the panic button. Plan for it and act according to your plan.

'A seed grows with no sound, but a tree falls with huge noise. Destruction has noise, but creation is quieter. This is the power of silence...grow silently.' Confucius

Part Two

The Art of Transformation

Transition From Scarred to Healed

Now that you have concluded reading my personal voyage, this part of the book will help you with your individual transformation journey. There is no prescriptive way to do this, you can either choose to follow the steps outlined in this section or alternatively use this to identify aspects of your life that you wish to enhance and work in your own format by capturing your transition in your personal journal. Find what works best for you. You may also consider a group session to discuss each section so you all can grow and transition as a group. Are you ready to move from the former and create a new state-of-the-art you?

A crucial aspect of life is learning what you do not know, but how can you know what you do not know in the first place? The more we learn, the more we discover just how little we do know. Life does not come with a 101-instruction guide. I personally felt like I was hit by a bus when the tribulations of life hit me hard. I had to scrape up the courage daily to live despite the circumstances. My thirsty soul was seeking healing and sadly, that is a process that I had to stumble onto by myself amidst my pain. I did receive the toss of a rare comforting word, a well meaning telephone call, focused prayer and the occasional invite to fellowship. Ultimately, I had to create my own path of healing and restoration.

I work as a professional in health information technology and in essence I implement medical software systems in the hospitals. A hospital has a complex grid of approximately two hundred different systems that need to network together and talk to each other. Most importantly, the system must prohibit the clinician from making a clinical error as this can be detrimental to the patient. My job is fast paced with a precise focus on detail – I excel at it, as my accolades and rewards would testify. In addition, I attend church regularly and sit under wise teachings. My personal realm seemed to be riddled with one saga after another, and it was not possible for me to excel in one facet and yet not see results in another area of my life. Thus, I took deeper dives into my personal facet.

The metrics of all the significant elements poured out to me at staggered intervals with no tangible connection to heal deep wounds was a starting point and it remained in this state for a prolonged time. Well intended random gestures did not heal all my deep wounds. The formula was incomplete. Most interactions were superficial in a well presented way. Even when a revelation enlightened my spirit from the pulpit, it lacked the **'show me how to do this'** insight. These revelations offered me a quick fix or sometimes no fix at all because the scar was so deep, and a band aid did not suffice. I had to embark on a journey to find the tranquil healing balm myself.

Obtaining key words of wisdom from church is only part of the puzzle. Healing and transformation are parts of a process and gaining awareness or revelation is not the goal. I was missing the key component of the formula: THE PRACTICAL APPLICATION, or the transformation journey map that could take me on the healing journey.

- ✓ Transformation from start to finish
- ✓ Transformation from unknown factors
- ✓ Transformation from scarred to healed

In this section, I have detailed a self-help guide with twenty five tools that will assist you to walk the journey of transformation from start to finish. These tools will address all facets of your life's mystery and guide you with instructional design to transform from your current state to your desired goal state. Once our basic needs like food, water and shelter are met in accordance with Maslow's hierarchy, we move on to the next levels: our psychological needs and finally our self-fulfilment needs. This transformation guide will focus on the second and third layers. Transforming your mindset is far more valuable than changing your circumstances.

Every now and then life can seem stuck, as if you are circling the same mountain for too long. Have you ever wondered if it is time to head in a new direction? It is a crucial moment to remember – a discerning milestone when you face a life changing choice. We can stay stuck, endlessly circling the same old place, or we can choose hope and head in a new direction. You can turn north. Contemplate. This is the perfect time to pause and introspect if there is anywhere you need to 'turn north' in your life.

Have you been circling the same muddles for years with no end in sight? Are there areas you need to change but feel like it will require too much sacrifice? We choose a rut because it is comfortable and requires no calculated risk. And getting out of it requires courage and a willingness to make hard hitting optimal choices. Instead of mindlessly following the crowd, seek your own clarity and path for your life and commit yourself to enhancing your life. Where are you heading? The Word says, *'Where there is no vision, the people perish.'* Proverbs 29:18. No better time to embrace the refining process and turn north. So how do we begin to turn north? In the Bible, Philippians 3:13 – Paul said: *'Forgetting those things which are behind.'* You have circled this mountain long enough. Now is the time to move on.

Excellence is not a skill; it is an attitude. Excellence is practised and targeted. Are you committed to establishing goals that create an example that is galvanised with fair minded prototypes? It is beneficial to plan, but we must allow God to direct our growth capacity. Don't expect God to ordain what you have not organised. Undeniably, I have been exposed to some unorthodox life gleans that broke me but also made me into a better version. You cannot accomplish anything of magnitude without planning. Majority of people are reacting to life and do not reach a target because they did not define a target. These tools will show you how to find your purpose and vision to live a strategically targeted life. *'Learning never exhausts the mind.'* Leonardo Da Vinci.

To get lost is to learn the way. How you finish matters a lot more than how you start in the race called life. Prepare to purposefully finish as an overcomer and not a victim. Your beauty is not defined by the number of people who smile at you but by the sum of people who you touch in a profound way, the ones that you help despite your own pain. As you now have some personal insight into my story and how God blessed me with clarity despite all the uncertainty and shattered dreams, rest assured He has the absolute divine clarity for your life too. So do not look back with resentment, look forward from a place of experience and growth. Try to master the art of resilience and use your past lessons to create a better version of yourself.

Nothing that you are holding on to is worth the space it is taking up in your life, so find a way to let go and transition to a new season. The research and facts confirm there is no one size that fits all. Humans are complex and we all respond differently. We all process trauma contrarily. Some need to effectively process the emotions before Cognitive Behavioural Therapy can be applied. Either path you travel on, take steps each day to process something and articulate in some positive way. Gradually the healing can begin and that gives you the ability to make choices and then refine your choices. This guide will help you find your authentic self and let go of fragments that no longer serve your welfare.

'Smart people learn from everything and everyone, average people from their own experiences, stupid people already have all the answers.'
Socrates

Mental Resilience

You cannot lead a positive life with a negative mind. In most cases we are unaware of the negative perils of our mind until they get triggered and manifest in our life. We all have internal monologues, so take heed to master your thoughts, and your life will take care of itself. Make micro changes in your life to keep adapting to a better version. It is an opportunity to grow and be better. Abide by your highest priorities, congruent with your values. Life is signed, sealed and delivered with all seasons, so don't expect just the good positive things in life. Be prepared for the season in the valley. Unpleasant times allow us to grow and develop new capabilities too. When it rains look for the rainbow, and when it's dark, look for the stars. Let your elated consciousness be on default mode in every season of life. Happy or sad moments: always look for the silver lining. Craft a life that is driven by greater purpose.

To identify any recurring pattern in your life is the first step, and then developing a plan to remedy those patterns is progress. Look at the words below and write the first thing that comes to your mind:

1. Wisdom _____
2. Weekend _____
3. Repair _____
4. Build _____
5. Thorns _____

Hypothetically if you had an hour to think about this and then write your responses, do you think your answers would be different? Clinical research confirms no. The above process you just completed is called WORD ASSOCIATION TEST. It essentially tests how word meanings are stored in our subconscious mind and where our mind may be at. We are often unaware of how people, words, situations and events impact our lives in both negative and positive ways.

Clinical research confirms that your mind stores data frozen at the point when the memory was created. This information may be stored in our mind with the associated event as a negative memory, and when you recall the event, it brings unaddressed pain to the surface. On a brighter note, clinical research also confirms that this information stored in your mind is not hardcoded (fixed data that cannot be altered), so in essence we do not have to live with these frozen memories. You have the ability to renew your mind.

Granted that we are now aware of this pattern, we can use it constructively to plant positive associations in our mind and, most importantly, to weed out all negative associations in our mind. We all need to reach a place where no word, event or situation has a negative impact on our mind. Even if you experience a bad situation, you can renew your mind to have positive feelings. The first step is to identify the negative impacts. Frequently we hear the phrase *'he pushed my buttons.'* What does this really mean? It means to draw a strong emotional reaction, usually a metaphoric one. It is targeted to make you feel weary and discontent. We reach a healthy plateau in life when we can cut the cords to these buttons. This button may be concealed in your past, in your reactions, or in unforeseen events, pain and trauma.

Whenever I smelled something or visited a place, it triggered both positive and negative memories and reactions. I was on an international holiday once having a ball and then the air waves was filled with a popular song at the time. Memories came gushing to me like a tornado and my mood plummeted instantly with no real cause – but the subconscious was all too alert and willing to succumb yet again. How many times will this happen? You have the ability to define your world – you and only you. Let the blast from the past be just that. Proactively carve out better triggers for both your conscious and subconscious mind.

You need to reach a point in life where words, buttons and situations have absolutely no influence over you and especially no influence over your mind. Just as the story that I related earlier when the wind blows the cap off the guy's head, he is not frazzled by the event. No matter who pushes what buttons, do not be frazzled. Just maintain your focus on your destination! In the book *A New Earth*, Eckhart Tolle depicts strategically how our heart can store up so much from an event that may seem insignificant to the other person. From the book, the tale of two monks:

Tanzan and Ekido were walking along a country road that was extremely muddy. A woman was trying to cross the road, but the mud was so deep it would have ruined her clothes. Tanzan picked her up and carried her to the other side. The monks walked on in silence. Five hours later as they were approaching the lodging temple, Ekido could not restrain himself any longer. 'Why did you carry that girl across the road?' he asked. 'We monks are not supposed to do things like that.' 'I put the girl down hours ago,' said Tanzan. 'Are you still carrying her?'

What are you still carrying from five hours ago, or five days, weeks, months, decade or a lifetime ago? The initial word association test was a generic test, just to get you acquainted to the novel process. Pray and ask God to help you introspect on what's heavy in the depth of your heart, and then delve deeper into your own world and life. What words, persons or events trigger pain and despair for you? Identify what's tender in your heart and then pray daily and ask God to help you to reach a place where your mind can store a positive reaction to this word, person or event in your life. Repeat the word association test a few months later to determine where your mind is at. Write down the first word that comes to your mind:

1. Discord _____
2. Hatred _____
3. Envy _____
4. Joy _____

5. Peace _____

6. Kindness _____

How to Renew the Mind

Train your mind just as you train your body at a gym. Create positive muscle memory. If you are not happy within you will not be happy with external factors. Intentionality characterises your life and recognise all telling patterns. Create enough emotional space to manage the products of your mind which defines life in a profound way. Completely explore the dramatic and buried effects of your life history – what brought you to this point? Go beyond your familiar identity. Identify what torpedoed your morale!

- ✓ Identify the location of the memory in your life. From all the responses outlined in the first tool during your word association test, examine which word and associated response bring pain to the surface.

- ✓ Create steps to untangle from the memory. Write down what you are going to do to reach a healthy balance in this area of your life.

- ✓ Pray and ask God for wisdom, discernment and courage to cut this cord in your life. Sometimes you cannot remove toxic people from your life, but you can control how you let them influence you. Plan your response so you can avoid reacting later.

- ✓ Things may bring you pain as you remove the scab to examine the root cause of the hurt. Let nothing entangle your mind as you start, continue and finish the process of renewing your mind. Persevere until the end.

- ✓ For example, if you had my name next to HATRED then that confirms you have an issue with me. Do what you need to heal from the pain I caused you. Create a routine every day to practise forgiveness towards me and resolve that you will not hate me no matter what. Practise this every day until your mind is renewed and you can now write something else next to the word HATRED in your WORD ASSOCIATION TEST.

Once bothered by the vexations and conflicts of life, still the schemes of your mind. Ralph Waldo Emerson, philosopher, said, *'We do not count a man's years until he has nothing else to count.'* Your personality, quality of your mind, your faith and your convictions are not substances of corrosion but rather assets to establish a better quality life. If your thoughts are chiefly positive, noble and good you will continue to be fresh and energetic irrespective of the chronological years. Society fears old age because they anticipate mental and physical deterioration. You become old when you lose interest in life, when you cease to dream, the appetite ends for innovative accuracies and the pursuit for different spheres to conquer is halted. Never let your mind be bankrupt of ideas.

'The capacity to learn is a gift, the ability to learn is a skill, and the willingness to learn is a choice.' Brian Herbert

Personal Journaling

Get real with yourself and create a list of your highs and lows in life right now. Discern what's heavy in your heart, things that you swept under the rug, things that make you toss and turn or simply ones you may be unaware of. Prompt God to remind you of situations where you may have been unaware of how your words or actions hurt someone. It is a vital milestone in life to mature to a point where you realise that you may have toxic traits as well.

Take ownership for the negative energy that you bring to the equation as well. Create a list of your personal words that you prefer to work on as your WORD ASSOCIATION TEST and confirm where your mind is at. Do a self-assessment every few months to measure how far you have reached from the time you started. This will take time, and the process depends on your willingness to transform. Be positive, patient and persistent. Create a list of words that are specific triggers in your life:

- ✓ Names of people
- ✓ Places
- ✓ Events

Your body, spirit and mind are affected by these words. You need to change these word associations in your brain. Renew your mind to live a restored life. You cannot become your best version if you cannot overcome the negative storage system in your mind. Do not get paralysed by something that you can regulate; rather, take the steps to develop in a wholesome way. Awareness and change are the best seasons of life. It is a celebration of your life to trade captivity of the mind for absolute freedom of the spirit. Awareness and change simultaneously shape our world with competitive alterations. As you reflect and journal your monitored growth, be sure to include your levels of gratitude. Count every blessing!

Romans 12:2 – Do not conform to the pattern of this world, but be transformed by the renewing of your mind

A cardinal rule to renew your mind is to be present. Let go of what the fairy tale should have manifested and work with the materials present in your life here and now. With reference to Wikipedia, 'eustress' means beneficial stress, either psychological or physical. **Eustress** refers to the positive response one has to the stressor. Journal the greatest advantages that you have learned from setbacks in your life, in what shape or forms did you grow and, most importantly, how are you going to use this lesson?

'If you fell down yesterday, stand up today.' H.G. Wells

Steps Towards Authentic Self-Assessment

The process of self-assessment is to look at oneself in order to assess aspects that are important to one's identity. Some of the components include actions, attitudes, performance and reactions. My first-hand experience with life qualifies me to dauntlessly share my life lessons with you. Please use the below mentioned lessons as a self-help guide to help you journey through your own season of wilderness. You do not have to walk the same perils in life as I did to learn from my mistakes.

'The same boiling water that softens potatoes hardens an egg. It's what you are made of; not the circumstances.' Unknown

Use these lessons to transform your life and enhance your personal growth. Pray and invite The Holy Spirit to help minister new growth in you. When you have a crystal clear picture of who you are, then you know precisely who you are not and then you can shake off any incorrect labels that others may have put on you. Know who you are, so that others cannot label you as they like when you are vulnerable. Life is not so much about getting on track as it is about persistently seeking and creating the next path that brings you joy and contentment.

My Lesson Learned	Factors That I Can Control	For Consideration
All relationships have disagreements and I had to acquire the skills to discuss my point without condemnation and without hurting the other person.	Decades later I cannot even recall what most of the meaningless bickering was for. I have learned to adopt the attitude of asking myself, 'Will this matter to me in a year's time?' If no, then let it go. Worthless bickering is in vain in the grand scheme of things.	I cannot control another person's conduct only my own emotions

Rigid expectations are the source of our assumption of failure. What are you setting or assuming as your personal benchmark?

_____

_____

_____

My Lesson Learned	Factors That I Can Control	For Consideration
It is the small foxes that spoil the vine as stipulated in scripture. I learned not to ignore the small things that suffocate life. These little issues that creep in almost unnoticed will kill the vine if not addressed and managed appropriately.	In life we need to be cognisant of our thoughts, words, deeds and actions no matter how small or insignificant we may think they are. These small actions do have a profound impact, so I learned to watch my small actions too.	During my visit to the tropical rainforest in Queensland, Australia, I saw the 'Strangler Fig Tree' a tiny little shrub that starts to grow besides a gigantic solid anchored tree. With the progression of time this Strangler Fig Tree consumes the host tree completely. There is no trace of the once gigantic tree. Take heed of the hidden stranglers in your life.

Examine your life and consider if you have small issues that cause big problems. Have you addressed them?

_____
_____
_____

My Lesson Learned	Factors That I Can Control	For Consideration
Do not try to copy another person. Be your authentic self. I know someone who copied my dressing style and my home decorations. I felt sad that she could not be herself and offer this world a unique flavour that is exclusively crafted by her.	Do not try to squeeze into a glass slipper just because it looks pretty. Maybe your style and comfort involve hiking boots or better still, maybe you are created to break the glass ceiling.	Discover yourself and live to your maximum potential. Refrain from following like a sheep. Be an unparalleled original that retains its value and not a cheap fake that has no substance. You were born an original. Don't die a copy.

Do you enjoy the original version of yourself? List some of the flavour and fun that you bring to this world. For example: maybe you cook the best lamb shanks in your family? Or get a bit deeper...

_____
_____
_____

My Lesson Learned	Factors That I Can Control	For Consideration
If you want an authentic friend, then be an authentic friend. We reap what we sow.	If you do not want superficial relationships, then refrain from being superficial yourself. Go the extra mile, jump that hurdle with a friend, cross the ocean to be there for that milestone.	Foster the tradition to be a blessing to someone else instead of spending on yourself again. Make sacrifices so someday someone will **not** think twice about doing the same for you.

Do you have authentic friends? Are you a dependable friend? Do you go the extra mile for others? What do you need to do to enhance your friendships and take your rapport to the next level?

_____
_____
_____

It is easy to be friends in good times. But how do you treat others in bad times? Do you support them? Do you take sides? What skill set and process do you use to handle differences?

My Lesson Learned	Factors That I Can Control	For Consideration
Method is the message. People can say they are there for you, but their actions can spell something different. I have learned to let my thoughts, words and deeds align.	If you are not there for me, then we can politely part. Be authentic and speak the truth in love and without jargon so people know where they stand.	Your silence, body language, tone, absence, selective fellowship, online post and social media meme speaks volumes too.

Do you support people who have supported you?

_____
_____
_____

My Lesson Learned	Factors That I Can Control	For Consideration
Remember you do not have to constantly be in top form with everything. Life, trauma and drama do not come with an instruction manual.	Be gentle with yourself as you learn the way of an altered path, the new norm or walk in a different season.	Be your authentic true self.

Do you speak candidly to your support network about your struggles? Do you hide some parts of your life? If yes, then talk to God about it. Describe what's heavy in your heart and why you feel this way and ask Him to help you with things that you do not talk about.

_____
_____
_____

'Failure is the opportunity to begin again more intelligently.' Hendry Ford

Self-Care Enhancements

Self-care is vital to maintaining a balanced relationship with yourself as it produces positive emotions and escalates your confidence and self-esteem. So leave no stone unturned to get your mojo back and bounce back with a vengeance. Here are some basic primary self-care tips:

- ✓ Cultivate a regular sleep pattern
- ✓ Eat healthy
- ✓ Go on that holiday
- ✓ Create memories
- ✓ Go for a walk

These are some self-care enhancements that I had to dispense to myself to bridge the gap to heal. So use the lessons to establish some deep dives in your life and inner health. We have to get real about who we are if we want to progress. When the same old ways of life no longer work, find new ways of doing things. Dig deep to uncover your wounds and give yourself plenty of time to heal and find new ways. I was used to sharing life with a husband, sharing fellowship, pillow talk, finances, a table, a home, a remote, a car and a holiday. Things changed, people changed, and I needed to change to adapt to my new circumstances. Become better, not bitter. ADAPTABILITY is the key.

Where is your life right now (current state) anchor yourself with reality and not an illusion? What is happening in your day today not where you want to be in the future? Remember a fish cannot climb a tree, so be strategic about your analysis and your capabilities. Don't dream of being a baseball player when you have never ever played sports.

_____

_____

_____

Where would you like your life to be (Goal State) in a week, month, year, ten years and this lifetime?

_____

_____

_____

How will you measure your success indicators? *(For example, I will monitor my success in my journal or get an accountability partner: this week I will reduce my sugar/ cigarettes / swearing, etc. by 10 per cent)*

_____

_____

_____

I did not move to a new realm of my life without purging and expanding the calibre of my affiliations. I constantly redefine the tribe that I hang out with, those that I share my heart with and those that I permit to influence my life. Surround yourself with people who nourish your soul. Remove toxic people if you have to. I owned my transformation with such confidence that every molecule in the room moved when I stepped into it. Rise up and live like a victor, not a victim; the choice is yours. Make new choices, dream new dreams and create new visions.

You are the limit, not the sky. We can find blessings everywhere when we zoom out of the negative mindset. Mindset is more valuable that talent. Change begins with you! Become the change. I constantly remind myself that others are experiencing painful situations as well. So I choose my words to be kind and positive. Words can speak life or death. Do not speak death every time you open your mouth. Words are the instruments that sculpt and harness the blueprint of life. Proactively choose to speak blessings, not curses. Spread hope, faith, healing, prosperity, favour, acceleration and abundance with your words. The method is the message here. What message are you sending with your words to yourself, to those around you and to the world?

_____
_____
_____

'Our greatest glory is not in never falling, but in rising every time we fall.' Confucius

Improve Your Radar

You may feel like you have reached your maximum limit and cannot endure another setback or more pain. You are feeling super saturated and burnt out when another thing happens. You are just beginning to understand the power of The Word and another peril hits you like a ton of bricks. It now feels like it is impossible to put The Word of God into action. This stage is the threshold of transformation to improve your radar so that you are aware when you are stepping into a new season. Do not give up in despair, thinking that this is a breakdown, and you need to surrender to the forces that test you. This is your test for promotion, so prepare diligently and pass the test. If you do not learn your lesson in private, then your confidence will be dashed in public. Recognise your plight and the situation you are in. Focus on how far you have come and not how far you have left to go. It's about the journey, not the destination.

Enjoy the transformation journey while being gentle and kind to yourself, it is perfectly fine to move at your pace, as long as you are moving. Choose to purposefully live a dignified life and walk away and shut the door from anything that robs your peace or drags you down. Focus on the power of now. Do not fret about the past as it cannot be changed. Learn from it and move on. Do not be anxious about the future as you may never reach that point! Therefore, make the most of the present.

Laugh even when you are hurting. Find things that make you laugh. Watch a comedy, listen to worship music and let your spirit be lightened. Seek the silver lining in every situation. Develop the habit to capture your happy moments that take your breath away, so that when the turbulence hits, you have good memories in your tank to keep you strong. Showing mercy and grace to others is a privilege. Develop the fine art to exhibit this capacity even when you have every reason not to.

What can you do from today to improve any facet of your life?

_____

_____

_____

Are you affiliated with real fellowship, where you can be your authentic self and be transparent? If you had to plan your last dinner party, who would you invite and why? If you do not have deep fellowships, then describe how you would like to enhance this area of your life.

_____

_____

_____

Mercy and grace are beyond love and forgiveness. What do they mean to you?

_____

_____

_____

'If your actions inspire others to dream more, learn more, do more and become more, you are a leader.' John Quincy Adams

Ascend Above the Predicament

One day I hurriedly dashed to the supermarket during my lunch break and while quickly slipping out, I saw a young gentleman by the exit of the store. He was a mute *(a person who is deaf and unable to speak as well),* and he had a donation box to raise funds. I had no time to stop and read his banner. I opened my purse and added some money to his donation box. He also had a table full of stunningly beautiful paper butterflies and he was in essence giving these to those who donated.

Nonetheless I thought I had no need for another dust collector in my home, so I politely declined to take a paper butterfly in exchange for my donation. But when I turned to walk away, he grabbed a butterfly and insisted through gestures that I take it, or he would refuse the donation. Having no choice, I took the butterfly he was offering and dashed back to work.

Days later I opened the packet, and he had a little note explaining how he had created these butterflies because he could not find work as a mute and did not want to rely on others or take their pity. He wanted to earn his living from his own efforts. I cried as his story touched me in so many intense ways. I encounter people who have no health limitations, yet they expect the world to hand them a carved life on a platter. I went back to the store a few days later to find him but it was in vain.

I still have that butterfly in my kitchen, and it is a constant reminder that life is how we respond to it and not what happens to us. So let this be a wake-up call to encourage you to live your best life. When life is punctuated with circumstances beyond you, rise above them – make lemonade with the lemons.

2 Timothy 1:7 - For God did not give us a spirit of fear, but of power and of love and sound mind.

Faith is born in uncertain times. Choose to activate your faith regardless of how overwhelming the circumstances are. When a difficult situation presents in life, God does not want us to just survive it. He wants it to strengthen us to have a deeper spiritual life, just like a tree with deep roots can withstand the turbulence of a storm and not get uprooted.

Anxiety originates when you do not have a plan, have not identified risks and mapped out a mitigation. Fear creeps in when your mind thinks what if...and why me.

The advantage of planning and making lemonade when you have lemons is that you can zoom in and mitigate most risks. Tweak the unfair shake for your benefit as your life evolves. In what ways do you give to the community or humanity despite your limitations?

_____

_____

_____

Do what you must to move from the current season, page or predicament that you are in. You cannot remain where you are forever. Use every experience as a stepping stone to launch into your next season. You define your life, the end of a job, a relationship or milestone. It is the beginning of your next experience and you have the keys to define when that begins and how amazing or mediocre it will be. Setbacks are there to teach us, not label or confine us. Make better choices with the experience and skills you acquired from the last season. If you have your eyes fixed on a beautiful destination, rest assured the road comes with challenges, so be ready.

What are the true objectives that you value in life?

_____

_____

_____

Let it go, let it be healed and let the fragments go. Get it together and do not let your brokenness rob you of a blessed future. Determine and cognitively declare that your will, cultural conduct, words, thoughts and actions will align to make you a person who has moved to the next chapter and season of life.

Change your challenge into an opportunity. Outline one thing you can implement to achieve this.

_____
_____
_____

Look at the colour of your heart and your deepest convictions and sins while introspecting the true calibre of your heart. The real attributes of your heart are unseen by society, such as: attitude, mood, disposition, tone, default reaction and response, level of integrity and method of communication.

How do you neutralise your response especially in awkward circumstances?

_____
_____
_____

Love is a verb; this is seared in my heart and I gleaned it the hard way. It does not alter with changing circumstances. It is a constant despite circumstances. You need to be content with your whole person, so you can add value to others. Love is about giving; not about taking and expecting others to fill a gap in you.

Mastermind your own vision and do not subordinate to another's person vision of love. Outline what kind of love you offer to yourself, your significant other and the world at large.

_____
_____
_____

Ignite with peaceful sanctuaries of the heart and be the voice of reason in the conversation no matter how difficult the conversation is. The method is the message. Deliver your key message with precision and a whole lot of class. Be real, as this is where you can lead by example.

Objective means even minded. Define how you deliver your key message especially when you are in the fire.

_____
_____
_____

Manage your money like a wise steward and do not despise the little you have. When you are faithful with the little you have, God will bless you with more.

How do you model generosity? How do you use the little you have to bless others?

_____
_____
_____

Nobody can take away what you have learned, so capitalise from it. Let it redefine you into a better person. The life you live is the one you create for yourself. Get strategic about it and aim to be productive.

How do you obtain balance and orientation every day?

_____

_____

_____

I did not have to wait for an apology to forgive. I released myself from the pain and stepped into the next season. I made the decision to forgive to start my own healing. You can do the same as well.

What does your life really demonstrate when you are in a catastrophe? What picture do you paint to the world?

_____

_____

_____

'Difficult roads often lead to beautiful destinations. Don't quit.' Deb Sofield

The Roaring Difference Between Change & Progress

Embracing change is a passive or active choice best depicted by Bob Dylan's words when he exclaimed: *'You better start swimming or you will sink like a stone, 'cause the times they are a-changing.'* Do you want the narrative of your life to be different than what's your reality? Only you can change this! How do you stimulate change in your life or your local community? Do you have the aspiration to foster change in the world? You can be anything you like...be gung-ho with facilitating positive changes rather than just leaving an inappropriate emoji. You do not need the world as much as the world needs you!

Accept change as part of the universal constant. Be acutely aware of the fact that the only person in the world you can change is you and that makes a world of difference. An idol is anything that becomes more important than God. I am not obsessed with my money, home, car, clothes, travel, stocks or loved ones. I have experienced the loss of it all. What really matters in the end is how I live, who I bless and how I use what God has given me. I am blessed to be a blessing to others. Cultivate the art of accepting and instigating change constantly.

No matter how hurt or broken you are, strive to get up and enjoy each day and live with purpose. You are the key element to progress in your life. I create waves of progress in my life when I:

- ✓ Connect with someone
- ✓ Bless someone
- ✓ Let go of something that is not edifying me
- ✓ Plan to enjoy the outside world

- ✓ Connect with God
- ✓ Express my creativity
- ✓ Take care of my body by exercising. If you do not, your body will prioritise this for you by manifesting ailments that you do not welcome.
- ✓ Take care of my mind and inner health
- ✓ Practice self-care
- ✓ Express my gratitude to others and to God
- ✓ Get off the online grid as a daily routine. Give your brain quality time to reboot and relax by doing nothing for at least an hour. Just recalibrate your brain.
- ✓ Read avidly. There is still so much I do not know.
- ✓ Learn something new. I am learning to ride a bicycle at the age of forty seven.
- ✓ Tackle my fears. I have snorkelled at the Great Barrier Reef despite not being a swimmer. I have also tackled my emotional fears in the realm of betrayal and abandonment.
- ✓ Help others to attain their dream or goal in life.

If nothing changed, there would be no butterflies. Change is inevitable; no matter how much we try to fight it, things are going to change. *'Change is the only constant.'* And 'The best way to predict the future is to invent it.' Alan Kay. Progress however is the result of conscious choice.

What aspects of your life would you prefer to change?

_____
_____
_____

Define how you would like to implement personal progress in your life. What are your waves of progress?

_____

_____

_____

Implementing Change in Your Life

If the monotony of life is currently not where you want it to be, then refrain from fretting with despair! Change begins with you, move forward and fix what you do not like about your life. Do not remain stuck on the past. Identify your dreams that are castles in the air. It may be a hard pill to swallow, but the sooner you accept that reality, the sooner your healing begins and the sooner you reach your goal. Use the tangible tools and skills you have right now to propel yourself into the next season.

Don't allow adversity and complacency to define you or the future. Don't just fly, SOAR. A well lived life has equity. Detach from what you need to, heading towards a balanced sustainability for yourself and the circle that you touch and do not touch but impact in a profound way – The Bible says it is better to remove your eye if it causes you to sin and get to heaven deformed than going to hell with a fully functional body. If your heart and mind cause you to create inequity, then realign your life as your actions affect people here and now and build the future that many depend on. Only you can transcend from self-deprecation to appreciation. In order to love who you are, you cannot hate the experience that shaped you. Nonetheless you can try to give both yourself and others a better experience from this point on.

Change Cycle Methodology

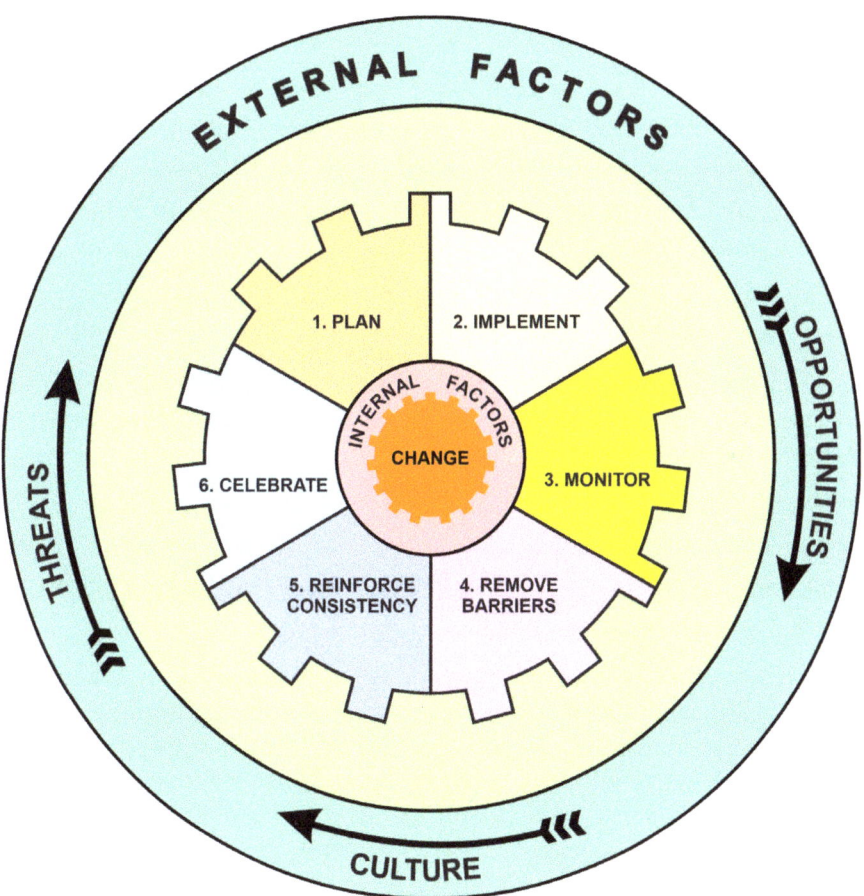

Our outer realm is a reflection of our inner sphere. To modify our situations, we must start by changing our internal factors, beliefs, attitudes and emotions. This diagram represents both the internal and external factors that we need to address in the circle of change.

Internal change factors

- ✓ Activities
- ✓ Decisions
- ✓ Behaviour

- ✓ Attitudes
- ✓ Weakness
- ✓ Strength

Plan: Create a plan of what you would like to change. Later on, I will guide you to create a vision plan that will incorporate elements of change.

Implement: It is vital to action your plan sooner rather than later. Set reasonable timeframes.

Monitor: Monitor your personal growth. I have included a growth matrix to assist you in the chapters that follow.

Remove Barriers: Identify any barriers that may hinder your desire to change. This may be a person, too much time on your phone or your favourite television show.

Reinforce Consistency: Develop ways to keep your goals in focus every day.

Celebrate: Celebrate small changes along the way as they build momentum and zeal for your secondary goals.

Respect the change that manifests in your life, even if you have to orchestrate it. Let it trek through in every element that it comes packaged. It may be placid, obtuse, sluggish, chastising, correction dripping, quick as lightning and everything in between. Be anything but afraid of change. Welcome it, embrace it, grow from it and awaken anew from it. Foster the art of change – the spike that conveys CHANGE can be lovely to create sometimes far more attractive than the process.

'One of the most difficult lessons to master as we struggle to create effective change is to learn not to label something as bad just because it is different from what we want.' William Glasser.

External change factors
- ✓ Culture
- ✓ Opportunities
- ✓ Threats

Do not let internal or external factors thwart your need to change. Identify how these factors limit your enhancement.

Wisdom to Know the Change Difference

'God, grant me the serenity to accept the things I cannot change, courage to change the things I can, and wisdom to know the difference.' Reinhold Niebuhr. Certainly a profound statement that has provoked thoughts worldwide. Progress is impossible without change. Permit yourself the psychological air to transcend to a healthy person to no longer accept the things that you cannot change. Be the bold and beautiful change agent and change the things that you cannot accept and do not represent your values with critical wisdom to know what can be changed! Continually monitor and adapt working to make proactive changes earlier on rather than having to take a reactive approach – This is progress.

Change Factors That You Can Control

- ✓ Your zeal and attitude.
- ✓ Your consistency and the length of time taken to change.
- ✓ Power to control barriers.
- ✓ Renew your mind – replace negative memories.
- ✓ The power to change inhumane policy and procedures that impact the world negatively.
- ✓ The power to change old patterns of history that do not serve or improve you or humanity.
- ✓ The ability to change the course of gossip and unhealthy banter when it reaches a wise person who has the ability to make a sager choice.
- ✓ The strength to let go of the twinge of regret and live your best. Only you have the power to change that.
- ✓ The power to change the world by setting a fine example.

One reason why people resist change is because they focus on what they have to give up rather than what they have to gain. Until you spread your wings, you will have no idea how high you can soar! You may not be able to change your situation, but you can certainly change your perception. You need to model the change if you expect to lead others to change. Acknowledge your emotions and validate them but never be reduced by them. Live by a higher standard. Compose your inner harmony on a source that is an ever-fixed mark. When our inward vision is clear and steady, we create an aesthetic inspiration. This in return gives us a vocation to create and command a technique of an appropriate art to live by. We realise an ideal when we hasten to embody the inspiration of building life with substance that does not change. Seek, build and rest on elements that don't change in life. Matthew 24:35 'Heaven and earth will pass away, but my words will never pass away.' It is true that life is about balancing the oxymoron elements that taunt us – despite the over exposure to the persistent fact that change is the only constant. You define your constant!

Change Factors That You CANNOT Control

- ✓ Elements beyond your control (e.g., a world pandemic).
- ✓ You cannot change others.
- ✓ You cannot change the past.
- ✓ You cannot change coherent legislation that protects the masses.
- ✓ You cannot buy time. Focus on the power of now, enjoy the present moment and season.

'Yesterday I was clever, so I wanted to change the world. Today I am wise, so I am changing myself.' Rumi

Work to Reach the Promised Land

We are three dimensional beings: Mind, Body and Soul. So be purposeful with what your plans are to enhance and edify each form of your core being. It is unwise to only focus on the needs of your body even though it is your temple and important since it is a vessel with a finite shelf life. The soul has an infinite shelf life. Are your efforts focused in correlation to reality?

- Mind – I practice prayer, rest, and solitude to unplug from the world and recuperate. Stop, unwind and listen to your own breath and heartbeat.

- Body – I eat healthy and exercise. I have regular health checks, pray for healing, follow a balanced lifestyle, take supplements and use nontoxic products on my body.

- Soul – Are you aware of the destination of your soul without a shadow of a doubt? Go on a self-discovery journey if you need to embark on one.

✓ It is your party, so cry if you want to. Take time out to heal and recover so you can bounce back stronger.

✓ In numerous occasions I choose to loan the other party my strengths and allow my compassionate muscles to set in instead of reminding them of their weakness.

✓ In uncertain situations I pray for God's will, not mine. He has proven to be the best direction for me.

✓ No matter how many mistakes I have made, God still forgives. I can follow the chosen path, or I can turn around. Just because I have wasted many years over a mistake, I don't have to continue

- ✓ with that mistake. It is a lesson. Turn, repent and sin no more. Free will is a great human blessing so use it.

- ✓ I look for opportunity in every situation that presents. This has closed and opened doors for new seasons and a path directed by someone greater than me.

- ✓ I read Nelson Mandela's autobiography and when he was preparing to leave prison, he said the likes of 'If I did not leave the pain, anger and bitterness behind I would still be in prison.' I cried when I read this. I was born in South Africa and visited Robben Island in Cape Town. I went into the prison cell that Nelson Mandela was held captive in for 27 years. I was not moved with emotions as I was when I read the above quote. I was emotional because I was in prison. Walls I created from unforgiveness and bitterness. I had to learn to break down these walls one stone at a time and release the pain until I was totally free.

- ✓ Sometimes God does not answer our prayers. I prayed with zeal for some things and God did not show up, He let my unborn child die and my marriage end in divorce. I learned that His ways are higher, and His vision of the master plan is better. Walking with God means I have to trust Him even when I do not get my prayers answered.

- ✓ Keep moving and keep living. I am not responsible for unprocessed pain and unresolved trauma that another person brings to any relationship. If people have unresolved issues, they will most definitely manifest in other ways in the relationship. We all have baggage, and we need to deal with it. We stop suffering internally and affecting people around us when we deal with these firmly rooted issues. Get help to resolve your pain. If the other person is in denial, then you need to establish healthy boundaries for yourself. I had to cultivate my own confidence, self-care, self-love, healing, transformation, renewing and purging.

- ✓ I had to learn to spot red flags and deal breakers. Discern who is wounded and suffering and has no plan to go on a healing journey. I wanted a soulmate that had my level of consciousness and was committed to growing and creating a healthy relationship. A healthy relationship starts with working on yourself. I did the hard yards so naturally I wanted to be yoked with a guy who did the same. So Dave and I took to each other as we both recognised the healing journey was over and we were both ready to create something wholesome. So the critical step is to work on your core healing journey first. Transform to the best version of yourself.

- ✓ There is so much satisfaction in living your best destined life. I had to learn to trust God and be assured He had the best for me. I saw Him honour and reward me. I had to become a kingdom builder and my heart desires and dreams slowly but surely came true. Sprinkle love and hope in all that you do and in due season you will reap the harvest. Sow wisely.

- ✓ Nurture yourself to dispense unconditional love. When you bless others with no expectations of a reward then the world is a better place. This encourages others to live an unselfish life too.

'If opportunity doesn't knock, build a door.' Milton Berle

Moving to the Next Level

My professional role demands extraordinary levels of efficiency – it's a complex environment implementing medical systems in the dynamic hospital landscape. Coupled with this, some clinicians have a god complex which contributes to the complications. I have worked on multiple projects and presented at several meetings, and I have sincerely lost count of how many times it was a classic case of jamais vu.

My first job in South Africa prepared me literally by baptism of the fire. A callow bud, I worked as an administrative resource at the local clinic that provided community health services. However, I assisted the nurse in charge of clinical tasks to complete the vast patient cohort for each day. Once a month, clinic was scheduled for geriatrics with chronic conditions. The nurse fetched these medications from the hospital in Stanger which was approximately thirty kilometres away. On one occasion, the medication was not ready when she presented to fetch it the night before as was custom. Thus on the day of the clinic she had to make the trip to the hospital.

I was holding the fort. Clinic to the rest of the community was unavailable – yet people still presented as most patients in the rural community were unaware of this. I was performing the patient intake, testing blood glucose levels and recording any adverse events for the patients. The geriatric clinic had approximately two hundred Indian patients. In addition, almost another hundred indigenous patients filled the waiting room, most in absolute dire need of medical intervention. I never had the heart to turn them away – every day we worked as a team to provide care to every patient. Some days we struggled to provide care to over a thousand patients.

To say we were swamped was an understatement. And then someone screamed for help from outside. I dashed out in my superwoman suit – not. A young indigenous woman was lying prone on the gravel in the yard, screaming. Zulu is not my first language but I knew enough to provide basic patient care. This was a critical patient and my limited vocabulary did not hasten the communication. Thankfully, she spoke some English – my heart palpitations increased as I could see she was heavily pregnant, and she announced that she was two weeks overdue.

My sister had a medical emergency book at home which I had flicked through years ago. It had some ramblings on how to deliver a baby and I took no real notice because I never dreamed that my job would demand it. I was only twenty years old in a mini dress and I could hardly bend over in that attire. Disclaimer – that was the last time I wore a mini dress, just in case I have to deliver another baby. This was South Africa in the 90's – the work phone was not cordless and fixed to the confines of the treatment room. I called the ambulance. They were in another town and could not get there in time – so he gave me the spiel that I have to deliver this baby – PHEW!

Rule number one is to wear gloves all the time – I was definitely not thinking logically and had no gloves on. The woman could not be moved – the treatment room was the gravel ground, requiring me to bend in that dress! Moreover, I was working to birth this baby in the public yard while dashing into the office each time to speak to the ambulance guy on the phone. Her gaze somehow finds me albeit the distractions and I know that she is counting on me to come through for her. Eventually the baby popped out. I was back on the phone because I had no idea what to do with the umbilical cord. He asked me, 'Is the baby stillborn?' In my panic, I first screamed yes, then comprehending the situation and what stillborn meant, shouted, 'No, the baby is alive! But the cord is still attached. What do I do now? What do I do?'

I did not get a medal – but I certainly got the stripes to deal with any drama or curve ball that was thrown at me at work or any other facet of my life since then. We all have the capacity to thrive in any situation, we just need to tackle it with zeal. Take nothing for granted. Nothing in life is guaranteed. Expect change and challenge and let adaptability be your default option.

Never evaluate your life based on the current situation. In one season David was a shepherd, the next season he was a king as recited in The Word. He was preparing to propel with his fight with Goliath. Take time to prepare for your destiny – be persistent about it:

What do you currently do very well in life/church/work/relationships?

_____

_____

_____

What do you currently do very badly?

_____

_____

_____

What requires improvement?

_____

_____

_____

'A river cuts through a rock not because of its power but because of its persistence.' James Watkins.

Discovering Your Purpose

Purpose is discovering the meaning to this one audacious life and determining how you want to impact this world in a positive way. It taps into your core values and your life ideals, the standards that you set for yourself. Most people never ponder on this. They just live a life with the cards that were handed to them or choose not to rock the boat of where life is presently anchored. They suppress authentic happiness with what they are currently living with.

Purpose is not static; it is rather dynamic. It is a constant enhancement of your life. Life rides the seemingly imperceptible edges of epochs to chronicle the point where the tide ebbed, often discovering riches hidden beneath. It's a lifelong skill that you have to honour in order to seek your purpose. Inherent curiosity ultimately leads us to uncover several notable trends that help define us unexpectedly capturing them at their pinnacle and troughs – find the meaning of your highs and low and harness something worthwhile from it.

Resolve to be persistent if you prefer the view at the top. There is no better time to introspect your life and make changes than now. Anything of value involves sacrifice. Nothing is pleasurable and uplifting all the time. Your threshold for struggle and sacrifice will determine your true grit to find your purpose. Most people do not understand that purpose is a result of action. Discovering your passions and purpose is a result of conscious choice. It is not a process that occurs by osmosis. Only you can make that cognizant choice to make the rest of your life the best of your life.

Romans 5:3 - Not only so, but we also glory in our sufferings, because we know that suffering produces perseverance, perseverance character and character, hope.

According to statistics, the average person checks their mobile phone one hundred and thirty times per day. People spend their time and energy on their phones rather than harness love and connection of a real soul sitting with them. The proverbial question is – what do we gain from this? More importantly, how often do we check the quality of our life objectively? What are we putting our energy into? Is it cultivated habits that bring enhancements to our lives or do we just routinely do things that take up our energy with no real tangible results?

You can find your purpose no matter how old you are. Define your own version of success; your passions and basic values. Do not limit your dreams to just money, think outside the square of your current parameters. Consider injustices that both bother you and ignite passion in you. Breakup with the things that are holding you back and reach for the stars with your feet firmly on the ground! Go discover the world...and therein you will find yourself and your purpose.

In The Word we gather that Moses was running from so many things he could not reach his destiny while on the run. You need to stop running to find your purpose. He grabbed the snake by the tail and God turned it into a rod in his hand! Pick up the snake while you are petrified and nervous and God will meet you where you are. God called a man who could not speak properly to talk to his people. God used his weakness despite his incompetence. Moses's problem was unbelief.

What is your life's core message to the world?

'You may get the thing you wish for. But you will surely get the thing you work for.' Unknown

Purge List

Perhaps you are struggling to find your purpose and destiny because you want to do what is trending for now or you like to do something because someone you know is doing it. We are all different, so be your authentic self and find out what your destiny is. Your purpose is to seek your truth even if it rocks your world. None of us come out of life alive, so you have finite days to leave a legacy that will be forever. It is vital to process your raw unfiltered emotions because if traumatic emotions are suppressed, they will manifest in unhealthy and inconvenient ways in other facets of life. So wake up and address your deferred emotions before they taint every aspect of your life. In transformation there is stumbling, but stay on the path and persevere.

Describe the current constraints in your life. What factors do you need to take into consideration that will influence your destiny? These are factors that you cannot control but need to manage effectively.

_____
_____
_____

Writer James Chapman created a list of the most read books in the world based on the number of copies each book had sold over the last fifty years. He found that the Bible far outsold any other book with a whopping 3.9 billion copies sold over the last fifty years. This data attests to the fact that the world is both thirsty for wisdom and recognises this book as a blueprint for life. It is filled with pearls of wisdom. It gives us great insight into so many lives and so many calculated and uncalculated risks.

Do not let your future and destiny be dictated by chance. Be strategic, plan and commit, be targeted and driven. Write down a list of risks that you need to take in your life presently to reach your real purpose.

_____

_____

_____

Risk management in your life centres on being able to identify what might go wrong. These are the negative risks, otherwise known as threats to your life. It's important to identify and record them, so you know what might be waiting round the corner to weaken your chances of completing your purpose successfully. But identifying them is only the beginning. Once you have done that, you also need to work out what to do about them. Use the table below to help you identify your own risks and create a mitigation plan:

Risk description	Impact	Likelihood	Mitigation Plan
E.g. This is my fate I was born poor, and I will remain poor	High	Very	Get a good education and work on a career to afford a better life

'Faith can move mountains, but do not be surprised if God hands you a shovel.' Unknown.

How Content Are You With Your Life at Present?

The key revelation that Paul offers us from the Bible is to remain content in all seasons of life. This is easier said than done but it definitely can be done. It requires practice and planning. Most of us that work in corporate jobs adhere to our employer's contract of Standard Operating Processes and industry standards. We aim to perform to this outlined professional standard. This is a job that can cease at any given point and we may be at liberty to seek new employment. If you have the capacity to invest this much professional acumen in a job that can be replaced, then surely you can find the time to invest in the direction of your life which can never be replaced.

Circle one point that represents your contentment rank. How content are you with your life right now? **1** being least content, **10** extremely content.

1 2 3 4 5 6 7 8 9 10

Retrospectively, last year this time what was your level of contentment? If there is a difference, note down what the change element is.

_____
_____
_____

We survive because the fire inside us must burn brighter than the fire around us. However, life is not just about surviving and getting basic sustenance, but about thriving. It is about having that wonderful abundant life. Have you reached the point of abundance? If not, what is holding you back?

_____

_____

_____

'Don't wait. The time will never be just right.' Napoleon Hill

Setting Goals

Setting goals is important as it steers us in the general direction that we want our life to head in. The process of achieving our goals may not be a charming one but it is better to have a map in the jungle than no map at all. A goal gets us engaged with our destiny and pregnant with action to move towards both small and big responsibilities of life. Some key fundamentals when setting a goal:

Establish your priorities: We all make a greater effort when something is significant to us. So define what matters to you.

What are your values: Live your truth and find what makes you happy and what adds value to you and your loved ones.

Do you need further support: Do you need help from others to achieve certain goals?

What is your budget: Live within your means, never try to keep up with the Jones.

Are your goals attainable: Do not bite off what you cannot chew! Dream, but be discerning.

'This is the time to stop running on the spot going around and around the mulberry bush. Receive your destiny kissed with forgiveness, free as a bird not only to receive but to fly. Yes, there is pain being manifested as anger, look at the root causes, deal with them, and go forward. His banner over you is love bringing restoration. Love never fails! The time is now, no more self-pity nor procrastination but asserting on a willingness to flow and grow. A salmon goes up stream against the current to give birth safely. You too are required to be different to make a difference. Never fear: it's all mapped out and you are guaranteed to make it. Enjoy this precious season and make the most of it, you won't come this way again. Shalom, The Father walks with you.' Pastor Gilyean Levick

Ecclesiastes 3:1-8 – To everything there is a season, a time for every purpose under heaven:

A time to be born,
And a time to die
A time to plant,
And a time to pluck what is planted
A time to kill,
And a time to heal
A time to break down,
And a time to build up
A time to weep,
And a time to laugh
A time to mourn,
And a time to dance
A time to cast away stones,
And a time to gather stones
A time to embrace,
And a time to refrain from embracing
A time to gain,
And a time to lose
A time to keep,
And a time to throw away

A time to tear,
And a time to sew
A time to keep silence,
And a time to speak
A time to love,
And a time to hate
A time of war,
And a time of peace.

This scripture highlights the spiritual contract we have. It makes us acutely aware that it is normal to experience both good and bad times in life. So why do humans assume that living to the highest ideals would be smooth sailing? The above scripture confirms that we should never assume a constant as there is no constant. It is easy to hold on to hope when life is dandy. However, we need to be so deeply anchored that changing circumstances do not cause us to falter. We need to align our priorities to give us buoyancy in every season and facet of life. Ground yourself to always deal with both negative and positive times. Gain clarity of your perceptions and what you can and cannot control. Get objective and make a decision to sink, swim or scream. Create a list of actions or tasks.

Having a priority or goal to retire with a pronounced nest egg is great, but that's just the beginning of the vision. You need to put your priorities in motion. People who have foresight accomplish more that those who wait for the cosmos to hand it out. Take charge and control what you can about your life with targeted precision. Prioritise the things you can control. Think like Thomas Edison through trial and error, find your spark and discover your intrinsic drive. Create daily tasks and actions that will align with your macro goal to retire with that huge nest egg.

We remain in status quo mode when life is hopeful and positive. When life travels south, we are challenged. This is the time to get innovative and discover new norms instead of getting swept away by the storm.

Come up with creative ideas to adapt. When we have established goals and priorities, then we know the general direction our life is heading in. Brilliance is the pivot of seeking the highest values that stimulate you. Identify your primary purpose and strategically prioritise both your macro and micro goals.

'You are never too old to set another goal or to dream a new dream.' C.S. Lewis

Strategic Vision

Why You Need a Vision Plan For Your Life

I grew up playing darts with my brothers and I am not bad for a lass! Recently, during one of my rather stressful work projects, my manager resolved to introduce the team to a session of dart games to help us destress and relieve pressure by just having some simple fun. I was the only female in the team so they all looked down on me thinking I will not excel at this game at all. Well, to the contrary, I whipped them real good! The moral of this story is that you cannot hit your target if you lack focus and experience. You will hit nothing if you target nothing.

Therefore, prepare a vision plan for your life. You do not need to overanalyse this. Keep it as simple as you prefer, and as you mature, change your goals and purpose as well. This offers you a bird's eye view for where you are and where you want your life to head. While you may not be able to control all the factors guiding your life, you most definitely can influence the direction in a fundamental way. In the previous chapter you identified your purpose – now build a plan for attaining your purpose.

As mentioned in The Bible God did not create the ark for Noah, and he could not just buy it and neither did he stumble upon it! No, he had to build it with his two hands even though he had never seen one before and he had no clue about the future or even knew if he would ever get to use it. In the same way we cannot just live life aimlessly, hoping that one day we will stumble onto our vison, purpose and destiny. Oh no, we have to plan. Failure to plan is planning to fail. So do not wait for the burning bush moment where God will direct you on the path you need to walk.

God will direct your path, but you need to plan. If you fail to plan a vision for yourself, there is a high probability that your life will get engulfed in someone else's vision. Noah had to store up food in advance for his family and the animals. We are called to prepare for our future. If you do not sweat in practice you will bleed in battle. When mayhem hits, it is too late to prepare; this is when you rise up with resilience as you know how to respond. Things may not go exactly as your vision plan, but at least you have a rebuttal at hand for a potential situation that may arise.

Proverbs 20:4 - A sluggard does not plough in season, so at harvest time he looks but finds nothing.

Key Benefits for a Vision Plan

- ✓ When we have a plan for life, we can deal with catastrophe with more finesse
- ✓ Failure to plan is planning to fail
- ✓ A vision plan gives you a high-level plan detailing what you need to strive for
- ✓ If you have no target, then you will have no zeal to aim at anything
- ✓ Personal growth is harnessed with an active dynamic plan
- ✓ Be blessed to be a blessing, as you cannot impart to others what you do not have yourself
- ✓ Knowledge and transformation are infinite, so do not stop the process
- ✓ You have some degree of control when you have a plan
- ✓ There is an element of security in a plan with God's direction
- ✓ You have a sense of control about what you can do

- ✓ Confirmation that you cannot make others do what you want when you want
- ✓ It is your blueprint for making decisions

Let the Vision Begin

'A flower does not think of competing with other flowers next to it. It just blooms.' Iris Murdoch. No one but you are responsible for how long you let your hurt haunt you. I share my journey gleans from a place of experience. I am confident as this is not based on an ocean of theory; it is practiced resilience lived out loud. So use my lessons to grow and get wiser from your own life experience as well. Life has no manual, but we do need to plan our lives. Life turns out the best for those who make the best of the way things turn out. You do not have to have all your life figured out but plan ahead and be flexible and tune in to the Holy Spirit.

Most people go through life without considering an outcome for their life. Do not live a life that someone else has dreamt for you if that's not your destiny. Find your own purpose and a tribe of supporters that are as committed to it as you are. Let us now define some life directions that relate to the way you operate as a person. This outlines what needs to be done to meet a purposeful need in your life and to identify the weight of other people's expectations, and what you should stop doing to align with your destiny. Use the table below to create your list of visions / goals.

Legend

- **MUST have:** This is a mandatory factor. You cannot function in the absence of this.
- **SHOULD have:** You should have this element to make everyday life easier.
- **NICE to have:** These are **NOT** mandatory prerequisites. They are nice to have bells-and-whistles features for your life
- **Compliant:** This simply means are you currently achieving this in your life

Life Direction	How to Achieve	Category	Compliant YES/NO
E.g. I want to hear from God and want Him to direct me	Read the Word of God and spend time talking to God in prayer	Must	Yes
E.g. I want to help more people.	Work hard and save. Be wise with your time and resources	Should	Yes
E.g. I want to leave a better and brighter legacy behind	Create tangible ways to instil and implement love and hope when I can	Nice	Yes

A gap analysis is a method of assessing the differences in performance between where your life is currently at and where you want it to be in order to determine whether life directions are being met and, if not, what steps should be taken to ensure they are met successfully. *Gap* refers to the space between 'where we are' (the present state) and 'where we want to be' (the target state). If you expect any probable hurdles, then prearrange the eventualities to address these issues, gaps and risks. Create a list of Gaps in your life, then identify ways to resolve these gaps. You may need to talk to your mentor or seek professional help to find a remedy if you prefer.

Identified Gap (present state)	Solution (target state)	Proposals to Bridge the Gap
E.g. I feel over worked and lack the time to do things for my kids and I spend very little quality time with them	I want to be a better mother	Redefine my priorities and find new ways to balance my life. Cut out the noise from my life to focus on what is important to me

Vision Plan

Create a vision plan for your life describing what you would like to accomplish in the next week, month, year, five years, decade, and lifetime and what legacy you want to leave behind. Now include some dates for each milestone. How much time do you need to take to move from your current state to your target state? Create a list of simple everyday **'to do tasks'** to implement and manage your vision plan. Bring the plan to life by taking small steps each day. Your vision will come into fruition! Set SMART goals and consider these points:

S = Strategically plan your micro goals

M = Maintain your plan diligently

A = Accountability is the key to success

R = Reward yourself for reaching your micro goals

T = Time is of the essence. Use it wisely

Ensure to address these facets of your life:
- ✓ Spirituality
- ✓ Community
- ✓ Family
- ✓ Health
- ✓ Relationships
- ✓ Personal
- ✓ Financial
- ✓ Career
- ✓ Recreation
- ✓ Factors that you are unable to control (e.g., a global pandemic)
- ✓ Experiences
- ✓ Accomplishments

- ✓ Skillset
- ✓ Qualification
- ✓ Humanity

Finally the day arrives when confidence matches know how, remain poised with the process for your season of bounty – someday you will transform into a butterfly remain loyal to your developed self-confidence as your experience grows to new levels. Edit your plan as you and your vision evolve and update your actions and values as you grow deeper moving from strength to greater strength.

The company Kodak was in full glory in its hay day selling film cameras. It was the market gorilla. Kodak played a pivotal role in creating the digital camera however they were too concerned to lose the current market share with sales of films, so they did not market the digital camera. Kodak missed the boat on the digital front not once, but at least three times. Consumers, the market and photography has evolved to a new dimension now and it is a tragic fact that Kodak invented the digital camera but lacked the acumen to capitalise on this revolutionising invention.

The most direct lesson from the collapse of Kodak is ill-fated, don't be fearful to rejig your industry in the name of advancement. The story of Kodak highlights what happens when you stick to your lane and refuse to see the horizon of the future and thus plan in accordance. A giant organisation used all its powers to stay in the game but refused to look beyond and it was shaved to nothing eventually. Let this Kodak story expand your horizons. Do not limit yourself based on your scope of finite knowledge. Do not map your future based on current trends.

'There are three ingredients in a good life: learning, earning and yearning.' Christopher Morley

Process the Unprocessed Pain

Write a letter, pour your heart out and speak about what is heavy in your heart. Talk to God about the things that you may not have shared with anyone else before. Include all the gaps you currently have in your life. Now for each gap write down what will help you reach your solution state – that is where you want to be – your target goal.

Read the letter out loud a few times after a few days until you have processed all the pain and reach a point where you are happy to leave it with God. Then talk to God and tell Him how difficult it is for you to carry this around all the time and that you want Him to have these issues. Then leave it with Him and rip the letter up. Remember not to carry the burden like the monk as mentioned in the mental resilience chapter. Take steps to address the difficult situations that you need to heal from. You may need to create muscle memory for this to work.

Subsequently establish what works best for you to renew your mind from all these memories that bring you pain. My personal trauma was a struggle. Each season presented its own agony that contributed to change the disposition of my soul and mind. I read the scripture in Isaiah 61:3 that confirmed God will trade my spirit of heaviness for a garment of praise. I read it, lived by it and believed it. The tangible reality is I tossed and turned at night, I had no one to change the light bulb, and I had no companion, no plus one to RSVP on invitations. I had to make hard decisions with no pillow talk reference and that's a tough road in a foreign country all alone. So here's what helped me.

I have a fetish for pyjamas, quite an impressive global collection. I can attest to the fact that there is nothing on this planet like a comfortable pair of pyjamas to chill in like a second skin. I got out my favourite pair and I prayed the above mentioned scripture and I literally told God, here I am trading my garment, I am putting this item that I love into the bin, so show up and help me with this. Much to my delight, I got out a brand new pair to add to my collection of wearables. Every time that I felt heavy about my past pain, I quickly remembered that I had paid the price with my favourite pyjamas and God is helping me to move to a new season and renew my mind.

I also wore the new garment – nightwear that was traded and anointed with scripture. Strangely it brought me comfort even when sleep eluded me at 2 a.m. Confession, I did throw away many pairs, but I reached the place that God promised in His Word. Faith without action is dead. We do need to do some work to bring The Word to fruition. Do your part and God will do His portion. Find what readily works for you.

'All of our dreams can come true if we have the courage to pursue them.'
Unknown

Love Map

Create a love map. What does love look like for you as a woman, mother, man, father, confidant, teammate, wife, friend and kingdom builder? Now create tasks to practice channelling this everyday vision of yourself. Model the level and calibre of love you want to receive by exhibiting it in all your relationships first. Here are some points to consider:

L = Love is a verb and love is as love does
O = One thing at a time. Use one hat at a time with focused quality on that person or task.
V = Value your weakness and develop from it. Become better and not bitter
E = Emphasise your strengths
S = Statement! Yes, make a statement but be sensitive about it

Make a list of all your predicable behaviours. For example, you cannot pass a store that has a sale. You know this is not helping your budget if you are trying to save a deposit for a home. In addition, write down how you are going to stop your predicable behaviour. Consider these factors:

R = Responsibility is the key ingredient
E = Evaluate your progress
V = Victory is the target
I = Impossible is nothing
E = Evade all temptations
W = Wishful thinking will get you nowhere

One of the greatest priorities is finding a service that you can contribute to. Find a way to help others and be sober about pursuing it. Do you fear losing something that you are attached to? Why are you afraid to lose this? What can you build within yourself to help you transition from this state? Take steps to detach from what's binding you to fear. Create a healthy balance to model to others and to live by. Let your life exhibit how you fight your battles and not how you get crushed under them.

'Someone once told me not to bite off more than I could chew. I said I'd rather choke on greatness than nibble mediocrity.' Unknown

Proactively Discover Your Blind Spot

Create a list of five people who you trust, those who confidently support your welfare. Arrange to have some authentic fellowship individually with each member of your super tribe of support. Perhaps organise a coffee date. Then ask them candidly if they have noticed any blind spots in your character. These are negative traits in your character that they can clearly see but you cannot.

Disclaimer: this may get heavy for you, so pray first and ask God to confirm who to select as your super tribe. Keep it real and do not select people who you know will only tell you good things. Also, refrain from creating tension with those that are honest with you. This exercise is to identify the negative traits from all facets of your life. So once you obtain the data about your character, create a plan of what you are going to do to improve in this area of your life.

Find your Achilles heel rather than developing the paranoia of assumed perfection. Anything that needs to grow will change. Be more discerning about when it is time for new realisations. Objectively seek to enhance yourself. It's our challenges that trigger innovation. Your capacity for improvement depends on your ability to really look beneath the surface. A blind spot is a side you are unwilling to see. It's not necessarily a weakness. Discover it and use it to your advantage.

What are the things you can control in your life once you glean all your blind spots?

'In the hardest times we grow the most.' Unknown

What Does Utopia Look Like for You?

Write a letter to your 80 year old future self. What do you want to thank yourself for? What does your best life look like? Thank yourself for making wise choices. Magnify the lessons you learned. Describe all the life-changing circumstances you were presented with and how and why you made the choices that you did. Some points to consider:

- ✓ What have you accomplished?
- ✓ What have you lost?
- ✓ What was your best experience?
- ✓ What was your saddest experience?
- ✓ What is the greatest lesson that you learned?
- ✓ What is your character like?
- ✓ What is your level of contentment?
- ✓ What are your regrets?
- ✓ What will you change if you ARE given the opportunity?
- ✓ What is your health assessment?
- ✓ Have you made peace with your past?
- ✓ How long did it take you to reach the best season of your life?
- ✓ Are you well travelled?

Now use this letter to enhance your vision plan. For example, if you think you will end up with a bad health assessment report when you are 80, then fortunately you now have the time to plan a better and healthier lifestyle. Your espoused vision plan is dynamic and will constantly change as you evolve as a person, so remain abreast and focused to edit your plan and march forward with confidence and do not panic when a curve ball comes your way.

Read this every day and carve out your ideal world until you can perform this on autopilot mode. Change starts with you, so create your ideal world according to your Utopia. Now all you have to do is tap into that plan and respond to the situation with God. You have done the work and God is the faith factor. **FAITH + WORKS = VISION**

'You must learn a new way to think before you can master a new way to be.' Marianne Williamson

Elements for Success

Your life success is defined only by you. You measure what is valuable to you. Someone may measure success by the accolades they receive as a mother. This gauge is futile to me as I do not value the same things as this mother. So the primary objective is to find your primary values and the secondary task is to measure your values over the long term. Only compare yourself to yourself. You are not in competition with anyone.

You are striving to be the best version of yourself. Some factors to consider:

- ✓ What matters to you? Are you living that truth?
- ✓ What legacy do you want to leave behind? Are you actively creating that now?
- ✓ Implement daily healthy routines for your body, mind and soul.
- ✓ Never stop learning.
- ✓ Work towards your goal even in the dormant season
- ✓ Take charge even in the most difficult time, even just a small step like sleeping, eating and resting well.
- ✓ Show gratitude; if not, life will teach you how to be humble.
- ✓ Resolve your emotions and heal. Do not pretend it does not hurt.
- ✓ Establish a routine to manage your goals.
- ✓ Commit to execute your personal growth, no one else will prioritise your refinement.
- ✓ Be focused and flexible with your goals.

- ✓ Maintain the right to disagree. Find your true north.
- ✓ Do not expect to change overnight. Change is a process.
- ✓ You always have a choice. One mould does not fit all.
- ✓ Whatever your stance in life is, are you growing to be a better version of yourself?

Success does not denote that you are perfect; it simply means that you are consistent and that you continuously attempt to learn and improve. You lead with compassion despite imperfections. I am strong because of the limitations that I have endured. I am attractive because I am acutely aware of my mistakes. I can laugh because tears have featured in my life oh so often. I have experienced more setbacks than a duck has quacks. I am now proficient as I have absorbed the lessons of my audacious life habitually in concert with God.

One evening in 2004 Mr. Ex and I were at church and a visiting prophet from USA was preaching and then he brought a few prophetic words to the eager congregation. I was a new converted Christian, and it was all new and foreign to me. People were soaking up every word like a sponge. I was trying to camouflage myself. I had no desire to be a leader or reach out to the masses. I was content with my personal agenda. The preacher walked right up to me at the rear, where I was standing next to Mr. Ex, he looked me squarely in the eyes and said, 'you will sing the Song of Solomon from hilltops, you will preach and teach to masses, you will lead and be a pace setter.' Everyone around me was marvelling. He then turned to Mr. Ex and said, 'you really need to shake up to catch up and keep abreast.'

I honestly was in shock and I did think the preacher got his wires mixed. Mr. Ex sent out vibes that he was the poster boy for Christianity, and I was the rooky on the block. Mr. Ex constantly confirmed this to me and highlighted to me how I did not stack up. Confession – I had no clue what the Song of Solomon was! The gentleman on the sound desk recorded the prophesy on a cassette (hope you know what that is) and handed it to me. He asked me to listen to it often and hugged me saying what a great word. I took it and slipped it into my handbag still a bit baffled. It was an impetuous walk back to our car as Mr. Ex seemed rather annoyed with something. Still a tad wet behind the ears about all of this I enquired what was wrong. He called me gullible for believing all that I just heard. With a bemoaning attitude he said, 'do you really believe I will need to catch up to you?' I was lost for words – I was not in a competition. I was just trying to live. We reached home and he said 'I don't want that cassette in our home.' I tossed it in the bin.

I did not understand the implications of all this then. But with the progression of sixteen years I can now see this prophesy coming into fruition in my life even though I tossed that cassette in the bin. God's Word is everlasting, stands the test of time regardless of human intervention. He alone is sovereign so don't bother about how humans view your potential and your future. All my failures are internal reckoning to establish a better character by development to grow wealthier. Thomas Edison the American inventor said I have not failed – 'I just found ten thousand ways that don't work.' Insightful when we comprehend and live this.

Apply the inspiration into your daily application of life. Recalibrate your thinking for the long term and be ready to endure pain on your path. When you learn and grow from your setbacks that's the recipe for an extraordinary future. Your soul beats better when you strive to improve your own deficiency rather than copy someone's projected perfection. Create and repeat affirmations that you want to live out loud in your life. We write a script by default for our lives, be aware of the default impact and how it maps out your life. The dread that we refuse to tackle becomes the restrictions we live with.

Transformation is a process. It is a conviction of your spirit. Some people transform faster than others because the seeds of their wounds may not be planted as deep as in others. **Do not let anyone tell you that your journey is slow, especially when they do not have metaphoric thorns embedded in their flesh, heart, mind, spirit and soul like you do!** People love to judge when they have not walked your path and lived in your shoes. Only you can walk the healing path and be healed in His time. Do not grant consent to others to voice unsolicited opinions about your care plan. Do not let people derail the progress that you have made. Be steadfast – it is not how far you still have to go; what counts is how far you have already progressed. Celebrate that!

Life is not what happens to us; it is our perception of the events we face, the way we handle setbacks and how creative we are when the down in the valley moments present. What lessons have you learned during your unfavourable time?

'We need to accept that we won't always make the right decisions, that we'll screw up royally sometimes – understanding that failure is not the opposite of success, it is part of success.' Unknown

How to Monitor Your Personal Growth

Transformation is an ongoing process. No one has mastered it and graduated from the University of Transformation with a PhD. Perhaps the butterfly did, but we are a different species. Newsflash – we are all works in progress! Wisdom is progressing today to a better version of who you were yesterday.

Growth Matrix

Use the matrix below to help you with things that you want to STOP, CONTINUE and START in your life. Take daily actions and document your accomplishments every day, both the big and small wins. Measure your growth and progress every four months by entering the status for each thing as per the legend. The matrix is just a sample model. You can use the same process in your personal journal.

Legend

- **Work in Progress:** You are still struggling with this issue.
- **Nailed It:** You have made significant progress in this area.
- **Mastered the Art:** You can now do this with no effort required.
- **Quarter:** Measure your progress every four months.

Things That I Want to STOP	1st Quarter	2nd Quarter	3rd Quarter
I want to stop unforgiveness in my heart	WIP	WIP	Nailed It
Things That I Want to Continue			
I want to continue being a blessing	Mastered	Mastered	Mastered
Things That I Want to START			
I want to start taking better care of my mind	WIP	WIP	WIP

The joy of twenty twenty hindsight is that someone has learned the lesson already, the hard way. So I'm sharing my lessons with you to shield you from the same pain. Glean what you can and grow in whatever way you can, just do not stagnate! Go forward. In a complex world, let the simple but impacting decisions reign supreme.

Just as we do not drink only milk all our lives and move on to solid foods, the dimension of our character must also graduate to the next level. Consistent diligence can pave the way for the future like a four-leaf clover. Stabilise your mind with an anchor to grow in some small way each minute, each hour, each day, and the enhanced version of your character will emerge like a phoenix. Pick up the pieces without getting cut and soldier on. Sunshine all the time makes a desert, so create your ideal in the rain too.

How do you govern and manage your emotions? Outline some examples of life on a rollercoaster when you have to change to a different role (e.g., from a mother to a manager). How do you adapt? **Learn the art to interpret your emotions before they ruin you.**

How do you find your rhythm and consistency in life and what do you do to maintain it?

'Never apologise for creating your life around what you know about yourself. Your people will understand. Many won't. But your greatest gift to yourself and the world is authenticity.' Unknown

Balancing the Equation of Sowing and Reaping

None of us are created to be a masterpiece by default. We have to grind something to shine later, and we need to develop the art of challenging our limits. Redefine how we rise after falling. Ensure that we adopt criticism seriously, but not personally. Nail it or learn from it – no defeat in the equation, period. You got to plant something to reap a harvest. Where ever you go, go with all your heart.

Getting the blessings of God is not written in Morse code and locked up in Fort Knox. It is written in the blueprint of The Word in simple language that you can understand. In the book of Deuteronomy chapter 28, the blessing of obedience is outlined as: **'if you fully obey the Lord and all his commandments'** so do not expect to get all the blessings when you have not read all the conditions in chapter 27. You need to master chapter 27 first to reap all the blessings that are outlined in chapter 28.

This is our spiritual contract. You can use the same principles to define what you sow and reap in your **personal and professional life** as well. The only limits are the ones you create.

I find it entertaining how humans naturally compare harvests with each other's when they have never propagated the same seed and toiled the same soil. The metaphoric cup is filled or empty by what you put or do not put in the cup and the alignment of your cosmos. We get out what we put in – artless equation. I have a testimony of a spectacular harvest because I honour the principle of tithing. I give more than ten percent to the store house. It is my lifestyle to give. Sleep does not elude me when it comes to finances as I know what my infinite source is.

Don't Just Fly, SOAR

If you sow in one season, then rest assured you will reap in another season. What do you sow? Examine your harvest. If your harvest is not what you would like it to be, then realign what you are sowing. To assist you in mapping out your current and future state, refer to the diagram and confirm what you put in verses how much you get out of life.

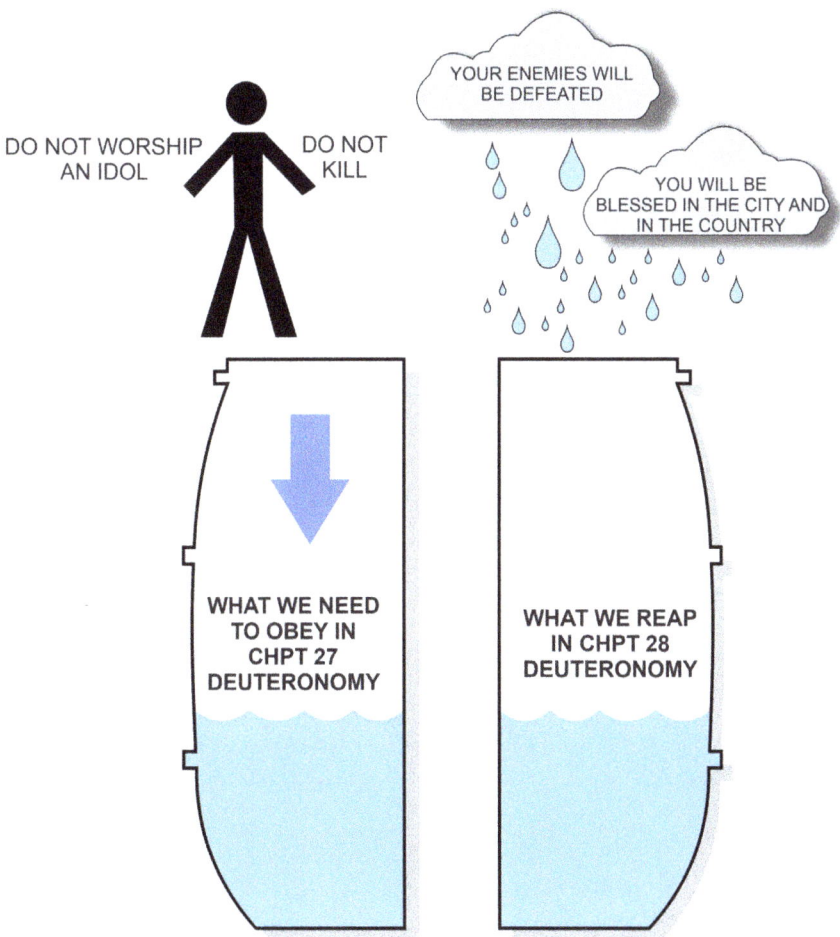

This is a diagrammatic representation of scripture from the book of Deuteronomy that depicts the analogy of sowing and reaping.

I have attached the table below. Please feel free to include additional areas that you would like to sow and reap in your personal and professional life. This matrix is populated from the above mentioned scripture as an illustration guide. Complete the matrix below:

Blessings for Obedience	I Am Dreaming of This	This is Tangible in My Life
Blessed in the city and in the country.	I am not dreaming of prosperity.	This is absolutely evident in my life
The fruit of your womb will be blessed, and the crops of your land and the young of your stock.		
Your basket and your kneading trough will be blessed.		
Blessed when you come in and blessed when you go out.		
Your enemies will be defeated before you.		
Everything that you put your hands to will be blessed.		
If you walk in obedience God will establish you as Holy and grant you prosperity.		
The Lord will open the heavens, the store house and send rain in season to bless all the works of your hand.		
You will lend to nations but will borrow from none.		
The Lord will make you the head and not the tail.		

Now that you can visibly gauge what you are putting in and what you are getting out in terms of your blessings, identify where the gaps are. Create a list in your journal or vision plan of the areas in which you would like to grow, so you can move to seeing all these blessings manifest **tangibly in every facet of your life.**

If you had a list of 101 objectives for sowing and reaping (giving and taking), what would be the top five on your list?

'There is no exercise better for the heart than reaching down and lifting people up.' John Holmes

The Ladder of Ascent to Transformation

Transformation is a process by which you are converted and changed in form or nature. This process of change can be either negative or positive. You and I can change for the better and sadly sometimes for the worse. The sun transforms nuclear energy into ultraviolet, infrared and gamma energy – a positive transformation. Our bodies convert chemical energy from food into mechanical energy to allow us to live and move – another positive transformation. The distinct difference between **change** and **transformation** is that change utilises external influences to modify actions, whereas transformation modifies beliefs, so actions become natural and thereby achieve the desired result.

You have now embarked on the journey to discover your blind spots, created your vison plan, listed your current gaps and discovered what utopia looks like for you. Using all the longitudinal information you now have, you ought to have a vivid picture of what aspects of your life you would prefer to transform. Transformation is an ongoing process, and we should all be constantly working on transforming to a better version of ourselves. Let's take a deeper dive into our transformation.

A diagrammatic representation of the ladder of ascent to transformation – RHS.

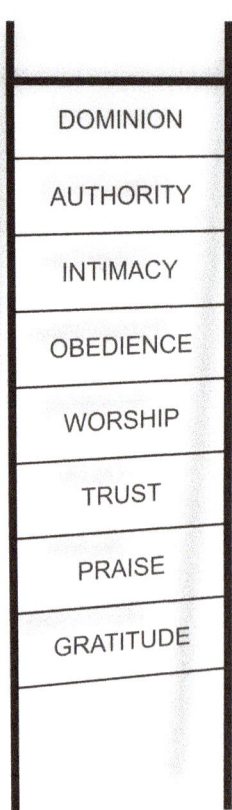

Gratitude: Thank God for the basic, seemingly small things in your life such as food, clothing, shelter and good health. Become acutely aware of all the good things in your life. Gratitude is pausing to notice and appreciate the things we often take for granted in life. A thankful heart will lead to praise.

Praise: We praise God by lifting our hands in the sanctuary, singing, with our words – let the fruit of our lips give thanks to his name and by sweet fellowship with others. When you praise God, you learn to trust God.

Trust: Trusting God means that whatever suffering we endure can be used for our – all our – ultimate good. When you trust God, you will become a worshipper.

Worship: To worship God is the act of attributing reverent honour and homage to God (e.g., having a non-curated and non-memorised prayer or conversation with God from your heart or starting a prayer journal). When you worship God in spirit and in truth, then obeying God comes naturally.

Obedience: This is when a person yields to explicit instructions from authority. Obedience breeds intimacy.

Intimacy: This is how close we are willing to get to the Lord and plunge in deeper dives. Intimacy with God cultivates authority.

Authority: This is the extent to which you can regard the scriptures as authoritative over human beliefs. Authority allows the power of God to flow through you in every facet of your life. When the authority of God is flowing via you, this enables you to have dominion.

Dominion: This is the use of power supremely over something. To rule over a negative circumstance.

Personal Ascension to Transformation

Reaching the place where you have dominion is a cultivated process. Dominion is attainable over yourself, circumstances and even the elements. Jesus rebuked the wind and said to the sea, 'Peace! Be Still!' so the wind ceased and there was a dead calm in The Gospel of Mark.

Complete the matrix below to ascertain the state of your transformation and which part of the ascent process you are stuck at or need to actively work on.

Personal Ascension to Transformation	This is a Cultivated Habit in My Life YES / NO	What Can I Do to Improve
How often do you express gratitude to God and others?		
Is praise part of your lifestyle?		
Do you have trust in God?		
What does worship mean to you?		
Where are you on the obedience scale?		
How intimate are you with God?		
What level of authority do you display in life?		
Have you cultivated dominion in your life?		

Each of us was created as a beautiful soul and we are capable enough to withstand anything that comes our way. I am a testament to victory despite my circumstances. Consequently life is not as perplexing as we perceive it. A situation is as authentic as we are. You were created to have dominion, so leave no rock unturned to find that dominion and live congruently to your values in every facet of your life. Your true priorities will help you to create your equilibrium. Your destiny is not controlled by the outside world. During catastrophe, strive to align with your priorities rather than succumbing to the vibes of the outside world.

You may need to recalibrate your life to eliminate all the noise from your life. Allowing you to rocket in on your emotional journey with just you and learn to know your heartbeat, smile and tears of the person in the mirror. When you discover who you really are then your values become much clearer. You cannot live with somebody else's values so don't expect others to live by your values. I noticed this on twitter *'the real GLOW up is when you stop waiting to turn into some perfect version of yourself and consciously enjoy being who you are at present.'* There is merit in enjoying the 'power of now', however the purpose of life is to grow deeper not stagnate. No one wants to arrive at the final destination with regrets. Those that hated me, broke me, hurt me, betrayed me or did not believe in me gave me a zeal to realign my values; to become wiser and upgrade to a newer version of myself. I am thankful and no, I will never be content with just accepting the cards that fall on my lap and let cobwebs grow all around me.

Outline what you do to shut off the outside world's noise and distractions. How do you obtain dominion in your situation?

'Nothing happens until the pain of remaining the same outweighs the pain of change.' Arthur Burt

Beauty or Afflictions? You Choose

'Some people grumble that roses have thorns; I am grateful that thorns have roses.' *Alphonse Karr.* Acknowledge that life comes packaged with thorns as well. Hone the art of focusing on the beauty of the rose and all the positive elements of life. May healing and transformation be ever so real in your life!

Sometimes we need to step out in faith. We don't know what we can overcome until we step out. It is petrifying to step into the unknown. However, it is at this point that we encounter Jesus. Just as Joshua had to step out in faith first then the Jordan River receded with reference to The Word. Faith is coupled with action, so do the work diligently to see your faith grow with remarkable changes and solutions for your life.

When a police officer stops you or gives you a command, he does not have to beg or plead with you to adhere to him. He simply exercises the authority invested in his badge, uniform or title. In the same way, when we come to God we do not need to beg or plead with God. God has given us the authority in accordance with The Word. We need to know the scriptures so we can approach the throne with confidence and exercise our God given authority.

Do not have a pity party and beg God to heal you. Pray according to His Word. Believe that you are healed by the stripes of Jesus. A ring on our finger is a constant reminder of our earthly love. Calvary is a brilliant reminder to us of Jesus's love. His love represents both our finite life on earth and our infinite realm of the soul. So do not let the predicaments of life be the death of you. Let them simply be the stepping stones to attaining a better version of yourself. His blood washes you as white as snow so start afresh right now. Leap forward with joy and expectation.

Life issues will not move from doom to gloom beset in Shekinah glory by wishful thinking. You have to put targeted energy and effort to focus on transforming your mind and life. Practice the target state goals and tasks that you defined in your journal from the previously mentioned exercise for three months and monitor your progress. If you are failing to reach your scheduled goal, then edit your plan and life in accordance and then try again. It is better to try and fail that fail to try. After three months you will love the smallest positive change. Then implementing change and transforming your mind will become a natural norm. Renewing your mind is a practice, not just a prayer. It is faith with works, so do the work as well. With the progression of time you will see worthy enlightened revelations and transformations in your life. Some aspects of you may still be fragile, so set your own pace for recovery and ultimately define your road to recovery.

The choice is yours. You assess all the acquired knowledge and gathered information, reject what does not improve your spirit and then implement what will help you enhance your character. We all have limited time on earth so use each day wisely. Take time to heal if you need to recover but never stagnate. As each day trickles by, develop an internal compass to check these vitals in your life.

The above illustration defines a daily circle of mantra

- ✓ Do you pray every day?
- ✓ Have you got a plan for the day?
- ✓ Are you transforming in some way each day?
- ✓ Are you bouncing back from issues better than the past days?
- ✓ Did you forgive who hurt you yesterday?

'God makes you unshakable as you abide in Him. He clothes you with favour and honour because you bear His name. He is a true father parenting with delight. Even right now your faith is being ignited so you don't feel bowed down, you stand straight as an arrow to do His will. Go forward with shouts of victory. He is alive, you are not forgotten. Those accusations have been squashed by the blood. Stand in His authority with eyes fixed like a flint on Him. You are going to the other side, that is certain. Hola with delight and victory!' Pastor Gilyean Levick

I trust that reading about my journey and working on your personal enhancements enabled by the tools in this book has helped you begin your transformation. I trust your mind is renewed beyond your uncertainties and you now have more power to navigate change with resilience. For you to bloom to your full capacity, it is vital for you to heal first, thus chase after your healing and let it prevail in every facet of your life.

What does hope look like for you? Have you found it? For me Jesus' defeat over death captivates my pain and gives me hope. No book, story or mistake defines me. Hope defines me and that hope is in Jesus. We may plan but God directs our paths, so invite the Holy Spirit to direct your life, decisions, emotions and choices as you live your best life. Life is like a camera, focus on what is important. Capture the good times and develop from the negative. If the picture is a boo-boo, then take another shot. A drop of practice is better than an ocean of theories and good advice. Sovereign trust does not just appear in our lives but grows as we take steps of faith and experience God's faithfulness.

Proverbs 3:5-6 Trust in the Lord with all your heart and lean not on your own understanding and in all your ways submit to Him and He will make your paths straight.

My net worth = extraordinary memories. I encourage you to go create some fine memories and leave a legacy that will outlive the impressive assortment of your picture archives. Trust the healer and go forward with newfound joy and master your journey of life with no abandonments. Die with memories, not with dreams. No one can negate the experiences you have with a supreme force, so cultivate a real relationship so God will continue to prevail. It's okay not to have all the answers, just live your best life and the answers will come. What does not challenge you will not change you. Give your disillusionments time and you will see that when you thought God did not care, in fact He was closer than you felt, directing your next season as He prepared your character.

When we operate optimally in both good and bad times, we create the catalyst for our best self-development. This means soaring in bad times too. How do you soar in bad times? How do you adapt to a new agenda? You design the agenda. Design it to SOAR. No matter how hurt, broken or distraught you are, never build a wall around you. Instead build a bridge. Always reach out and help someone despite your pain. Love is the greatest tool, so ensure you use it profusely. When you dispense unconditional love selflessly then you spread HOPE, and hope is the best antidote. Lead by example of LOVE, not hate. Don't just fly, SOAR.

'You will never do anything in this world without courage, it is the greatest quality of the mind next to honour.' Unknown

Reducing Learning Cycles

In 1957 the Soviet Union stunned the world with the launch of Sputnik 2. On board the satellite was a small dog – Laika, a Siberian husky. She was a rescue from the streets of Moscow. So why did the Russians do that? At the time, our knowledge of space had many gaps, and the dynamics of gravity were not conclusive. They were still experimenting, so they selected the poor unsuspecting dog to be orbited in space. Unfortunately Laika's trip to space was only one way. Sputnik 2 burnt up in space. Laika had no future, her life cut short by an experiment.

Thankfully, your life is not an experiment. You do have a future and the fundamental difference is that you can plan for your future. Yet most people live life as if they are in an experiment and have no control of their future. Sure, you do not have a crystal ball to glean all aspects of your future, but you can plan for a better tomorrow and most importantly you can learn lessons from others and your own experience. Life is never about what happens to us, but how we handle what happens to us. It is carved by what we say yes to and most significantly how we handle the no's in life. Edification occurs when we stop repeating the same behaviour, when we have matured enough to learn the lesson the first time around and move forward in life with a wealth of experience.

Learning the crucial lesson from each predicament not only helps us survive but it also enables us to thrive. When we learn lessons and use them to make better choices, we develop an anthem of triumph. To say yes to life you have to say yes to life's experiences, and to flourish abundantly you have to remember the lessons that you learned and refrain from repeating the same cycles of behaviour.

Both time and energy are limited commodities in life. We need to be very strategic with how we use them, ensuring that we don't waste either our and another person's time and energy. I beseech you to take heed of the lessons that life has given you. Refrain from allowing life's lessons to constantly slip through the noose of predictable behaviour. Train your brain to genuinely examine your life, your patterns, your wins, and your setbacks. Below is a guide to help you along the way.

Reducing Learning Cycles

	You	Spouse	Parents	Friends	University	Work	Hospital	Church
Roles & Responsibilities	You	Spouse	Parents	Friends	University	Work	Hospital	Church
Process & Inputs	List the top five issues that fills your day and what you do to manage these issues.	How much of time does your spouse spend on helping you with these issues each day?	How much of time do your parents spend on helping you with these issues each day?	How much of time do your friends spend on helping you with these issues each day?	How much of time does your university spend on helping you with these issues each day?	How much of time does your work spend on helping you with these issues each day?	How much of time does your medical staff spend on helping you with these issues each day?	How much of time does your church spend on helping you with these issues each day?
Values & Principles	List the values and principles that you use in your life everyday	List the values and principles that your spouse aligns with in your everyday life	List the values and principles that your parents aligns within your everyday life	List the values and principles that your friends aligns within your everyday life	List the values and principles that your university aligns within your everyday life	List the values and principles that your work aligns within your everyday life	List the values and principles that your medical providers align within your everyday life	List the values and principles that your church aligns within your everyday life
Metrics Measured in cost	How much does it cost you each day to address your top five issues	How much does it cost your spouse each day to address your top five issues	How much does it cost your parents each day to address your top five issues	How much does it cost your friends each day to address your top five issues	How much does it cost your university each day to address your top five issues	How much does it cost your work each day to address your top five issues	How much does it cost your medical providers each day to address your top five issues	How much does it cost your church each day to address your top five issues
Outcomes	Describe how you resolved your problems	What did your spouse do to help you with your issues	What did your parents do to help you with your issues	What did your friends do to help you with your issues	What did your university do to help you with your issues	What did your work do to help you with your issues	What did your medical providers do to help you with your issues	What did your church do to help you with your issues
Did the issue reoccur	What issues reoccurred after you addressed it the first time **+** How much does it cost you each day to address the same issue again **=** **?**	How much of time does your spouse spend to readdress the same issue **+** How much does it cost your spouse to readdress these issues **=** **?**	How much of time does your parents spend to readdress the same issue **+** How much does it cost your parents to readdress these issues **=** **?**	How much of time does your friends spend to readdress the same issue **+** How much does it cost your friends to readdress these issues **=** **?**	How much of time does your university spend to readdress the same issue **+** How much does it cost your university to readdress these issues **=** **?**	How much of time does your work spend to readdress the same issue **+** How much does it cost your work to readdress these issues **=** **?**	How much of time does your medical provider spend to readdress the same issue **+** How much does it cost your medical provider to readdress these issues **=** **?**	How much of time does your church spend to readdress the same issue **+** How much does it cost your church to readdress these issues **=** **?**

This diagram is a generic sample overview. Feel free to streamline your response to reflect your own life with some of these guidelines that are specific to you – when reducing your personal learning curves.

Inspect who makes up your support network. Establish what principles and values they align in your life. Outline an estimated cost of time and money each person invests in helping you with your issue. Highlight how the issue was resolved, then list how many times the issue reoccurred in your life. If it cost your friend two hours plus $20 to help you each time and your problem happened five times...do the math. Each role will contribute differently so finally add all the costs. You know have an overview of the cost of each person's investment plus the total cost to your network. The results will compel you to act.

Once you have completed the exercise, you can now see the cost, resource, time, and effort it takes you to manage the current issues in your life. You can also see how much it costs to re-manage the same issue. When the lesson is not grasped the first time and you have to repeat the cycle, then you can use this to predict the cost of repeating each cycle several times. Aim to not live your life like a victim to history but rather use the everyday information to master your destiny.

This is not a blanket approach to ensure that you never repeat or re-manage an issue. Some things in life are inevitable such as an illness or accident and you may not have a choice. This is meant for addressing behavioural change. If you have an accident ten times due to driving while intoxicated, then the issue is that the behaviour of driving drunk needs to change. This exercise is to assist you to objectively look at the cost of repeating your behaviour cycles and what it costs your tribe of people to help you.

Take notice and make an informed choice to learn the lesson from the first cycle of events. Remember, a learning curve is also a status – provided that you learned a valuable lesson and do not repeat the cycle. Focus on the solution, not the problem. Outline how you become part of the solution with issues in your life. Look for the blessing in everything that life throws at you to grow. How can you grow from the current setbacks in your life?

'Life is full of lessons. You are free to make choices, but you are not free from the consequences of those choices.' Unknown

Consecrated and Concrete Standards

When I began school after a few weeks my teacher took me on a visit next door – to a class that was a year ahead of me. The kids were in groups sitting on the floor as their teacher called each one to recite ABC – A for Apple, B for Ball and C for Cat. It was rather daunting for me who was only in school for a couple of weeks. I felt so unequipped, and my heart pounded right out of my chest wondering if I would ever reach a point of true capability! Life took me on a journey to facilitate my growth and transformation – I am now equipped with knowledge and experience. Honestly, nothing terrifies me these days.

The same analogy is applicable to our prayer lives. We start in class one and we need to graduate from primary school into the real world and live out experiences. I am certain when you examine your threads of growth and fellowship – you will find times where you grew and reached new horizons. You will also find times in your life where you stagnated and remained in your comfort zone.

If we reach the age of fifty, seventy or ninety and we are still in class one mode – terrified of ABC then this journey is drastically distorted. We have not grown rich with experience.

If you want to build anything of power and might that stands the test of time – it is done by prayer and a tangible relationship with God. Consecrated prayer and a tangible healthy relationship are practiced lifestyles. There are numerous examples of deep and consecrated enlightenments in the Bible. I am going to zoom into just FOUR examples that model consecrated relationship to me:

1. Hannah Pours Her Heart to God in Prayer (1 Samuel 1-15)

What a supreme model of consecrated prayer when we come into the presence of God and lament – the meaning of lament is to weep passionately. Hannah cried so passionately that she was called a drunk. We are bombarded with the enlightenment of Abraham offering Isaac on the altar. Long before Abraham was even born – Hannah lamented in prayer for a son – God answered her prayer, and she offered her child to God. Which mother can offer what she lamented for? Only prayer gets us to this milestone! Hannah was a barren woman – but the power of consecrated prayer changed her narrative, and it changed the world forever. She became a mother, and she facilitated the lineage of Jesus's birth. The Messiah came through her blood line. Imagine how different the world would be if she just stayed stuck praying her class one ABC prayer every day?

I have lamented prayers to Jesus as a barren woman and Jesus in his wisdom did not answer my prayers – that does not make me a lesser human. God blessed me in other facets of my life. The fundamental point to note is that I reached a place where I offered the very thing that I lamented for on thee alter. I resolved in my heart and soul – Jesus, Your will not mine. I had peace about it and Jesus placed my feet upon a rock…he has literally blessed me beyond measure, to a point where both men and woman covet me. But they don't know the price I paid.

2. The Wrestle of Jacob (Genesis 32: 22-32)

All of us feel like we just can't live without some things in life – for many of us these might include Wi-Fi, smart phone, internet, and coffee. In reality, there are very few things we cannot live without – oxygen, food, water, shelter, and clothing. But the next character we encounter from the Bible – the book of Genesis, shows us something that is just as vital as those life essentials. Jacob models to us – a critical event in his life in Genesis 32 and reveals something that neither he, nor anyone, can live without. In particular, three fundamental life lessons emerge from his experience as brilliant life morals:

1ST Moral - Jacob grasped God's blessing was what he desired most.

This mindfulness did not come easily for Jacob. He knew there was something outside himself that he needed so he spent the better part of his life looking for it. In fact, his search began even before his entry into the world. Jacob had a twin brother named Esau. According to Genesis 25:22, the boys struggled while still in the womb. When Esau was delivered first, Jacob emerged right behind him 'grabbing his heel' So he got his name, Jacob which means 'heel holder,' 'grabber,' 'one who strives.' Why was this sort of delivery significant? Simply because the firstborn received a double portion of his father's assets by law. From all signals, Jacob wanted it and strained to get it.

2ND Moral - Jacob obtained God's blessing by clutching onto the Lord.

According to the text, a 'man' wrestled with Jacob until daybreak. Knowing that this 'man' was not of human origin, Jacob held on for dear life. Even amid great pain and agony, Jacob held out for what he now knew was most vital: 'I will not let you go unless you bless me.' (Genesis 32:26). We need additional 'Jacobs' in the world today. People who will hang on to God at all costs. God's blessing is experiencing the very presence of the Lord – God is the blessing. It is about who we are after, not what we are after. Like Jacob, we must be ready to do whatever is necessary to secure the Father's blessing. God's blessing is free but it's not cheap. There is a price to be paid. The cost reveals our genuineness. Are you willing to give up a few minutes of sleep or social media be with Him?

3RD Moral God's blessing totally improved Jacob's life.

No longer was Jacob a conceited schemer, now he was a humble servant. It's as though he laid down as one man and woke up as another. In fact, that's exactly what happened. Note the power of zeal and transformation! Jacob is now to be called Israel. The name Jacob described who he was – striver, grabber, deceiver and cheater. But now with the name: Israel, it is an indication of who he is – 'struggles with God or God rules.' Jacob was trying to acknowledge and even repay his stolen blessing when he approached his brother Esau. It's what happens when someone gets true with God – they seek to get right with others. We are blessed to be a blessing. We are forgiven so we can forgive. But Jacob was changed in another substantial way – he now limped. What happened to Jacob is a 'crippling victory.' His limp served as a reminder of WHO was in charge of his life. Instead of being self-reliant, Jacob was now God-reliant. And this perspective made him stronger, not weaker despite the limp.

3. *The Revival Prophesy of Ezekiel (Ezekiel 37:1-14)*

If you was the first on the scene of an accident and you saw somebody lying stock-still on the ground, you may think perhaps there's hope. You would probably even do a CPR – try to revive the person and call the ambulance. But if you saw a skeleton lying in the road, you wouldn't even consider mouth-to-mouth resuscitation. You'd think, 'It's just dead bones. There's no hope.' Imagine the Valley of Death. Have you walked this journey of spiritual and literal death? Ezekiel was surrounded with a countless number of dry bones from a slain multitude. God can breathe vitality through His Spirit and through His Word into our lives. Have you fostered consecrated prayer and a tangible relationship for the dead parts of your life? Prayer can revive all.

4. *Jesus Sweating Blood (Luke 22:44)*

Hematohidrosis is a rare, but very real, medical condition that causes one's sweat to contain blood. The sweat glands are surrounded by tiny blood vessels that can constrict and then dilate to the point of rupture, causing blood to effuse into the sweat glands. The cause of Hematohidrosis is extreme anguish. In the gospel accounts, we see the level of Jesus' anguish: He says, 'My soul is overwhelmed with sorrow to the point of death' Matthew 26:38 and Mark 14:34.

Thee intense anguish and sorrow Jesus felt was undoubtedly comprehensible. Being God, Christ knew 'all that was going to happen to Him' He was betrayed. He knew He was about to undergo several judgements. He knew the prophetic words of Isaiah spoken seven centuries earlier that He would be beaten so badly that He would be disfigured. He trusted the disciples to pray but they fell asleep. Certainly, these things factored into His great anguish and sorrow, causing Him to sweat drops of blood. Personally, I have experienced abandonment so I can relate to a fraction of emotions Jesus felt and yes indeed it is more intense than physical pain! There are no words to describe the anguish but we have a medical condition that manifests it in a visible way. I am unaware of any human in history that endured what Jesus borne.

Demise was credited in concrete victory. Although God's plan was calculated before the creation of the world, we must never overlook that its execution came at a pronounced cost. Ultimately, then, we are the ones responsible for the blood that dripped from our Saviour as He prayed in the garden. And we are the reason Jesus' soul was flabbergasted with sorrow to the point of death. Indeed, these bloodied sweat drops came at a great cost, let us certainly not forget that.

Personally if I am on a project and when my effort equates to me sweating blood and the rest of the team rock up with no real zeal – rest assured that I feel a tad frazzled. Moreover ponder how Jesus felt when He was in the garden of Gethsemane sweating blood during prayer; shut your eyes and ponder this – Jesus sweating blood for you and me, He is overwhelmed by anguish – and our rebuttal is, I am too busy. I will scrape up some time to pray while on the run, I am on a journey and I will stagnate in class one as long as I want. Are you actually paying a price during your prayer time? Does your prayer correlate with what Jesus prayed in the Garden of Gethsemane, does it compare with the Prophesy of Ezekiel, does it relate with the wrestling of Jacob and does it connect with the lamenting of Hannah?

Are you still on a journey at class one ABC level? Yet you expect responses the same way Hannah's prayers were answered, the same way Jacob's wrestle was blessed, the same way Ezekiel's prophesy was ignited, and we expect resurrection in all facets of our life just like Jesus, but we don't sweat blood like Jesus. You have a blueprint for your life. If you have aligned your life to your conveniences ONLY then you have created an addendum to the Bible and there is no merit in following your book of convenient choices that suits your schedule, plan and purpose.

Decades ago I visited a friend in New Zealand. She had a frame of JESUS in the lounge. He was kneeling and praying in the garden of Gethsemane. I was a newly converted Christian with no deep revelations of Jesus and the Bible. I have seen numerous depictions of Jesus but none like this. This picture had a dramatic impact me.

Jesus with blood sweat drops on him. To date I have not encountered a similar picture or experience:

- ✓ This picture gave me a revelation of what Jesus did for me in the garden of Gethsemane, in addition it gave me a revelation of what Jesus's prayer life looked like.

- ✓ It compelled me to seek the blueprint of revelations on prayer. It propelled me to honour Jesus with my prayer time – it's the least I can do when He was so overwhelmed with anguish for me that He had to sweat blood.

- ✓ When we get in the spirit like Hannah – the spiritual warfare helps us to deal with infirmities that we may not even be aware of. No one can stop you from reaching your promised land – but you. How consecrated are your prayers? A tree is known by the fruit it bears. Hannah, Jacob, and Ezekiel give witness to this.

- ✓ The more intersessions that you embark on the greater connection you create with God to bridge the gap to your promised land. No matter how dead the situation is. Let Ezekiel's revival reign in you.

- ✓ Learn from Jacob and discipline yourself to NOT reach for things that you should not moreover you do not have to wrestle in the dark to overcome and then walk with a limp.

- ✓ Prayer is the power that guarantees our favoured future. If you do not sweat in training, then you will bleed in battle. For me to be focused and targeted in my prayer I need to zoom in on Jesus and connect like Jesus connected in the garden so when the battle arrives, I can endure the terrain with clout. It is profound and I am going to honour Him with all my being.

There is a lot to foster in our lives and if consecrated prayers and tangible relationship is too daunting for you then start with the sample prayer of the Lord's Prayer and grow. Jesus and life are about the vine of growth. Lament the abundance of your heart. Wrestle until you are blessed. Speak revival to every dead facet of life. Never ever forget the anguish Jesus felt when He prayed and sweat blood – our efforts do not even come adjacent but be willing to be a vessel that can forever change just as Jacob was forever transformed. It is vital that you grow and cultivate deeper. Tap into the fostered art of consecrated prayer and tangible relationship. Begin your own journey – step out in confidence and create a list of how you are going equip yourself and what dimensions of your life you seek to improve.

'Your attitude, not your aptitude, will determine your altitude.' Zig Ziglar

Conclusion

What you have read here is my journey in just a nutshell. There is so much more than what is transcribed in this book. What is the greatest lesson you have encountered in your life? How long did it take you to decipher this? Are you certain that you offer the world the best version of yourself? As these questions loom, I am met by the significant day that originated healthy self-introspection in my conscious. The significance casts my mind to recall a day of my life in secondary school.

We careened into the physics laboratory griping loudly about our next lesson. Our physics teacher was somewhat eccentric with the most outrageous and outdated fashion sense but a true guru in chemistry and physics – Mr. Gangapasadh was a true physicist. We had just completed the mid-year exams and were enthusiastically awaiting our results. Mr. Gangapasadh walked in with a stern face, looking like he was ready to kill us – let me enlighten you to the fact that corporal punishment was well and truly alive at my high school, and poor exam results could lead to bleeding and crying in class.

The class banter stopped, and we could feel the silence amplified. One brave soul from my class enquired about our exam results, and he screamed, *'You want your exam results? Yes, I will give it to you.'* He started calling each pupil's name followed by a loud roar: *'FAILED!'* The entire class had failed the mid-year exam – no big deal, as that was only the half-yearly exams and we would pass the finals, which was what really mattered. The fact that we all failed the most difficult subject on the curriculum is not the reason I remember this day so fondly. I could not care less about physics and chemistry – I don't acclaim to have used these subjects in any way, shape or form.

Mr. Gangapasadh proceeded to give us the proverbial shake-up lecture of our lives. It was a long lecture, and I will spare you the details as you did not fail his class. The component that still remains infused in my mind is: *'None of you planned your outcomes! Not one of you took time to study for this exam. You all want good results but have no desire to do any work to get good results. So in essence what you are really doing is cooking beans curry, then when it's dinner time you open the pot, and you expect to find mutton curry. Did you cook mutton curry? No, but you have great expectations to eat mutton curry.'* We all burst out with laughter and thank goodness the lesson was over.

It was the basic message of we all reap what we sow delivered in such a simplistic and profound way that it was truly one of the best forms of advice I received in my youth. It created an internal compass that defined the core of my being. It became my subconscious guide, compelling me to constantly introspect on what I am cooking and what to expect as a result. It gave me the profound grit and courage to make choices, and the cognitive realignment to discern how my choices and behaviour would affect my results. Thus I consciously always had the acumen to make choices by understanding the direct correlation to great results.

My rollercoaster life was abbreviated with courage. Despite all the pain, I had joys too and my heart still beats because I had to find that bravery with audacity. I still retain the capacity to love fervently, and I still believe in the goodness of humanity. How can any of us be salt to this earth if we do not leave the saltshaker – go venture out. Experience is the best teacher, and there is no formula to master. Nothing is ever a mistake, it's all just an experience to glean from.

I received one of my greatest lesson when I failed an examination, and that helped me navigate my life and that's all that matters – the positive outcomes that propel us to the next season in life. My journey took me, and continues to take me, across many international borders and gave me extensive platforms to be salt and light to this world. I may not be everyone's cup of tea, but I am here to be me, and you are here to be your true self. We have enough space to co-exist and paint this world with our best flavours. My heart will always be filled with agape love to see others become victors and not victims.

This world that we share sadly enslaves many merely due to colour, gender, finance, mindset and perception. We reach considerable latitude when we are not the privileged in the room, take nothing for granted and appreciate what binds us then liberates, and thus freely extend grace and unconditional love to others. Do not let your potential to dispense auspicious grace remain uncultivated. I trust that my journey has given you greater insights and fundamentally changed the prime of you to never let transformation and unconditional love vanish in your hands. The mystery of life is often in our mindset, and the secret is revealed when we change our perspective. It is my choice, it is your choice, and it is all our collective choices. Do you have the capacity to change and bring forth a better tomorrow? Your resolve!

It is winter in Sydney as I write this. The chill of the season lingers and the COVID-19 lockdown rules still prevail into the uncertain future. I have already taken steps towards authentic self-assessment. Regardless, courage is the significant bedrock for my destiny. I make the choice every day to live my dream with every step I make and every breath I take. It is the platinum standard for building sensational cathedrals of life – the I pinch myself moment. DESTINY = boundless LIVING. The limit is the restriction you place on yourself and certainly not the circumstances that come hurling our way.

A visual vista to our fish tank lights the way to tranquillity as our pets swim blissfully. I ponder on the fact that they have no clue of the perils of the world right now! Would I trade places to be in a protected bubble? I can say in a heartbeat – ABSOLUTELY NOT. I love living my life to the maximum, and experiencing my journey, my sojourns, my stories, my style, my transformation, my courage and my passion. I love injecting my personal flavour and touch to this world as I chase the sun daily, catch the waves of constant change and meet every challenge with courage. Death loses its license to threaten those that are certain.

What I have endured to date is surreal and I make the grand effort every day to enhance my character. If life is going to turn a corner for us all, then we need to choose between an unfair world and a world of progress, ultimately at our pace. It is better to try and fail than fail to try. Therefore, live well and finish strong despite where you and your mind have dwelled in the past. Circumstances do not make us; they simply reveal who we really are. Our greatest deeds should not be succeeding at the expense of others yes indeed you can chop someone to be the tallest poppy in the field. Give credence to the fact that when you chop someone, it kills literally, and it most certainly is a death transaction. This is my fifth decade on earth living my best life without carrying my heart on my sleeve, yet I have been labelled: black, emotional, social butterfly, high achiever, intimidating, competent, weak – as if they know me and everything in between, but I let none of those label stick to me. The fact that an Indian female escapes as a salient character is frequently met with astonishment. Deflecting incoming arrows as easily as summer gnats is not an afterthought. It is a precision skill that beckons kudos.

My concern is not what others deem of me, but I marvel at the sheer resilience life has ignited in me, reminding myself to not cry about the worn-out shoes on my feet as some have no feet at all. I am eternally grateful for all the outcomes in my life. One of the constant criticisms I endure is that I am too generous, and I get categorised with a basketful of adjectives. I give people the benefit of the doubt and an opportunity to prove themselves. Sometimes my empathy is abused, and I reconcile with that, as I would rather get hurt than treat people in the same fashion that I was treated in.

Someone has to stop the cycle and the buck stops with me even if I pay the highest price – it matches my ideals and that's all that matters. What matters is the compassion I dispense and not the incompetence of the other party. I am not tainted by what significant or insignificant people say. I am graced to be a Solomon amidst society by personal experience and I brim with confidence as I embark on the next challenge. I had no intention of writing a book but I was compelled to write this during COVID-19 lockdown so we can all reflect, refine, and redefine our rhema *(Derived from the Greeks it literally means an 'utterance' or 'thing said' – it is a word that signifies the action of utterance)* to transcend. Do not sweat over acquiring and maintaining perishable things. It is unfruitful when you focus your energy and theory to pursue delight however in practice your behaviour spells misfortune. *(Don't say you want to lose weight but eat a whole cheesecake everyday – focus your energy on what favours your goal)* If the mountain feels too big today, then climb a hill instead.

Literature is the defying creation of self-expression. You just read the unapologetic account of my life, and some may resort to Bible bashing me, others will react, few will respond, and multitudes will be stirred and touched. In whatever fashion this art of mine resonates with you – transcend to search for your advantage point of standing in your state of controversy rather than remaining asleep in your status of convenience. Bustling forward with inspirational growth hacks that will erupt questions to confirm where you stand in times of challenge rather than where you live in times of comfort. I have gleaned that sometimes the gloomiest experiences can usher us forth to an optimistic place.

I have learned that the most toxic people can teach us the most significant lessons. I have gathered that the most excruciating struggles can offer us the most crucial advancements. Simon Sinek posted on Instagram: *'There are only two ways to influence human behaviour: you can manipulate it, or you can inspire it. Manipulation is much easier, but the impact is short lived and breeds no love or loyalty. Inspiration may take more effort, but it's worth it. The results can last a lifetime and generate intense love and loyalty along the way. Inspire on, I say.'* My dear readers you have two choices to leave your streak of influence – choose sensibly. The inoculation against behaviour that corrodes life concludes we are on a quest for a better world. This does not just happen by wind pollination. We all need to collectively foster an environment that values truth no matter how angst provoking it maybe. Living our truth out loud in a positive manner strengthens behaviour around us. If you think you are living up to your highest values, then by all means run it up on a flagpole and see who salutes you. If you are happy with those endorsements, then you are aligned to your true north. Equally important is to discover which way true north is. We are all hardcoded for struggle by birth nonetheless we are all worthy of pronounced love and support.

A journey of a thousand mile begins with a single step. Steps in a positive direction enable one to grow to one's full majesty. Progress is a culmination of small but significant steps. If you feel like David staring at the giant, then travel forward shaken, rattled and victorious, and grow as you revel in the fact that all David had was a stone and he knew how to work it for victory. Don't stop your transformation if you do not exhibit true and immediate proclaimed progress. I have lived through many dangers and snares, giving my best and continuously learning to still do better. The most difficult thing is the decision to act. The rest is mere perseverance. Transformation is not a place of sheer visitation; instead, it is a place of habitation.

'How wonderful it is that nobody needs to wait a single moment before starting to improve the world.' Anne Frank

Acknowledgements

My sincere appreciation to...

My parents for raising me to be more than a conqueror. For inculcating values and principles in me that surmounted my character, awakened boldness, and enabled me with determination and confidence to forge a life. My dad for remarkably and benevolently modelling true generosity in me since I was born. Your spirit lives in me. My mum, I am fascinated by your powerful character of rampant inspiration, radiating calm and powerful resilience. My super saturated soul smiles through your unconditional heart and I am blessed to have both your genes. I love the vivacity and charm that the pair of you procreated in me!

My blood sealed sisters for sculpting suppleness and moulding competence in me, as if it was a regular commodity. Our birth bonds form a collection of characteristics that are finely tuned to dispense abundant bonuses.

My pair of brothers who ignited a healthy zeal for endurance and the tenacious spark to never quit. For adding punches of colour to my life that brings ambience to Stayin' Alive vibes that will make John Travolta sweat!

My rainmaker, my North Star, my anchor, my strong tower: my husband, Dave Markey, for transcending our lives from vow to wow. Marvel made flesh, LOVE made literal, Utopian. You are the quintessence of support and love in every facet of our blessed lives, thank you for selflessly helping me to read and edit my manuscript. In addition, THANK YOU for creating all the diagrams to illustrate my points in this book.

My dear friend Maureen Dowdell who held my hand in the storm and walked with me until I safely reached the other side. The ongoing chinwags both propelled and inspired me during this book editing and other times as well.

Nicole Vinson Bingaman, Carol Seeto, Uluaipouomalo Aiono, Azita Abdollahian and Dr Samuel Ekundayo: thank you for penning a beautiful endorsement for my book. I appreciate the time you spent on reading my manuscript despite your hectic schedules.

Additional taproots to my life and daily inspiration are my besties Elaine Naidoo and Penny Hayes who have walked the journey of life with me for decades and continue to sow into my transformation of becoming the best version of myself.

Pastor Gilyean Levick, thank you for your time, guidance, and pearls of wisdom, I appreciate the cherished advice.

From my book club, Kerrie McGibbon thank you for reading my manuscript and your valued feedback is greatly appreciated. Ann Hunter, Beverly Golder and Cheryl Barnett sincere gratitude to you ladies for proof reading my first printed book.

To both my dear friends Jan McIntyre and Katrina Garen, I am grateful for the part you both played in introducing me to Emily Gower. I cherish all the connections and sweet fellowship that we share as we journey in life. Emily thank you for the publishing lessons.

Liz Naidoo, gratitude to you for scripting a heartfelt foreword that brings life to my words. Your faith inspires me intrinsically in so many profound ways.

My friend Gabriel Chibomba all your efforts are well appreciated, especially to drop everything and read my manuscript as a priority in its entirety. You take zeal to the next level, thank you!

To the publishing team at Ultimate World Publishing, my sincere appreciation for your professional acumen and working in a highly organised fashion. It was a dream to be part of this team.

My unconditional friends the luminaries that I look up to, I am blessed to have numerous to tally. You all continue to quell the chaos in my soul, and I absolutely love the tranquiliser with no side effects aka 'laughter' that you all so generously dispense into my life. It is profound that you are all still a constellation of stars in different countries, yet still burn ever so bright in my heart.

I am truly grateful to you the reader – the open-minded historians that will transform to an audacious vision and thus be a speaking picture to this world. Practical enhancements are mutually exclusive and profoundly beneficial – a piquant journey to embark on.

ABOUT THE AUTHOR

Composed like the rock of Gibraltar Kelly Markey generates an inspirational witness as a stimulus made human. Her life spells resilience and speaks of sensational encouragement. A sassy South African native transitioned to a proud citizen of New Zealand and now happily domiciled in Australia. Markey's life and knowledge has touched and conveyed remedial to souls globally.

Her usual candour will hasten your level of connection as you practically bond to her life and experience. Markey's passion is to help others to create an enhanced version of themselves and thus impact humanity in a positive fashion. She frequently travels the world sustaining more enriching and valuable life morals. She writes from experience acquired personally and shares her insightful gleans knowledgeable from a place of confidence. Kelly has travelled over 200 cities around the world and experienced life through many different lenses.

A virtuous woman, bold speaker of truth, a valued confidant, loving wife, cherished daughter, valued sister and esteemed professional. Markey has carved out a stellar career in the corporate sphere as an expert in Health Information Technology. A trailblazer for inspiration and an epitome of zeal. She is a powerful character that is not defeated by any challenge. A multi-layered treasure to draw from, the superpower of: a nurturer, motivator, entrepreneur, philanthropist and a visionary. Ample in experience – a book and life that shatters genre boundaries.

Through her words, we see her come into resilient consciousness as she evolves from new immigrant to citizen, from a grieving woman to a triumphant woman. Kelly is a maven beacon that harnesses life from personal experience of working and living in four different countries, speaking five different languages, and sharing life with a divergent global demographic. The power to transcend lies within you and you can do this with panache despite distressing circumstances. Her narrative will dare the reader to self-introspect and self-regulate this one audacious life as you heal and restore your heart, soul and ultimately humanity.

My book created waves well and truly before it was published.

For keynote speaking and inquiries, visit:

Facebook @KellyMarkeyAuthor and Instagram Author_Kelly_Markey

I am honoured to obtain a cover feature on Women of Faith Magazine. The founder of the magazine was reading my manuscript to pen the foreword when she contacted me and said: 'Wow Kelly, I cannot put your book down, can we do a cover feature on you?'

I am humbled by such a profound acclaim from such a distinguished periodical. THANK YOU, Woman of Faith Magazine. Digital Magazine available at womanoffaith.co.za

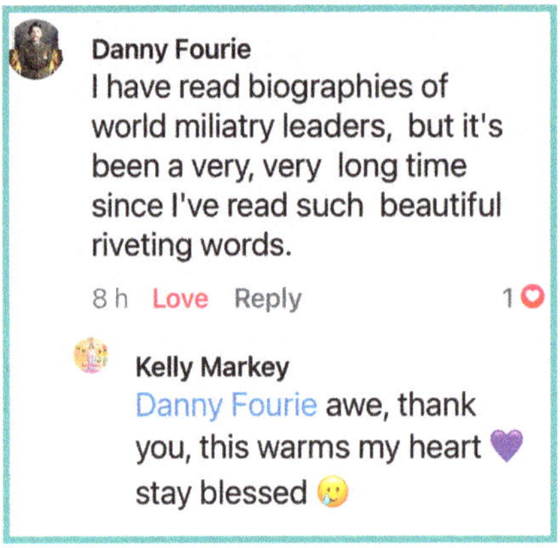

Danny Fourie
I have read biographies of world miliatry leaders, but it's been a very, very long time since I've read such beautiful riveting words.

8 h   Love   Reply   1

Kelly Markey
Danny Fourie awe, thank you, this warms my heart 💜 stay blessed 🥹

One of the many profound book acclaims from an exuberant reader

Social Media
2021

References

Preface

1. **Quote 'If...die':** unknown, Instagram, 2018.

Introduction

2. **Proverbs 29:18:** Zondervan, The Holy Bible, New International Translation (NIV), United States, Harper Collins, 1973.
3. **Reference to the card game Thunee:** a card game played by the Indian community in South Africa, especially in Durban, and also by Indian South African emigrants in North America and Australia, published electronically.
4. **Quote 'Valour...soul':** Michel de Montaigne, the essays of Michel de Montaigne, 1580.

Part one – My voyage

Chapter one - Resilience

5. **Jeremiah 12:5, Romans 8:31 and Psalm 120:1:** Zondervan, The Holy Bible, New International Translation (NIV), United States, Harper Collins, 1973.
6. **Quote 'Strength...will':** Mahatma Gandhi, Mahatma Gandhi quotes, published electronically.
7. **Quote 'I...it':** Maya Angelou, letter to my daughter, United States, Random House, 2009.
8. **Quote 'Success...it':** Marva Collins, return to excellence in education, United States, Jeremy P Tarcher, 1990.

Chapter two – The vicissitudes of life

9. **Romans 8:28, Acts 16:31, Ecclesiastes 9:10 and Proverbs 18:24:** Zondervan, The Holy Bible, New International Translation (NIV), United States, Harper Collins, 1973.
10. **Quote 'What...do':** Timothy Ferriss, the 4 hour body, United States, Crown Publishing Group, 2010.
11. **Quote 'Be...cloud':** Maya Angelou, I know why the caged bird sings, United States, Random House, 1969.
12. **Quote 'If...welcome':** Anne Bradstreet, the tenth muse lately sprung up in America, England, Woodbridge, 1650.
13. **Photograph:** of Joycinda published with consent.
14. **Quote 'The...mistake':** Ralph Nader, breaking through power, San Francisco, City Lights Publishers, 2016.
15. **Quote 'If...come':** unknown, Pinterest, published electronically, 2018.
16. **Photograph:** of Maureen published with consent.

Chapter three – Internal Fortitude

17. **Numbers 17:18, Luke 8:17, Acts 3:6, Reference to the story of Lot from the Bible and John 3:16:** Zondervan, The Holy Bible, New International Translation (NIV), United States, Harper Collins, 1973.
18. **Wilson drifting away:** author narration from the film Cast Away. Paraphrased a scene of Tom Hank's movie.
19. **Quote 'If...silenced':** Vincent Van Gogh, quotes.com, 1888
20. **Quote 'You...head':** Martin Luther King Jr, speech, 1960.

Chapter four – Prototypes for deeper connection

21. **Matthew 7:2-3 and Matthew 5:9:** Zondervan, The Holy Bible, New International Translation (NIV), United States, Harper Collins, 1973.
22. **Quote:** William Glasser, Choice Theory, New York, Harper Collins, 1998.
23. **Photograph of the lads:** published with consent from John, Ross, and Dave.
24. **Reference to peacekeeper and peace maker:** definition published electronically @ https: //wikidiff.com.

25. **Men of genius paragraph:** unknown, daily devotion, 2015.
26. **Quote 'Don't…crucified':** Charles Spurgeon, Instagram, 2020.
27. **Photograph:** of Jan published with consent.

Chapter five – A virtuous woman

28. **Quote 'An…stone':** William Prescott, the world of the Incas, United Kingdom, J.M. Dent & Co, 1950.
29. **Quote 'Nothing…change':** unknown, Instagram, 2020.
30. **Quote 'Although…ending':** Carl Bard, quoteland.com, published electronically, 1985.
31. **Quote 'Right…it':** Saint Augustine.
32. **Proverbs 31 woman – scripture reference and Matthew 14:8:** Zondervan, The Holy Bible, New International Translation (NIV), United States, Harper Collins, 1973.
33. **Quote: 'The…rainbow':** unknown, positive quotes, published electronically, 2018.
34. **Reference to the song The Rose:** Bette Midler, United States, 1979.
35. **Quote 'Hold…grip':** Charles Spurgeon, Instagram, 2020.
36. **Photograph of card:** Published with consent from Joycinda.
37. **Quote 'When…strong':** unknown, daily inspirational quotes, published electronically, 2020.

Chapter six – You cannot give a shattered heart

38. **Quote 'Doing…result':** Misattributed to Albert Einstein, second strongest match printed on a pamphlet by the Narcotics Anonymous in 1981.
39. **Quote 'Don't…circus':** Dan Nielsen, Be an Inspirational Leader, New Zealand, 2017.
40. **Spiritual power of salt:** reviewed case study on the use and power of salt in the Bible and ancient times, published electronically.
41. **Numbers 18:19 and John 14:26:** Zondervan, The Holy Bible, New International Translation (NIV), United States, Harper Collins, 1973.
42. **Quote 'God's…mistakes':** Nicky Gumbel, The Bible in One Year, Great Britain, Hodder, and Stoughton, 2019.

43. **Reference to Shakespeare's sonnet 116:** Let me not to the marriage of true minds. By William Shakespeare. https://www.poetryfoundation.org
44. **Quote 'It...relationships':** Matthew Hussey, Get the Guy, Great Britain, Transworld Digital, 2013.
45. **Quote 'Every...better':** Steve Maraboli, Unapologetically You, USA, A Better Today Publishing, 2013.
46. **Quote 'I...decisions':** Stephen Covey, Decisions Decision Our 2017 Startup Roadmap, USA, Admass Publishing, 2016.
47. **Photography:** of Dave and Kelly published with photographer's consent.

Chapter seven – Litmus test for true alliance

48. **Quote 'There...life':** Stephen Covey, The 7 Habits of Highly Effective People, USA, Simon and Schuster, USA, 1989.
49. **Review of case studies on oxytocin:** published electronically.
50. **Quote 'We...parable':** Bob Goff, word for today, 2019.
51. **Quote 'Some...go':** Oscar Wilde, Instagram, 2020.
52. **Reference to the song that's what friends are for:** Dionne Warwick, United States, 1985.
53. **Quote 'Friendship...care':** unknown, Facebook, 2014.
54. **Photograph:** of Elaine published with consent.
55. **Quote 'Those...live':** Paramahansa Yogananda, Autobiography of a Yogi, USA, Self-Realization Fellowship, 1946.

Chapter eight – The Rollercoaster Extravaganza

56. **Quote 'We...affairs':** Charles Spurgeon, Citizenship in Heaven, New Zealand, Titus Books, 2013.
57. **Hebrews: 11:1:** Zondervan, The Holy Bible, New International Translation (NIV), United States, Harper Collins, 1973.
58. **Quote: 'Do...try':** Yoda line reference from the movie, George Lucas, The Empire Strikes Back, Unites States, 1980.
59. **Quote 'Some...joy':** Amy Weatherly, podcast, published digitally, 2019.
60. **Quote 'Fear...decision':** Sir Winston Churchill, My African Journey, London, Hodder & Stoughton, 1908.

61. **Quote 'If...going':** Sir Winston Churchill, The World Crisis, New York, Scribner, 1923.

Chapter nine – Highlight your core beauty

62. **Quote 'Do...again':** Nelson Mandela, A Long Walk to Freedom, South Africa, Little Brown & Co, 1994.
63. **Quote 'Gratitude...mercies':** Charles E Jefferson, podcast, 2016.
64. **Reference to the Foxes book of Martyrs:** John Foxe, England, John Day, 1563.
65. **Reference to 'Diya':** This is a ghee or oil lamp, used for performing Puja according to Hindu customs and rituals. https://www.speakingtree.in/blog/why-hindus-lit-a-deepam-before-praying.
66. **Quote 'Don't...try':** .Jack Canfield, Chicken Soup for the Soul, USA, William Morrow and Co, 2013.
67. **Photograph:** of author's mum published with consent.
68. **Quote 'To...all':** Oscar Wilde, The Picture of Dorian Gray, England, Lippincott's Monthly Magazine, 1890.
69. **Quote 'You...shore':** Translated by J.M. Cohen, The four voyages of Christopher Columbus, United States, Penguin Books, 2002.
70. **Photograph:** of Zoey published with consent.
71. **Proverbs: 14:30:** Zondervan, The Holy Bible, New International Translation (NIV), United States, Harper Collins, 1973.
72. **Quote 'When...discounts':** Karen Salmansohn, Life is Long, USA, Potter Publishing, 2018.
73. **Included the ancient Greek word AGAPE:** from Wikipedia, published electronically.
74. **Quote 'Make...it':** Joel Osteen, Think Better Live Better, USA, Faith Words, 2016.

Chapter ten – We all have CHOICES

75. **Quote: 'It...abilities':** JK Rowling, Harry Potter and the Philosopher's Stone, Great Britain, Pottermore Publishing, 1997.
76. **Quote 'It...ourselves':** Edmond Hillary, View from the summit, New Zealand, Penguin, 2003.
77. Reference to astrology the name **'Dhanika'** by Vedic Astrology, published electronically.

78. **Diagram depicting reactive and proactive mindsets:** analysis and specifications by Kelly Markey and CorelDRAW illustration by Dave Markey, Don't just fly SOAR, Australia, Gowor International Publishing, 2021.
79. Author narration from the visit to the Titanic Museum in Las Vegas, personal visit, 2017.
80. **Excerpt from book:** Joseph Murphy, the power of the subconscious mind, United States, St. Martin's Publishing Group, 2019.
81. **Quote 'Values…birth':** Barack Obama, The Audacity of Hope, USA, Text Publishing, 2008.
82. **Quote 'When…Water':** Benjamin Franklin, The Autobiography of Benjamin Franklin, USA, Touchstone, 2004.

Chapter eleven – The unconscious bias

83. **Lane filtering legislation change:** Service New South Wales website, Australia, published electronically, 2014.
84. **Diagram of decision flow of Bias bites but beckons noting:** analysis, specifications and Microsoft Visio illustration by Kelly Markey, Don't just fly SOAR, Australia, Gowor International Publishing, 2021.
85. **Quote 'Loyalty…soul':** Mark Twain, The Quotable Mark Twain, USA, McGraw-Hill Education, 1998.
86. **Quote 'The…it':** Unknown, published electronically.
87. **Quote 'If…anything':** Ron Chernow, Alexander Hamilton, USA, Head of Zeus, 2017.
88. **Photograph:** Australian blood donor key ring of Kelly Markey published with consent.
89. Excerpt from Wikipedia on **South African Apartheid history**. The Hyperlink https://en.wikipedia.org/wiki/Apartheid
90. **Photograph:** public park signage prohibiting dogs and Indians, Richards Bay – South Africa, 1982.
91. Excerpt from Wikipedia on **Gandhi's history in South African.** The Hyperlink https://www.sahistory.org.za/people/mohandas-karamchand-gandhi
92. **Photograph:** public beach signage permitting only whites to use the beach, Durban – South Africa, 1980.

93. **Excerpt from the song Gimme hope Joanna.** By Eddie Grant. The Hyperlink https://www.azlyrics.com/lyrics/eddygrant/gimmehopejoanna.html
94. **Reference about Equity Theory:** Wikipedia, published electronically.
95. **Reference to the song we are the world by USA for Africa:** song writers Michael Jackson and Lionel Richie, USA, 1985.
96. **Quote 'You...world':** Arleen Lorrance, The Love Principles, USA, LP Publications, 2001.

Chapter twelve – The best has come and it prevails

97. **Quote 'If...effort':** Kamal Ravikant, Live Your Truth, USA, Fonderzen, 2013.
98. **Quote 'Try...value':** Alert Einstein, published electronically.
99. **Photograph:** of Penny published with consent.
100. **Photograph:** of Katrina published with consent.
101. **Joshua 10:12 and Isaiah 59:19:** Zondervan, The Holy Bible, New International Translation (NIV), United States, Harper Collins, 1973.
102. **Quote: 'A...silently':** Confucius, published electronically.

Part two – The art of Transformation

Transition of scarred to healed

103. **Proverbs 29:18:** Zondervan, The Holy Bible, New International Translation (NIV), United States, Harper Collins, 1973.
104. **Quote 'Learning...mind':** Leonardo Da Vinci, Brainy Quotes, published electronically.
105. **Quote 'Smart...answers':** Socrates, Wikipedia, published electronically.

Tool 1 – Mental Resilience

Word Association Test 'Galton introduced the first word-association test to psychology': Francis Galton and Carl Jung.

106. **Excerpt from book,** Eckhart Tolle, A New Earth, Australia, Hodder Australia, 2004.

107. Excerpt from the book, Ralph Waldo Emerson, Mastery of Life, audio book published on public domain, 2009.
108. **Quote 'The...choice'**: Brian Herbert, The sisterhood of Dune, Unites States, Tor Books, 2012.

Tool 2 – Personal Journaling

109. **Romans 12:2:** Zondervan, The Holy Bible, New International Translation (NIV), United States, Harper Collins, 1973.
110. **Quote 'If...today'**: H.G. Wells, Brainy Quotes, published electronically.
111. **Reference to eustress** from dictionary.

Tool 3 – Steps towards authentic self-assessment

112. **Quote 'The...circumstances'**: unknown, published electronically.
113. **Quote 'Failure...intelligently'**: Hendry Ford, Brainy Quotes, published electronically.

Tool 4 – Self-care enhancements

114. **Quote 'Our...fall'**: Confucius, Brainy Quotes, published electronically.

Tool 5 – Improve your radar

115. **Quote 'If...leader'**: John Quincy Adams, Business Journal, published electronically.

Tool 6 – Ascend above the predicament

116. **2 Timothy 1:7:** Zondervan, The Holy Bible, New International Translation (NIV), United States, Harper Collins, 1973.
117. **Quote 'Difficult...quit'**: Deb Sofield, public speaker, 2018.

Tool 7 – The roaring difference between change and progress

118. **Quote 'You...changing'**: Bob Dylan, Song – The Times They are a-Changing, United States, Warner Bros, 1963.
119. **Quote 'The...it'**: Alan Kay, Brainy Quotes, published electronically.

120. **Diagram of change cycle methodology:** analysis and specifications by Kelly Markey and CorelDRAW illustration by Dave Markey, Don't just fly SOAR, Australia, Gowor International Publishing, 2021.
121. **Quote 'One…want':** William Glasser, Choice Theory, 1998.
122. **Quote 'God…difference':** Reinhold Niebuhr, Serenity Prayer, United States, Wikipedia, 1932.
123. **Quote 'Yesterday…myself':** Rumi, The Essential Rumi, Iran, Castle Books, 1997.

Tool 8 – Work to reach the Promised Land

124. **Author narration from Nelson Mandela's autobiography:** a long walk to freedom, South Africa, Little Brown & Co, 1194.
125. **Quote 'If…door':** Milton Berle, Brainy Quotes, published electronically.

Tool 9 – Moving to the next level

126. **Quote 'A…persistence':** Jim Watkins, Brainy Quotes, published electronically.

Tool 10 – Discovering your purpose

127. **Romans 5:3:** Zondervan, The Holy Bible, New International Translation (NIV), United States, Harper Collins, 1973.
128. **Quote 'You…for':** unknown, Instagram, 2020.

Tool 11 – Purge List

129. **Statistics of the most read book in the world:** James Chapman, published electronically.
130. **Quote 'Faith…shovel':** unknown, Instagram, 2020.

Tool 12 – How content are you with your life at present

131. **Quote 'Don't…right':** Napoleon Hill, Brainy Quotes, published electronically.

Tool 13 – Setting goals

132. **Excerpt from blog:** Pastor Gilyean Levick, Facebook, 2018.

133. **Ecclesiastes 3:1-8:** Zondervan, The Holy Bible, New International Translation (NIV), United States, Harper Collins, 1973.
134. **Quote 'You…dream':** C.S. Lewis, The Chronicles of Narnia, Britain, Harper Collins, 1954.

Tool 14 – Strategic vision

135. **Proverbs 20:4:** Zondervan, The Holy Bible, New International Translation (NIV), United States, Harper Collins, 1973.
136. Reviewed several case studies **about the fall of Kodak:** published electronically.
137. **Quote 'A…flower':** C.S. Iris Murdoch, Brainy Quotes, published electronically.
138. **Quote 'There…yearning':** Christopher Morley, Brainy Quotes, published electronically.

Tool 15 – Process the unprocessed pain

139. **Quote 'All…them':** unknown, Instagram, 2020.

Tool 16 – Love Map

140. **Quote 'Someone…mediocrity':** unknown, Instagram, 2019.

Tool 17 – Proactively discover your blind spots

141. **Quote 'In…most':** unknown, Instagram, 2020.

Tool 18 – What does Utopia look like for you?

142. **Quote 'You…be':** Marianne Williamson, Brainy Quotes, published electronically.

Tool 19 – Elements of success

143. **Quote 'We…success':** unknown, Instagram, 2020.

Tool 20 – How to monitor your personal growth

144. **Quote 'Never…authenticity':** unknown, Instagram, 2018.

Tool 21 – Balancing the equation of sowing and reaping

145. **Reference to scripture Deuteronomy chapter 27 and 28:** The Holy Bible, New International Translation (NIV), United States, Harper Collins, 1973.
146. **Diagram representation of the analogy of sowing and reaping:** analysis and specifications by Kelly Markey and CorelDRAW illustration by Dave Markey, Don't just fly SOAR, Australia, Gowor International Publishing, 2021.
147. **Quote 'There…up':** John Holmes, Brainy Quotes, published electronically.

Tool 22 – The ladder of ascent to transformation

148. **Diagram representation of the ladder of ascent to transformation:** analysis and specifications by Kelly Markey and CorelDRAW illustration by Dave Markey, Don't just fly SOAR, Australia, Gowor International Publishing, 2021.
149. **Quote 'The…present':** unknown, Twitter, 2020.
150. **Quote 'Nothing…change':** Arthur Burt, Brainy Quotes, published electronically.

Tool 23 – Beauty or afflictions? You choose

151. **Quote 'Some…roses':** Alphonse Karr, Brainy Quotes, published electronically.
152. **Diagram representation of the daily circle of mantra:** analysis, specifications and Microsoft Visio illustration by Kelly Markey, Don't just fly SOAR, Australia, Gowor International Publishing, 2021.
153. **Excerpt from blog:** Pastor Gilyean Levick, Facebook, 2019.
154. **Proverbs 3:5-6:** The Holy Bible, New International Translation (NIV), United States, Harper Collins, 1973.
155. **Quote 'You…honour':** Unknown, Instagram, 2020.

Tool 24 – Reducing learning cycles

156. Reviewed case study **documenting Sputnik 2** – pioneering dog launched into outer space, published electronically.
157. **Diagram of workflow to reduce personal learning curves:** analysis, specifications and Microsoft Visio illustration by Kelly

Markey, Don't just fly SOAR, Australia, Gowor International Publishing, 2021.

158. **Quote 'Life...choices':** Unknown, Facebook, 2018.

Tool 25 – Consecrated and concreate standards

159. **1 Samuel 1:15, Genesis 32:22-32, Genesis 25:22, Ezekiel 37:1-14, Luke 22:44, Matthew 26:38 and Mark 14:34:** Zondervan, The Holy Bible, New International Translation (NIV), 1978.
160. Definition of Hematohidrosis from the Dictionary.
161. **Quote 'Your...altitude':** Zig Ziglar, Brainy Quotes, published electronically.

Conclusion

162. **Quote 'I...feet':** Helen Keller, Brainy Quotes, published electronically.
163. Reference from the Thesaurus of the word **rhema**.
164. **Quote 'There...say':** Simon Sinek, Instagram, 2020.
165. **Quote 'How...world':** Anne Frank, Brainy Quotes, published electronically.

Notes

Notes

Notes

www.ingramcontent.com/pod-product-compliance
Lightning Source LLC
Chambersburg PA
CBHW062030290426
44109CB00026B/2583